HOW
PEOPLE
GROW

Resources by Henry Cloud and John Townsend

Boundaries
Boundaries Workbook
Boundaries audio
Boundaries video curriculum
Boundaries in Dating
Boundaries in Dating Workbook
Boundaries in Dating audio
Boundaries in Dating curriculum
Boundaries in Marriage
Boundaries in Marriage Workbook
Boundaries in Marriage audio
Boundaries with Kids
Boundaries with Kids Workbook
Boundaries with Kids audio
Changes That Heal (Cloud)
Changes That Heal Workbook (Cloud)
Changes That Heal audio (Cloud)
Hiding from Love (Townsend)
How People Grow
How People Grow audio
The Mom Factor
The Mom Factor Workbook
The Mom Factor audio
Raising Great Kids
Raising Great Kids for Parents of Preschoolers curriculum
Raising Great Kids Workbook for Parents of Preschoolers
Raising Great Kids Workbook for Parents of School-Age Children
Raising Great Kids Workbook for Parents of Teenagers
Raising Great Kids audio
Safe People
Safe People Workbook
Safe People audio
Twelve "Christian" Beliefs That Can Drive You Crazy

HOW
PEOPLE
GROW

What the Bible Reveals about Personal Growth

DR. HENRY CLOUD
DR. JOHN TOWNSEND

Authors of *Boundaries*

GRAND RAPIDS, MICHIGAN 49530

We want to hear from you. Please send your comments about this book to us in care of the address below. Thank you.

GRAND RAPIDS, MICHIGAN 49530

www.zondervan.com

ZONDERVAN™

How People Grow
Copyright © 2001 by Henry Cloud and John Townsend

Requests for information should be addressed to:

Zondervan, *Grand Rapids, Michigan 49530*

Library of Congress Cataloging-in-Publication Data

Cloud, Henry.
    How people grow : what the bible reveals about personal growth / Henry Cloud and John Townsend.
       p. cm.
    ISBN: 0–310–22153-6
      1. Self-actualization (Psychology)—Religious aspects—Christianity.
    2. Christian life—Biblical teaching.   I. Townsend, John Sims, 1952–   II. Title.
    BV4598.2 .C56 2001
    248.2—dc21   2001045575

This edition printed on acid-free paper.

Published in association with Yates & Yates, LLP, Literary Agent, Orange, CA.

Interior design by Todd Sprague

Printed in the United States of America

02 03 04 05 06 07 08 /❖ DC/ 10 9 8 7 6 5 4 3 2

To all those who have sought God and his growth path,
and to all those who labor to help others grow.
We are grateful for your hunger for him and his ways.

For information on books, resources, or speaking engagements:

Cloud-Townsend Resources
3176 Pullman Avenue, Suite 104
Costa Mesa, CA 92626
Phone: 1-800-676-HOPE (4673)
Web: www.cloudtownsend.com

Contents

PREFACE

If you have picked up this book, it is likely that you have some interest in the growth process. It could range from being curious about the subject to a deep involvement in helping others grow. Whatever your reasons, welcome to *How People Grow!*

We would like to explain briefly the reasons for this book:

—To show that all growth is spiritual growth. Most Christians are aware of their need to grow. Some come to this point because they possess a hunger and desire to know God and his ways better. Others are interested through a problem or crisis that has driven them to seek his paths. We believe that getting to know God more deeply, growing emotionally, and having better relationships are all matters of spiritual growth. God has designed a path of growth that leads us to him and his ways. As we learn and experience that path, we enter his life. This changes our entire existence, encompassing emotions, behavior, relationships, career, and everything else in life. We want people to learn that way for themselves.

—To show that the principles of growth are in the Bible and its teachings. Many people are confused about the role of the Scriptures in their growth. They sometimes attempt to learn their religion and theology from the Bible, and growth and counseling from psychology. We believe that the Bible and its great doctrines teach the truths and principles people need in order to grow. The problem with many people is not that the truths aren't in the pages of Scripture, but that they have not understood what it really teaches about growth. This book leads back to the Bible as the source for teaching about growth and healing.

—To provide an overall approach to growth. Many people will get involved in a growth-based church, or start reading books about the subject. Yet there are few resources that provide a comprehensive approach to the growth process. As a point of background, we developed this approach over many years of biblical and theological study and have worked on it with people in all kinds of contexts, including

- Counseling settings
- Churches
- Denominations
- Parachurch organizations
- Businesses
- Psychiatric hospital settings
- Leadership settings

All of our counseling, consulting, writing, and speaking is based on this system of biblical growth. Each one of our books, for example, is about some aspect of life or growth that comes from the approach: a brick from the house, so to speak. After we had taught on these matters for a few years, people started asking us to write about the system of growth as a whole. They wanted to know what the architecture of the entire house looked like. We agreed with that interest, and this book is the result.

—To help those helping others grow. Not only do we want to see people learn about spiritual growth, but we want to provide a tool for those facilitating growth in others. This includes the following:

- Small group leaders
- Bible study teachers
- Disciplers and mentors
- Church growth and recovery leaders
- Counselors
- Pastors

In short, anyone involved in helping another down God's path. So at the end of each chapter you will find tips designed for growth facilitators.

We would like to thank the following people for all their help on this book: our editor, Sandy Vander Zicht; our agent, Sealy Yates; our publisher at Zondervan, Scott Bolinder; and all those who helped us think about these matters over the years.

Whatever your area of interest, we pray God's blessings on your life as you seek him: "But grow in the grace and knowledge of our Lord and Savior Jesus Christ. To him be glory both now and forever! Amen" (2 Peter 3:18).

DR. HENRY CLOUD
DR. JOHN TOWNSEND

PART I

PARADISE LOST

HARDER THAN
I THOUGHT

*I saw that everything I had been learning that helped
people grow was right there in the Bible all along.*

It was my first day on the job in a Christian psychiatric hospital. I
(Henry) was like a kid on Christmas morning. I had been taking
college and seminary classes and reading all that I could get my
hands on about Christian counseling for about four years, and I was
ready to put my knowledge into practice. I showed up at the medical
center in Dallas early that morning all geared up to teach the patients
how to find the life I knew awaited them as soon as they learned the
truth I had been taught.

I went up to the nurse's station and waited for the head nurse to finish writing in a chart so that I could introduce myself. The unit was
bustling with early-morning activity. I saw patients talking with their
doctors and visiting with each other. Nurses were taking patients' vital
signs as other people were beginning groups, completing homework
assignments, getting medications, and having therapy sessions—all the
typical activities of a busy psychiatric unit.

I looked down the hall, and a woman in a pink bathrobe walked out of her room. She extended her arms outward and exclaimed, "I am Mary, Mother of God!"

Now think about this. Here I am, brand new at Christian counseling, and thinking that all I had to do was come in and tell people God loved them, and if they would understand more of what he has said, they would be well. This was what was going on in my mind. But when I heard what this woman said, I thought: *This is going to be harder than I thought.* It was a thought I would have many times in the year to come.

FOUR MODELS OF HOW PEOPLE GROW

IN CHRISTIAN CIRCLES AT the time I was beginning training, there were basically four popular ways of thinking about personal growth: the sin model, the truth model, the experiential model, and the supernatural model.

The sin model said that all problems are a result of one's sin. If you struggled in your marriage or with an emotional problem such as depression, the role of the helper was to find the sin and confront you, urging you to confess, repent, and sin no more. If you did that, you were sure to get better. It was like many three-point sermons I had heard in strong Bible churches:

1. God is good.
2. You're bad.
3. Stop it.

The truth model held that the truth would set you free. If you were not "free," if some area of your life were not working, it must be because you lacked "truth" in your life. So the helper's role was to urge you to learn more verses, memorize more Scripture, and learn more doctrine (particularly your "position in Christ"), and then all of this truth would make its way from your head to your heart and ultimately into your behavior and emotions. Passages that emphasize knowing truth, renewing your mind, and how you "think in your heart" became a new theology of "thinking truth to gain emotional health."

The experiential model held that you had to get to the pain in your life—find the abuse or the hurt—and then somehow "get it out."

Proponents of the more spiritual versions of this model either took the pain to Jesus or took Jesus to the pain. In a kind of emotional archaeology, people would dig up hurts from the past and then seek healing through prayer or imagery or just clearing out the pain. Proponents of this model emphasized Jesus' ability to transcend time; he could be "there" with you in your pain or abuse and could change it.

The supernatural model had many variations. Charismatics sought instant healing and deliverance; others depended on the Holy Spirit to make the change happen as he lived his life through them. Exchanged-life people (those who hold that you just get out of the way so Christ can reproduce his life in you) as well as other very well-grounded students of the spiritual life trusted God to lead them and make changes in them.

While I saw value in all four models—and practiced all four to some degree—it wasn't difficult for me to decide which one made the most sense. After all, I was heavily into theology and studying the Bible, learning doctrine, and knowing everything I could about God and the faith. I have always been a big believer in the authority of the Bible. So I found the most truth in the truth model. I found enormous security in learning about God's plan for life, his sovereignty, my position in him, and the doctrines of forgiveness, justification, and the security of the believer. I believed in the power of the Bible and knew that God's truth could change any life. And I knew that if I could just teach others the same things and encourage them to know the truth as I was learning it, they would find the same kind of growth I had discovered.

Yet, at the medical center I saw people who had walked with God for years and many who knew more about God's truth than I did. These people, laypeople and pastors alike, had been very diligent about prayer, Bible study, and other spiritual disciplines. Nevertheless, they were hurting, and for one reason or another, they had been unable to walk through their valley.

The woman in the pink bathrobe was a missionary who had been called off the field because she was out of touch with reality—out of touch with who she really was and where she was in time. Although the realization I had had with this particular woman came in response to an extreme situation, I had the same realization over and over with hundreds of other more normal clients. To deal with marital, parenting, emotional, and work struggles, people had tried the things they had been taught, and they felt as though these spiritual answers had let them down. And I began to feel the same way. Again the realization hit me: This is going to be harder than I thought.

THE FAILURE OF THE TRUTH MODEL

I WOULD TEACH PEOPLE about God's love, but their depression would not go away. I would teach them about the crucified life, and their addictions would remain. They would focus on their "security in Christ," yet their panic attacks would be unyielding. I was discouraged about the power of "spiritual interventions" as well as my chosen profession. I wasn't finding anything I could feel good about giving my life to for the next forty years.

Don't misunderstand. It wasn't that people weren't getting better and gaining some relief from these methods. They were. I often saw people improve, and prayer, learning Scripture, and repentance were very powerful elements in healing many clinical conditions. But something was missing. The feeling that "there has to be more" nagged at me. Four things specifically bothered me again and again:

1. Spiritual methods didn't solve some problems.
2. Life problems were often "helped" but not "cured"; spiritual interventions often only helped people to cope better.
3. Sincere, righteous, diligent, and mature Christians hit a ceiling in some area of life growth.
4. Spiritual growth grounded in good theology should be helping to solve these problems a lot more than it was.

So I became disillusioned. I even thought about doing something else with my life. I did not see what I had gone into Christian counseling to see—namely, people's lives being transformed. But God seemed to be telling me to keep going, so I did. I went for further training.

Continuing to hang around and work in Christian settings gave me further opportunity to study how people grow. What I had seen *in* the hospital was repeated in the world *outside* the hospital. Sincere Christian people who had been very diligent about spiritual growth often hit an area of life that did not give way to their best spiritual efforts, whether that was prayer, Bible study, Christian service, or just "being good." And these were often very high-functioning people; they were pastors and people in the ministry or in business who had followed Christian methods of growth as best they could, but without success.

I knew there had to be more.

BEING BORN AGAIN, AGAIN

I CONTINUED TO WORK in Christian counseling, and something happened in the next four to five years that turned my world upside down. *I saw people grow past their stuck places.* I saw the things I had gone into the field to see. I saw real change. Instead of seeing depressed people coping better with depression, I saw depressed people become undepressed. Instead of seeing people with eating disorders cope better with their eating disorders, I saw them get over them altogether. Instead of seeing people with relational problems cope better with their relational problems, I saw them grow in their ability to be intimate and make relationships work. I saw processes that actually changed people's lives; I found the "something more" I had been looking for. People were growing past their "ceilings."

Sounds like a formula for happiness, right? After all, it would be great to find out that what you are called to do really works. And in one sense, it was. I was happy to be learning things that were helping people grow. But there was one big problem: What helped people grow did not seem to be what I had been taught was the "Christian" way to grow. What helped people grow involved paths of growth I had never been taught in all of my Christian-growth training or in my own spiritual life. It involved deep transformations of the soul that I had never seen. So I was faced with a dilemma.

It seemed to me that there was the spiritual life, where we learned about God and grew in our relationship to him, and then there was the emotional and relational life, where we learned how to solve real-life problems.

But it made no sense to me that there were answers other than spiritual ones. My theology taught me that God answers all of life's problems. We suffer because we live in a fallen world. God has redeemed the world, and as the Bible says, he has given us everything pertaining to life (2 Peter 1:3). How could there be spiritual growth and then other growth? I thought that all of life is spiritual and that God is involved in every area of life. Didn't it make sense that spiritual growth should be influencing these functional areas of life as well as the spiritual ones?

I did the only thing I knew to do. I went back to the Bible. I had to find the answer to this problem; I could not live a divided life. I could not live the life of a counselor helping people with problems, and then the life of a Christian, with a spiritual life that had value but did not solve the problems for which my clients were coming to me. Therefore I studied the Bible again to find an answer to the guiding question of my life: How does spiritual growth address and solve life's problems?

The only way that I know how to describe what happened at this point is to say that I was born again, again. Here is what happened: *I saw that everything I had been learning that helped people grow was right there in the Bible all along.* All of the processes that had changed peoples' lives were in the pages of Scripture. The Bible talked about the things that helped people grow in relational and emotional areas as well as spiritual ones. I was ecstatic. Not only was the Bible true, but also what was true was in the Bible!

For the first time in years, the world was the way it was supposed to be. God had said that he had answers to our problems, and it was true. I saw it as my mission to communicate what I was learning, so I began to teach workshops in Christian organizations.

About the same time, John Townsend and I began talking through some of the same questions. We had met in graduate school when I volunteered to help new students move in. Strangely, we became friends through our mutual love of rock music. At the time it was really un-Christian to like rock music, so we were both glad to find a friend who did not see the other as pagan. I found out that John was passionate about the same goal as I was (and, like me, was discovering that it was harder than he thought). He had been on a similar quest himself. We wanted to bring all of the issues for which people went to counseling back under the umbrella of spiritual growth, where they belonged. We were not against counseling. People need to get into a context where they can work on their issues in an in-depth way with an experienced counselor. But we had two emphases we cared about deeply.

First, when people came to us for counseling, we wanted them to understand that the issues they were working on were not *growth* issues or *counseling* issues, but *spiritual growth* issues. Spiritual growth, in our mind, was the answer to everything.

Second—and this is by far the bigger emphasis and the one that gets to the heart of this book—we wanted to bring the idea of working on relational and emotional issues back into the mainstream of spiritual growth. Spiritual growth should affect relationship problems, emotional problems, and all other problems of life. There is no such thing as our "spiritual life" and then our "real life." It is all one.

We began to develop resources that show how the Bible and the spiritual life speak to how people grow. We wrote books on how to apply the spiritual growth process to specific life problems.

As John and I shared our insights together, we saw a pattern in the Christian world we wanted to address. For thirty years or so the church had become increasingly interested in personal growth, the resolution of relational or emotional problems, and their integration into church life. In so many places, however, these issues were worked on with *either* spiritual disciplines, such as prayer, Bible study, and repentance, *or* in workshops that focused on the practical aspects of solving those problems. The spiritual and the practical were addressed, but not linked together with a biblical understanding.

We decided to address our concerns in three ways.

First, John and I wanted those responsible for helping people grow to know *how* the spiritual and the practical are linked. We wanted pastors to know, for example, how a small-group ministry that addresses people's emotional problems is an important application of the doctrine of the church, not just a good idea from secular humanism. And we wanted those who were leading divorce recovery workshops, for example, to know the theology behind those practices, not only so they could defend them, but also so they could make sure that what they were doing was truly biblical.

Second, we wanted those who were working with people to be aware of the things that deeply change people's lives. We wanted them to know the processes involved and be able to gain skills in all of them, not just a few. Many do a great job in working with people in the things they have been exposed to, but, like us, have a longing to know more of what the Bible teaches about what makes people grow.

Third, we wanted people who were growing to know not only how to grow, but that their growth was biblical growth. We wanted them to understand that "if you are getting better, it is because you are growing spiritually. You are doing what the Bible says to do." People need not only to grow, but also to understand where that growth fits in to a larger picture of God's plan for them and his plan of redemption. It is good to know that their growth is from him.

ALL GROWTH IS SPIRITUAL GROWTH

THEREFORE, IN THIS BOOK we would like, as best we can, to link the great doctrines of the Bible with how people grow spiritually, emotionally, and relationally. Everyone who is responsible for the growth of others—pastors, lay leaders, small-group leaders, teachers, counselors—is doing not only a spiritual work but also a very practical work. Most of them would like to do that in a biblical way. And we find many are doing so. But many people long for some links between the great doctrines of the faith and the reality of growth. So two of the questions this book will answer are these:

1. What helps people grow?
2. How do those processes fit into our orthodox understanding of spiritual growth and theology?

If we could answer these two questions, we thought that we would be doing a good thing. And then it occurred to us that one more thing is important. If those who want to grow as well as those who help people grow are reading this book, it would be good for both to understand what they each are responsible for. So we also will answer a third question:

3. What are the responsibilities of the one helping others grow (pastor, counselor, group leader), and what are the responsibilities of the ones who are growing?

Our desire is that the book be practical, that it help you understand how to help people grow. And more than practical, we want it to be a book that enlightens you on *how the growth process, at its very core, is theological.*

BACK TO SEMINARY

AS WE THOUGHT ABOUT the best way to write a book on how people grow from a biblical perspective, we remembered how helpful our early roots in systematic theology and doctrine were. In theology, as many of you will remember, the Bible is broken up into categories that teach the major doctrines of the faith. One learns about God, Christ, the Holy Spirit, sin, salvation, and the church, among other topics.

This seemed to be the best way to approach personal growth as well. We will go through the major categories of Christian doctrine, but we will spin them a little differently. We will not try to do an exhaustive study on all the doctrines, but instead we will talk about *how each doctrine applies to personal growth.* We won't even always call them doctrines, but you can rest assured that the major doctrines of the faith are the architecture of this book, as they are the architecture of all that we do. Here are a few examples of some of the major doctrines, disciplines, and themes that we will apply to growth:

- The Bible
- The theology of God
- The person of Christ
- The Holy Spirit
- The role of truth
- The role of grace
- The role of sin and temptation
- The created order
- The role of the Body of Christ (the church)
- Poverty of spirit and brokenheartedness
- Guilt and forgiveness

- Confession
- Discipline and correction
- Obedience and repentance
- Suffering and grief
- The role of time

At the end of this book we hope that you and the ones you help will be encouraged not only that growth can occur in very deep and signif-

---

TIPS FOR GROWERS:

- Examine your preconceptions about growth and your own model of how people grow. Look at the things you have been taught and see if you think they encompass all that the Bible says or that you want out of life.
- Examine your view of how spiritual growth and real life are connected. Is there a disconnect between the life of God and your "real" life? Are there areas of life you don't expect "spiritual growth" to affect? Make a commitment to God to be open to what more he might be able to give you.

TIPS FOR FACILITATORS:

- Make it safe for your growers to examine their preconceptions about how the realities of life and spiritual growth are connected. Find out where they are coming from and what they may have been taught, including their disappointments. Be prepared for the compartmentalization the chapter talks about, and create an expectation for the discovery that spiritual growth can deeply affect all of life.
- Find out what specific problems and realities of life your growers would like spiritual growth to affect. Focus on those and relate them to the discoveries in the following chapters.
- Take a specific inventory, if appropriate, of where they find themselves in the models of growth and also how familiar they are with the list of doctrines and topics. This will help you know where they are in their experience and knowledge and will serve as a good "looking back" point to show them how much they have grown.

---

icant ways, but also that those ways are the path of spiritual growth the Bible lays out for us. To us, that is an exciting journey—one that we relish every day. So join us as we take a look at what the Bible reveals about how people grow.

2

SEEING THE
BIG PICTURE

If we are going to deeply help people on the path to spiritual growth, we have to know where we came from, where we went from there, and where we are heading.

"Okay, how many of you have gone to seminary?" I (Henry) asked the group of professional and lay leaders I was training at a ministry conference. About a third of the hands went up in the large group of people. I wondered how much formal theological training my audience had had, for I did not want them to view my presentation as too simplistic. But as I thought about it, this is exactly why I was presenting it. I wanted to remind everyone, trained and untrained, of how simple the gospel is and how the gospel promotes human growth. I also always need the reminder myself.

Many times, in the process of helping people grow, we forget the big picture of what God is doing in the human race. We get caught up in the particulars of helping someone restore his or her emotional or spiritual health, heal a hurting marriage, or make life work, and we lose sight of the bigger picture.

But there really *is* a big picture. It is the story of God and his creation that was lost, and of his work to restore it to himself. This big picture is very important as we think about entering into the specifics of people's lives; we must not lose sight of what God is doing in the world. As the apostle Paul said, "All this is from God, who reconciled us to himself through Christ and gave us the ministry of reconciliation: that God was reconciling the world to himself in Christ, not counting men's sins against them. And he has committed to us the message of reconciliation" (2 Cor. 5:18–19). This "message of reconciliation" is at the heart of the gospel. In salvation and in the growth process, God is reconciling things, bringing them back to the way they should be.

Many times we forget the way things should be, and we forget what we are trying to accomplish in helping people grow. We focus on the wrong issues. We zero in on the "problem" that someone needs help with, such as depression or intimacy, as though this problem were the main issue. Or we hammer in on a pattern of behavior we think is the sin behind the struggle, and we think that if we can get the person to be good enough (for us), then we have helped him or her.

This thinking happens not only when we help people with personal problems in the counseling arena, but also when we preach, teach, disciple, or encourage people to engage in spiritual disciplines. We speak to problems and "symptoms" or try various religious formulas, and we miss the real life-changing dynamics of this "ministry of reconciliation." After all, it is far easier to focus on a particular problem in someone's life, or to focus on his or her particular way of "missing the mark," than it is to figure out the ways that the Fall is still operative in the person's life and discover a redemptive path that will "reconcile" his or her life. We focus on the symptom and not the root issue.

But the call to address the root issue is exactly the call we have received. We are not just to help others "feel better" or relate better or perform better. And God forbid, we are not just to try to get them to "do better" either. This is the essence of the pharisaical life. But, as Paul said, we have been given this "ministry of reconciliation," and we are to be working with God as he reconciles all things "to himself."

The question then becomes "What are we trying to reconcile?" First, we are obviously trying to get people back into a relationship with God.

Almost everyone who desires to grow as a Christian works on this. But beyond that, we generally see only two other emphases: one is to reconcile people to each other, and the other is to reconcile people to the idea of holiness and pure living. For many, these three emphases constitute the ministry of reconciliation. And, to be sure, great life change and healing are to be had when these three things occur.

But there is more to be done. Spiritual growth is not only about coming back into a relationship with God and each other, and about pursuing a pure life, but it is also about *coming back to life*—the life that God created for people to live. This life of deep relationship, fulfilling work, celebration, and more gives us the life we desire and solves our problems. As Paul says, we are "separated from the life of God" (Eph. 4:18). We must be reconciled to life the way it was created to work.

In the rest of this book we will talk about how we believe this process works. But to get us started, let's take a look at the way God created life to begin with, what happened to that life, and what God has said about getting it back.

In this chapter I would like to look at three big acts in the cosmic drama: Creation, the Fall, and Redemption. If we are going to deeply help people on the path to spiritual growth, we have to know where we came from, where we went from there, and where we are heading. We have to know the answers to three big questions:

1. How was life designed to be lived? What is it supposed to look like?
2. What happened in the Fall to change how life was designed? What is the problem we are trying to fix?
3. What is redemption and what does it do? How do we get there?

ACT ONE: CREATION

Big Idea Number One: God Is the Source

In the beginning there was God, and God created the heavens and the earth. *Everything starts out with God as the Source.* This is point number one in the Bible, and this is point number one in our theology of growth as well. Nothing was in creation before God, and everything that exists came from him. This includes all the "stuff" of life—the resources, the principles, the purposes, the meaning—everything. He is the Source, period.

After making the "stuff," God made humankind; he created Adam and Eve. And he breathed life into them (Gen. 2:7). So as you think about restoring life, remember that life came from God. We all think we know that, but we tend to mean by it merely that God created life from non-life. We understand that living things came from him. But if we are in the process of helping people grow, we have to take the realization deeper than just creation. We have to understand it to mean that it includes his bringing life to dead situations in our lives. God is not only Creator but also re-creator of life. Helping other people becomes an issue of the life they are trying to create and also the life God is trying to create in them. It becomes the theology of how one overcomes a depression or heals a marriage or rescues a failing business career. In other words, "How do I bring this marriage or this business career back to life?"

The Bible's answer to all these questions is "God." There is a Person behind it all who will create and give us life and growth. We will talk more about this later, but it has been our experience that many Christian systems of growth have many principles—even a lot of biblical principles—about God, but little or no God. Remember, God is the source of life. He is the source of growth as well.

Big Idea Number Two: Relationship

The second big idea is that when God created humans, he put them into relationship, first with him and then with each other. God made people for himself and also for one another. We have already seen that Adam depended on a relationship with God for life. But even with that relationship, he needed human connection as well. As God said, "It is not good for the man to be alone" (Gen. 2:18). Man was incomplete with God alone. So we see at the outset that relationship was at the core of the way things were created.

An important aspect of this relationship is that there was no "brokenness" in either Adam and Eve's relationship with God or in their relationship with each other. As the Bible says, "The man and his wife were both naked, and they felt no shame" (v. 25). They were laid bare before one another, and there was neither shame nor hiding. There was no fighting or bickering. There was harmony and vulnerability between the man and the woman. Relationship experts speak of this state as "intimacy," where people are "known" at deep levels. We will talk more about covering and shame later, but one of the aspects of genuine, healthy relatedness is that people don't hide their vulnerability from one another and are not ashamed of who they are before each other. But for now, the important thing to see is that relationship as it was created to be was vulnerable and open, without duplicity and without brokenness or breach.

Big Idea Number Three: God Is the Boss

Relationships were not just tossed in a bowl like a salad. There was an order to them. First of all, in the relationship between God and humans, God was the Boss, the Lord, the Authority. Not only was he the Source—as he had placed the couple there on the earth—he was also in charge. He gave both positive and negative directions. He spelled out what the people could do and enjoy, and what they shouldn't do, and likewise what they would not enjoy if they did. He wanted them to take care of the garden and have a good time. But he did offer a warning about exceeding the role he had given them:

> The LORD God took the man and put him in the Garden of Eden to work it and take care of it. And the LORD God commanded the man, "You are free to eat from any tree in the garden; but you must not eat from the tree of the knowledge of good and evil, for when you eat of it you will surely die" (Gen. 2:15–17).

Adam and Eve's order and position in creation was to take care of the Garden and obey God. It was a high position, but it also had limits. They were to work in the land that God had given them, they were to enjoy it, and they were to submit to God and his limits. Early on, creation involved a "good life" and a "prohibited life" (which is an oxymoron, since the prohibited life was really not life at all, but would result in the absence of life, or death). We were to live life, but to live it in submission to God, or we would not have life at all. Life and submission to God were one and the same.

Thus the Bible begins with the ideas of God as Source, relationship as primary, and God as the authority. As we will see throughout this book, the implications of this theology for how people grow are enormous.

Big Idea Number Four: Roles of God, Roles of People

God is the Boss, and we are to obey. But there is more to this structure than just "who's on top." We were to have distinctly different roles in this order of creation. Let's look at those roles.

1. GOD'S ROLE WAS TO BE THE SOURCE OR PROVIDER; OUR ROLE WAS TO DEPEND ON THE SOURCE. God originated life, and we were given life. Therefore we depended on God for life and for all that we needed. God's role was to provide; our role was to receive. God gave breath; we took it in. God gave the garden; we lived in it and ate from it. God gave us relationship; we received intimacy and relatedness. Our role was designed to be a dependent one. He provides; we depend and trust.

If God is the Creator and we are the creation, we have to depend on him for life and provision. Independence is not an option for us. God existed without us, not vice versa. So the role that we must take in life is not only *for* dependency, but also *against* self-sufficiency. Our role is to recognize our limits and to transcend those limits by looking *outside of ourselves* for life. We are limited creatures, not the Creator, and therefore we are not self-sustaining as God is. Thus we are limited in our ability to live alone, apart from God.

The same limitation applies to our relationship with each other. We are limited in our ability to provide what we need for ourselves without another person to relate to. So self-sufficiency from God is not the only relational limit we have. We also need other people and cannot live independently from them either. The results of trying to live apart from our need for others is disastrous and never works. *We must depend on the outside for love.*

2. GOD'S ROLE WAS TO BE IN CONTROL; OUR ROLE WAS TO YIELD TO GOD'S CONTROL OF THE WORLD AND TO CONTROL OUR SELF. God had done the creating; Adam and Eve could not control that. God had placed them in the garden; they did not control the environment in

which they found themselves. God created the animals and the various trees and their fruits; humans did not. In other words, God was in control of the universe and what happened. He was in charge of the big picture. So many of people's problems come from trying to control things outside of their control, and when they try, they lose control of themselves. It is no wonder that praying "the Serenity Prayer"*—knowing the difference between what we can change and what we cannot—leads to people regaining control of their lives.

So, not only were we dependent on God for these things, but we were not in any particular position to run the universe either. As God said to Job later, "Where were you when I laid the earth's foundation? Tell me, if you understand" (Job 38:4). Our control of the big picture was limited. In fact, we had none. But we did have control of our own behavior, and we were to exercise that responsibly. God's role is to be in control of the big picture, and our role is to be in control of our self and our responsibilities. In short, to maintain "self-control."

3. GOD WAS THE JUDGE OF LIFE; WE WERE TO EXPERIENCE LIFE. Another role that belonged to God was to know good from evil. He had that role and did not want it passed on to humanity. He sat in the judge's chair, and he did not want humans to "know" what he knew about evil. The role of the judge of the universe was already taken. So God commanded Adam and Eve to stay away from the tree of the knowledge of good and evil and to let him be God. We were not to judge, but to live the good life apart from judging it. Imagine that: doing good, enjoying good, and not even thinking that we were "good." Instead of being concerned with "Am I good enough?" we just lived and experienced life.

We were to experience all that God had given us in pleasure, work, and relationship. Live it to all the limits, but don't try to become God and judge it. We were to remain innocent and not even know that we were innocent. God alone was judge, and in essence he said to us, "Don't assume that role."

---

*The "Serenity Prayer" is of uncertain origin although it has been attributed to various persons, including an eighteenth-century theologian named Friedrich Oetinger and the well-known twentieth-century theologian Reinhold Niebuhr. The prayer reads, "God grant me the serenity to accept the things I cannot change, the courage to change the things I can, and the wisdom to know the difference."

4. GOD MADE THE RULES; WE WERE TO OBEY THEM. The roles were clear. God designed life the way it was supposed to be and the rules on how to live it. We were to obey them. God did not consult us on setting up the rules and the design of life. He did not ask us if our ruling over animals was a good idea or not. He did not ask us if he had chosen the right trees to give us to eat or not. He did not ask us if we thought man and woman was a good idea. He did not ask us whether having to work was a good idea or not. He just made the reality and then told us to obey it.

The Whole Package

If you think about it, this was pretty much the life everyone is looking for: a great place to live, the perfect mate, lots of good things to occupy your time, and a job that fits your makeup.

If these things had remained in place, there would be no need for this book. We would not need to think about how people grow or how to overcome life's problems. We would still be in the garden experiencing life as it was designed, and we would not even be aware of what life would look like any other way. But this did not happen. Instead of remaining the innocent crown of creation, we took a great tumble, which brings us to Act Two, where we try to gain independence, take control, become the judge, and make our own rules.

ACT TWO: THE FALL

Reversing the Order

The next act in the cosmic drama happened after Creation. Adam and Eve did not continue in the design that we saw earlier. They decided that God's design was not for them and that they would do things their own way. Specifically, in one fell swoop they reversed the entire created order.

The Tempter came along and got them to undo the entire created order by rebelling against what God had said. He questioned the truth of what God had told them and told them they would not really die if they ate of the fruit from the tree of knowledge of good and evil. In fact, they would do well by rebelling against God. They would become like God himself. In essence, they could ascend the throne. They could live apart from God, have control of their own lives, and have it their own way. They could be to themselves all that God was to have been to them.

But, as we all know, this was a lie. The man and woman did not become like God at all. *Instead, in trying to become God, they became less of themselves.* And this is why we need spiritual growth. We have become less of what we were created to be.

Although they were still human, Adam and Eve "fell" from the perfect state they were created in, and they became less than perfect. They now were in a strange state that the Bible calls "sin" or "death" (Eph. 2:1). To sin means to "miss the mark," and death means to be separated from life, especially "separated from the life of God" (Eph. 4:18). In the Fall, Adam and Eve became separated from Life and missed the mark of all that life was created to be.

In short, they lost it all. They lost themselves, each other, and the life they were created to have. They overturned the entire design. And look at what happened.

1. THEY BECAME INDEPENDENT FROM THE SOURCE. When Adam and Eve ate from the tree, they moved away from God and tried to gain life apart from him. They were trying to become like him, to possess godhood for themselves and gain life outside of their relationship with God. They thought they could get knowledge and wisdom apart from the Source. They no longer needed him and had taken a step away from their role of dependency.

2. THEY LOST THEIR RELATIONSHIPS. In addition to becoming independent from God, they lost their relationship with him as well as with each other. This is what death is. When God said they would die, he meant that they would be separated from him who is life. They lost their relationship and went into a state of what the Bible refers to as "alienation," actually becoming "enemies" of God. As Paul puts it, "Once you were alienated from God and were enemies in your minds because of your evil behavior" (Col. 1:21). The relationship and intimacy they had with their Creator was lost; they had become separated from him.

They also lost their other primary relationship, the one with each other. Instantly they became "naked and ashamed" and covered themselves with fig leaves. Their intimacy and vulnerability had been lost, and their ability to trust each other and have good relationship was lost also. From that point on, we see humans trading trust, fairness, love, and honesty with each other for alienation, unfairness, adversarial relationships, and dishonesty. Love became much harder to find and sustain.

3. THEY REVERSED THE STRUCTURE AND ORDER. In the creation, God was on top, and Adam and Eve answered to his authority. He was the lord, the ruler. But in the Fall, humans tried to usurp that structure and become their own lord. They tried to become "like God." Adam and Eve's goal was to take the place of God in their lives. They wanted to be on the throne, so they rebelled against his authority over them. In short, they became self-sufficient, controlling people who were judgmental and lived by their own rules.

4. THEY REVERSED THE ROLES. Here are the roles as God created them:

God	Humans
God is the Source	We depend on God
God is the Creator	We are the creation and cannot exist unto ourselves
God has control of the world	We have control of ourselves
God was the judge of life	We are to experience life
God designed life and its rules	We obey the rules and live the life God designed

In the Fall, humans tried to reverse this created order in their attempt to become like God. We, as the offspring of Adam and Eve, stopped depending on God and tried to become the source of life for ourselves. We stopped seeing ourselves as creatures and acted as if we could live apart from our Creator, independent of him. We desired to control things we could not control, including each other, and we lost control of ourselves. We tried to become the judge, and we ended up being judgmental instead; we lost our ability to experience life and each other by exercising the very judgment we desired. We stopped obeying God's design and rules and made up our own.

In other words, Adam and Eve tried to become God, and in the process they lost themselves. In trying to become what they could never be—God—they lost their ability to be what only they could be, themselves. And we have been searching for ourselves ever since.

Here is a snapshot of how the roles changed after the Fall:

The Desire	The Result
We are the source	We depend on ourselves
We are the creator	We exist unto ourselves
We have control of the world	We try to control our world and each other, losing control of ourselves
We become the judge of life	We judge ourselves and each other and cease to be able to experience ourselves and each other
We design life and the rules	We live any way we want to

So life began with a particular plan, and this plan was usurped by rebellion against God. And life was lost.

But God did not allow things to stay that way. He had another plan.

ACT THREE: REDEMPTION

GOD IN CHRIST IS "reconciling" all things. He was, and is, bringing it all back to the way it is supposed to be. He redeemed, or got back, his creation and is putting it all back in place. How did he do this?

God paid the price to gain it all back. The holy God required the death penalty for the sin of humankind. And as the Bible tells us, he laid all of this sin upon Jesus (Isa. 53:5–6). This paved the way for God to have it all back and return everything to its rightful order. And this is what redemption does for each and every human who applies it to his or her life. This application of redemption is the process of growth itself: It is the returning of everything to its rightful, "righteous" place before God. *This is why, in our view, to solve life's problems and to grow spiritually are one and the same thing.* Let's look at what the return to the rightful place looks like and what the path of how people grow will look like as well.

Return to the Source

In redemption, we come back to God as the source of life. We retreat from our independence from him and our attempt to be "self-made." We see that to make life work, we must turn to the One who makes life work. As we "seek first the kingdom of God," we see that all the things of life are "added unto us" (see Matt. 6:33). God is the one who adds life.

Also, we find that God is the source of healing and growth. How many self-improvement paths end up in despair until someone finds God? In redemption, we find that God will be the source of healing and growth if we will turn to him. And true growth begins with realizing that we are "poor in spirit" and from this humble position reaching out to God and receiving all that he has for us (Matt. 5:3). When we realize that God is the source, we realize that we are impoverished, and this puts us into a position to receive from him.

So redemption helps us get to the end of our attempt to provide for ourselves. Instead, we turn to God for strength, truth, healing, care, correction, and a whole host of other things that we will see later. But none of these are available to those who are still trying to provide them for themselves.

Return to Relationship

To return to the created order means to get back into relationship with God and with each other. As Jesus said, all of the commandments can be summed up in the two greatest commandments of loving God and loving others (Matt. 22:37–40). Everything in life depends on these two relationships.

Redemption puts us back into those two relationships. First, it reconciles us into a relationship with God through faith and forgiveness and the re-establishing of a connection. Second, redemption brings us back to the rightful restoration of connectedness with others as it stresses love, identification with each other through the Golden Rule, caring for one another, forgiving one another, healing one another, teaching one another, correcting one another, and so on. Without restoration of relationship with each other, we would still be in a state of alienation and not able to have the connections that provide the things we need to live and to grow. Redemption reverses our alienation and isolation from each other and gets us rightly reconnected.

Return to the Order

Redemption is also a surrender to God as Lord. As Jesus said, the first and the greatest commandment is to love God first. It is the commandment that makes all the others work, for it is the one that ensures I am going to do it all his way. And if I do it his way, life will be better. To reverse the Fall means to live under submission to him and to reverse the rebellion against his rulership in my life. So, when I want

---

TIPS FOR GROWERS:

- Gain a perspective of where you and your life issues fit in with the overall story of the Bible and what God is doing in the world. Get past today's struggles, and relate them to the bigger drama in which we all play a part. Ask God to help you see these issues in your life.
- Develop a perspective of your "theological" responsibility. Determine how important it is for you to understand the whole of the Bible and what God is doing.
- Take an inventory of how you relate to the specific issues discussed, such as God as Source, relationship, God as Boss, and the various roles. Determine how those overall ideas relate to your belief system and your life.

TIPS FOR FACILITATORS:

- Determine how you define spiritual growth. Determine if that view fits in or is inclusive of what God is doing in the whole cosmic story. Find where you might be getting lost in one of the points and might be missing the "big picture."
- Figure out how you are going to communicate the "big picture" and how you are going to implement that understanding into your growth environment.
- Look at the specifics of what you are doing and see if all the elements are included in your teaching, small groups, or other experiences of growth. Are all of the elements mentioned—seeing and experiencing God as Source, relationship as primary, God as Boss, and the roles—given a time and place for your "growers"? Determine how you are going to make sure that all of God's created order is addressed in the growth experiences you are providing.

---

to do destructive things, he tells me not to do them. Being redeemed, I listen and obey. And since this is difficult on my own power, redemption gives me two new sources of power to help me in this newfound obedience. I have God as a source of power, and I have others to support me. It is no longer just me and my sinful, rebellious nature. I have a new nature in me, one that is empowered by God to follow God and submit to him, and I have a body of people to help me to do that as well. For the first time since the Fall, I am in a position to obey God and submit to him.

This gives me the power to stop ruining my life. To disobey God is basically to ruin my life, for to disobey him means that I by definition am doing something destructive. If God says to be kind to others and I disobey, I will ruin my relationships. If he says to be honest and responsible and I am a liar and a cheater, I will wreck all that I try to build. So, in redemption, I no longer have to destroy my life by doing things other than God's way. In spiritual growth, we stop doing the "deeds of death" and begin to do the things that lead to life.

Return to the Roles

In the Fall we reversed the roles of humankind and God. We tried to fulfill his roles and then lost our ability to fulfill the ones we were created for. In redemption we reconcile things to the way they were supposed to be.

- We become dependent and give up our independent stance before God and others.
- We give up trying to control things we cannot control and yield to and trust God's control. Also, we regain control of what we were created to control in the first place, which is ourselves. We regain the fruit of "self-control."
- We give up the role of playing judge with ourselves and others by giving up judgmentalism, condemnation, wrath, shaming, and so on so that we are free to experience ourselves and others as we really are. So, by not being God, we are free to be who we truly are and allow others to be who they truly are as well.
- We stop redesigning life and making new rules and instead live the life God designed us to live. For example, God

designed marriage, but humans rewrite the rules to make cohabitation or serial monogamy a new design with disastrous consequences. In redemption we begin to do it God's way.

What Does It Look Like?

SO THAT WAS MY version of Theology 101. What God does in redemption and in our growth is so simple. At the same time, it is complicated and profound. And often we don't even recognize these simple issues as they play out in our lives and relationships. What does it look like in real life to try to be one's own Source? What does it look like to be in control or to be the judge or to make up the rules and change the roles? How does that destroy a life or a marriage? More importantly, how does the Fall's effect change things?

That is the question we want to answer. How does the fall of mankind cause our problems, and how does the redemptive process God set up cause us to grow and resolve life's issues? In the next chapter we will take a look at a real-life situation that illustrates this for us.

3

HOW THE BIG
PICTURE AFFECTS
THE SMALL

*Although they were active in God's work, Rich and
Stephanie were cut off from God as a source of living life
day to day, and they didn't turn to him to help them
resolve their bigger problem—a deteriorating marriage.*

Rich was pastor of one of his denomination's largest churches in
a major metropolitan area. For ten years he had shepherded
enormous growth in this church. Going into a city where
people said "it couldn't be done," he had answered the challenge and
had grown a small church into a body of thousands. "Success" was all
around his ministry, and many others looked to Rich to see how he had
done it. From the outside, all was well.

So I (Henry) was shocked to get the call from the head of Rich's
denomination. He asked if I would see Rich and his wife, Stephanie, in
marriage counseling. I had read articles Rich had written on marriage,
so I was surprised to find out the trouble their relationship was in.

And the trouble was not small. While keeping a full preaching schedule and fulfilling his other duties, Rich had been able to find time to
devote to a growing sexual addiction. At the same time, the distance

between him and his wife was growing. All that was holding the family together was their three kids, for both parents were highly committed to the children.

But this commitment finally was not enough for Stephanie to stay. Since they both had problems with each other, there had been enough blame to go around. But Stephanie's discovering that Rich was acting out sexually was the last straw. She might be a "nag" (as he called her), but infidelity was way over the line. So she decided to separate.

I agreed to see them for an evaluation and to help them make a plan. I did not have the time to take on a new couple, so originally I was going to see them for only a few sessions. In addition, I had seen my fair share of leaders who were popular on the outside but who had little or no relational abilities to make a marriage work, and I did not have the energy to deal with such a leader at that time. They were a lot of work. But I could at least make a good referral.

All of that changed, however, after a few sessions. I did not encounter what I had expected to encounter. Instead, I felt deeply for them and their misery, and I felt much empathy for how hard they had both tried to make their life together work. This couple, who had led many others through discipleship and spiritual growth, were unable to make it work for themselves, and I could tell it was from no lack of effort.

They had become believers in their early twenties, met in the church, committed themselves to ministry, married, and set out on a path they were passionate about. The early days of finding out about God and growing spiritually had been so invigorating that they looked forward to a lifetime of leading others down that same path. The future was going to be bright.

Then, as they poured themselves into the ministry, the skies darkened. They worked hard over the years. They started programs that helped many people. But as time went on, they were not finding the life they were communicating to others. They were becoming disillusioned and distant from each other, and they were anything but happy. They began to feel hypocritical.

Their spiritual life had consisted of standard evangelical fare: prayer, Bible study, spiritual warfare, and worship. They could talk about faith, avoiding sin, and the importance of the Bible. They had diligently walked paths of spiritual growth for twenty-five years. If they were to take an exam on the basic Christian life, they would have passed with flying colors.

What saddened me about all of this was that, although they had for a number of years grown spiritually and helped other people grow, they had ended up in such a mess. They expressed very little real love or affection for each other. Their relationship was anything but a safe haven; in fact, it had gone from a battleground to detached co-existence. And then there was Rich's obvious lack of sexual self-control.

As I got to know them better, I saw their growing disillusionment with the faith they were professionally administering. They had little positive feeling about God anymore and little faith that his ways were going to be the answers to their problems. I could see that they hoped that psychological counseling could do for them what their "spiritual" life had not. It broke my heart to see two people so committed to God feel as if his ways of living hadn't influenced their lives more deeply than they had. They had followed him and had ended up in a miserable place.

In fact, at that point they had little personal connection to God at all. Rich was avoiding God, as the guilt over his behavior was making him feel unacceptable. Stephanie was so into her pain and disappointment that God seemed a million miles away, and she felt that, although she was praying, God had done little to help.

Early on in our counseling sessions, I asked, "Where is God in all of this?"

Rich just shook his head and said, "I don't know."

Stephanie nodded.

"What do you mean?" I asked.

"Well, I don't know where God is," Stephanie said. "I mean, we are still doing all the things we normally do—going to church and all that. We are strong believers, but I don't really know where he is in our mess. I guess beyond praying, I don't really know where he is."

I assured them that it appeared to be God's doing to have them seek counseling. "I think you are going to find that he does have some things to say about what needs to happen," I said.

"I'm a little skeptical, frankly, of all the Christian stuff," Rich said. "I have seen too much and heard it all."

This happened many years ago. And while it is too long a story to tell in detail, the good news is that Rich and Stephanie came back together and are now living the marriage they had always wanted. They are also very fulfilled in their work, and his teaching is thriving.

What their story will reveal, however, is how healing occurs when we do what we talked about in the previous chapter: reconcile life to the way God created it, to the created order. It also gives us some insight into how people can be involved in "spiritual growth" for years without significant areas of their life changing.

A RETURN TO THE CREATED ORDER

WHEN I FIRST MET Rich and Stephanie, they modeled all the things we talked about in the previous chapter under Act Two. The Fall reigned in their lives. They were not overt, rebellious sinners—far from it. But the growth processes they had been involved in—Bible study, prayer, and the rest—had not done enough to reverse the problems of the Fall in their lives. They were not being "reconciled" to the way things were supposed to be. Much biblical growth was missing. To understand what makes reconciliation effective, let's look specifically at what was missing in their lives.

God as Source

Rich and Stephanie had certainly begun their spiritual journey by seeing God as the source of all life. In the early days they lived a moment-by-moment faith and turned to God for everything. Humble learners, they depended on him for everything. But slowly something happened. Without realizing it, they turned away from depending on God as the source of everything they needed toward depending on themselves instead. Subtly, the Spirit was slowly shut out.

In their ministry they had stressed the supernatural aspects of God's work, and they had prayed for many people. But they stopped turning to God and depending on him moment by moment for everything they needed. They did not, for example, leave an argument and ask God to show them what had happened and how to resolve it.

Rich and Stephanie were cut off from God in other ways as well. Rich, for example, was not acting out sexually in a vacuum. He was under huge pressure from his denomination to be a leader, and he feared that he was not going to make it as big as he wanted. He was a visionary, but some leadership weaknesses put him into situations in which he was in over his head. He turned to his wits over and over again, but not to God. He prayed to God for the whole of his work, but not for the little day-to-day things he struggled with. In the pressure of it all, he turned for relief to sexual gratification, when he could have gotten strength, comfort, and answers from God.

In the sexual area, Rich was not leaning on God either. He knew that what he was doing was wrong, but he did not see God as a partner in helping him to rid himself of the behavior. It never occurred to him that he could turn to God to show him the *source* of his behavior and heal him of it. This was to come much later.

So, although they were active in God's work, Rich and Stephanie were cut off from God as a source of living life day to day, and they didn't turn to him to help them resolve their bigger problem—a deteriorating marriage. The best thing they had going for them was that Stephanie was praying for their relationship. She knew they were in trouble, and even though she was not plugged into all that God had for her day to day, she was asking him to heal their marriage. But as a couple, Rich and Stephanie never got down on their knees together as a main strategy to ask God to heal their relationship, believing that he could or would.

Relationship as Primary

I began to see in Rich and Stephanie's lives something that happens all the time in Christian circles. They were connected to a lot of people, but their relationships were not changing them or helping them to grow up. Most of the time they spent with others was in Bible study or prayer. While these things were important, they lacked other relational ingredients that both of them needed for growth. They did not see friendships with others as a key ingredient of the growth process. They saw them as a context for ministry.

The model of growth operating in their lives was one of learning more truths and working hard in ministry. If people were involved in some kind of Christian service, or attended Bible studies or conferences, or taught a group, people assumed they were growing. The amount of service someone did was equated with his or her level of maturity.

This model of growth, however, left out something fundamental: *Rich and Stephanie needed people in their lives to connect with them not only for spiritual fellowship and activities, but also for growth and healing.* We will look into this much more deeply in chapter 7, which deals with the role of the Body of Christ, but suffice it to say here that this couple was not getting the things that the New Testament says we should be getting from each other.

Much of the quarreling in their marriage came from insecurities each had from childhood. Rich had come from a particularly harsh background, and he strongly feared criticism. Whenever Stephanie criticized him, he would react so defensively that nothing good could follow. If he had been getting loved at a very deep level from others in the Body of Christ, these insecurities would have been healed. In addition, he would not have had the shame he had about his leadership weaknesses or his sexual temptations. If there were others with whom he could have shared these parts of himself, he could have been healed (James 5:16), and the marriage crisis very likely never would have happened.

Stephanie had come from a chaotic background, and she feared not being in control. When she felt as if things were spinning out of control, she would get very controlling of those around her, especially of Rich. If she had related deeply with others and had been in a community where she could have shared those fears, she would not have been so controlling of Rich. But her insecurities drove her to be anything but loving with him, and he ran to other women for comfort. He saw her as a source of distress, not companionship.

Deep, abiding, healing relationship was not part of their growth model. Their relationships revolved around studying the Bible and ministering together. What they needed was deep relational healing, the healing power of love from other people that administers God's grace (1 Peter 4:10). This kind of healing community could have saved them as individuals and saved their relationship.

God as Boss

In the big picture, both Rich and Stephanie were committed to God as Lord of their lives. They had given their lives to him and were doing their best to obey his call. There was little doubt in their minds to whom they answered.

The problem was that *they submitted very little to God in their day-to-day internal lives.* In the midst of their disconnection, or in their attitudes toward each other, or in the way that they handled their own stress, they pretty much answered to themselves. They indulged attitudes and patterns they knew to be wrong, if only out of desperation.

It was, however, their submission to "God as Boss" that saved their marriage.

In one of our first meetings, after I had gotten a picture of how bad things really were, I said, "It's time to get honest. I do not think there is enough love between the two of you to make your relationship work. Do you think that's true?"

They both looked stunned. But they both finally nodded. I think they thought that they were admitting the marriage was over and the next call we made would be to the attorneys.

Then I said, "There is not enough love between the two of you to make it work, but I do think that you both love God. You are willing to walk out on each other, but I don't think that either one of you is willing to walk out on God. Is that true? Are you still committed to God, if not to each other?"

"Of course," they said in unison.

"I think that's true as well. And because that's true, I believe that to love God with all your heart, mind, and soul is to obey him and to make the changes he wants you to make inside yourselves. I promise you this: although I don't think you can make these changes for each other, as you do not love each other enough, I do think you can make them for God. If you do what God wants you to do for him, then you will find each other again, and your marriage will be good. But it will have to be an obedient act of faith. You will have to let God be the boss and do what he says."

What I was asking Rich and Stephanie to do was not unlike what God had asked Adam and Eve to do in the Garden of Eden. God had asked Adam and Eve to obey without knowing why or how their obedience would be significant in their lives. Rich and Stephanie did not know how obeying God was going to be significant in their marriage, and they would have to do it on faith.

From that point on, when I asked them to make tough changes, they had a foundation on which to make them. They did it for God. They allowed God to be boss in their lives, and they obeyed him. As a result, their marriage was saved—and so were their lives. God as Boss ultimately made everything else possible.

RESTORING THE ROLES

God as Source, People as Dependent

Rich and Stephanie had drifted away from God as the source of life and into a will-power model. They did not depend on God, and they basically tried to run things themselves. But they had also assumed an independent role in other aspects of life. Remember that we were created finite, not self-sustaining. Therefore we have to look outside of ourselves to get the things we need. This includes depending on God for everything and depending on others for what we cannot give ourselves.

In the beginning of their Christian life, Rich and Stephanie were dependent and growing. Older, wiser people discipled and mentored them. Maybe because they were new believers, they thought it was okay to look to others for help.

But not too long after achieving leadership positions, they did more giving and serving than "depending." They listened to others' problems more than they poured their own hearts out to those who cared about them. They were caught up in the business of all they had to do, and as a result, they failed to carve out time to lean on others and get their own needs met.

And they both had significant needs. As is often the case with leaders, talent and abilities can be confused with maturity. Rich and Stephanie had real unfinished parts of themselves that were in grave need of healing and growth. While each had their own "support system" of people in leadership, most of that support centered on the work they were doing. They did not really have people to nourish their souls and sustain their lives. They did not have anyone to call on when they were afraid, tempted, or hurting.

When they hit the wall in their crisis, this had to change. We designed a system that returned them to their proper human role of dependency. Both of them had to plug in to a small group of people who would be there to meet their needs. We structured it in such a way that it could not be a social club, but rather a support group in which they could share their deepest fears, hurts, and temptations. They could be vulnerable with the areas in their lives and souls that needed healing. Although I was still available to help them, I referred both of them to individual counselors who supported this spiritual change, and Rich joined an addiction support group.

Being involved in this group was a major turning point in returning Rich to a dependent position in life. He learned that it was impossible to stay clean without remaining in a humble, dependent position. This is the way addiction recovery works. He also learned that getting out of the dependent position was getting into a state called "denial." And then he learned that to depend on the group and its members when he was tempted was a new way to live. He did not have to resist temptation by himself, as he had once thought. He could get help, even in the moment, by a phone call, and his support group members would understand. And meeting at regular intervals during the week provided him with the stability and sustenance he did not have within himself.

In the same way, Stephanie depended on her own support system, learning to lean on them and work through her anxieties without bringing them into her marriage and acting them out on Rich. The life that they were getting from outside themselves was beginning to supply them with the resources they needed for their lives and marriage.

In short, dependency saved their marriage.

In the beginning it was difficult for Rich and Stephanie to see that they had to depend not only on God, but also on these support systems. They did not understand this to be the theology of change the New Testament supports. But gradually they came to understand that the Body of Christ is a big part of the delivery system of healing and growth that God has in store for people.

We will talk more about this later in the book, but suffice it to say here, that life in the Body of Christ can only heal to the degree that someone can reclaim the dependent role for which he or she was created. Many people see others as only people to be "given to," or served. They do not see that others are to be "depended upon" as well as given to. The Body of Christ is a "give and receive" entity. We serve and give to others, but we also have to receive from them in a dependent role. For the Body to truly function in a healing way, we all have to reclaim dependency as well as serve. We were created to be dependent, on God and on each other.

God in Control, People Yielding to His Control and Developing Self-Control

When Rich and Stephanie first came to me, they mostly saw themselves as nice people who were hurting. It surprised them one day when I said, "You know, for a couple of nice guys, you two really are control freaks."

"What?" They stared at me.

"You are a couple of control freaks. You really are controlling of each other."

"How do you mean?" They were more intrigued than defensive. They had never seen themselves in that light before.

"Well, when Rich does not perform, you [Stephanie] go into an all-out effort to nag him into doing what you think is needed. That is really controlling. And you [Rich] do all sorts of things to try to appease her and make her feel better so she won't get mad at you. You're trying to control how she feels, and that makes it worse."

"But," Stephanie protested, "if I don't keep after him, nothing will get done."

"And how has it been working, your being in control of him? Are you happy with that system?" I asked. "And, Rich, nice going on controlling Stephanie into a happy wife. She almost left you. Good job."

I was glad they had a sense of humor. Their sheepish smiles let me know we had broken through.

As I mentioned before, Stephanie had come from a chaotic background with parents who were out-of-control addicts and had a high need for structure. Rich was a creative, visionary type, and structure was not his strong suit. (This is a common dynamic in couples where the wife has a high need for structure.) He would do the really important things and let other, less important things slide until he thought they needed to be done. However, Stephanie's panic button would get pushed a lot earlier than Rich's, and then she would move into control mode, nagging him, getting angry with him, and accusing him of not caring for her enough to do the task that was making her crazy.

Rich had his own control dynamic as well. He could not stand for Stephanie to think negatively of him, so he felt the need to control how she viewed him. He could not just let her be displeased with him. He had to "fix her," so he would make promises to calm her down, or argue with her, or make excuses. At first he did not see this as controlling behavior. He thought she was the one with the problem. But gradually he saw how controlling it was to try to make sure that someone is happy all the time.

Stephanie had to get to a point where she gave up her need for structure and let God have control of the chaos. She had to get comfortable with not being able to control Rich and to see how her actions were opposed to the created order itself. The real eye-opener was how out of control of herself she had become in trying to control him.

One day in my office, she lit into him. "Yeah, you bet I was mad at you! You're just so irresponsible, it's ridiculous! You're such a child." She was angry and venomous. "You should have known I needed help with the kids. You should have known. . . . You should have known. . . ." She had a long list of how "bad" he was.

I interrupted. "I think if someone talked to me that way, I would call for an emergency psychiatric team. You sound psychotic."

"What?" She looked stunned.

"Listen to yourself. Listen to your voice. I wish you could see the expression on your face. You look like a witch. It really is ugly. If you could see a video of yourself, you would be embarrassed."

I glanced at Rich, and he had a sheepish but gloating grin on his face. "Stop gloating." I said. "We'll get to you later. But, Stephanie, no one in her right mind would want to sound like you do. Listen to how out of control your anger is."

"Hmm," she said. She went silent. No one else spoke. Stephanie sat there quietly listening to the echo of her poison in the room. We could all hear it, and for the first time Stephanie could see how out of control she had gotten. When I got her to focus on how she sounded, she was surprised she had been reduced to such a maniac. In trying to control Rich, she had lost control of herself.

As Stephanie limited her control behavior with Rich, took her anxiety to her support group, and trusted God to be in control of it all, she calmed down and backed off.

But then something else happened as well. She got in touch with some of the sources of that drive to control and was healed at a deeper level than she thought possible. In the end, she became much less anxious.

Rich was doing his own control work as well. As I mentioned, he was always trying to make her happy. This attempt to control what she thought of him turned out to be tied to a fear that she was going to leave him. So, in effect, he had been trying to control her into thinking things were great so she would stay. We worked on this, and he began to give God control of what happened in their lives and their marriage. He saw that he could not control her into staying. If she wanted to leave him, she would, and there was nothing he could do to stop her. He had to give up control. He had to leave it all in God's hands.

Something incredible happened, as is always the case when we return to the way God created things. When Rich stopped trying to control Stephanie and moved out of feeling as if he was controlled by her, he regained control of himself. When he gave up what he could not control, he regained control of what he was designed to control: himself. Self-control was the fruit of his giving up the God role and regaining the human role of yielding.

Rich was also amazed that by giving up control, he was for the first time seeing victory in controlling his sexual behavior and other important areas of life. He stopped his outbursts toward Stephanie and worked in a more disciplined way. He saw himself regaining the freedom to order his life in the way that he always knew he was supposed to. And as a result of his growing sense of autonomy and self-control, Stephanie trusted him more and tried to control him less. The growing freedom both of them gained by giving up external control and regaining internal control revolutionized their relationship.

God as Judge of Life and People as Experiencing Life

Sometimes in evaluating dynamics of change, we are tempted to point to one issue as more important than any other in someone's healing. When I think of the role of judgment in Rich and Stephanie's lives, I feel this temptation. That is, until I remember how powerful all of the dynamics we have already talked about were. In reality, the Fall was complete, and all of the dynamics are present in every situation.

The book of Genesis does not deal completely with what the "knowledge of good and evil" really means. We know that it has something to do with discerning the effects of sin firsthand. We also know, however, that it has something to do with usurping God's role as the One and Only Judge. Jesus clearly told us that we are not to judge one another. But what does this mean?

Jesus' command "Judge not that you be not judged" (see Matt. 7:1) confuses many Christians because they get it mixed up with evaluation of behavior and other aspects of life. We are to evaluate ourselves, test ourselves, measure each other and ourselves by God's standards, and always be striving to do better. In fact, Paul even tells us that we are to judge one another as believers, and Jesus tells us to confront one another's sin and show each other's faults (1 Cor. 5:12; Gal. 6:1; Matt. 18:15). So what does it mean to "judge not," and what is the difference between this and evaluation?

Ultimately, judging has to do with "playing God." When we judge someone, we do three things. First, we place ourselves above another as if we were his or her God. Second, we condemn another. And third, we create the standard for another. When we evaluate someone, we do not do these three things. First, we do not place ourselves above the other person. Instead, we identify with the person as a fellow sinner and struggler, humbling ourselves as we realize that we are subject to temptation also (Gal. 6:1). Second, we do not condemn another person and damn this person with the guilt, shame, and wrath of the law. We as sinners are just as guilty and do not have that privilege (Rom. 2:3).

Third, we do not make up the standard. We humbly bow to God's standard in evaluating each other and call each other to repentance. Therefore the three elements of helpful evaluation are humility, forgiveness, and correction. None of these entail playing God.

When we do play the role of God, our ability to experience and live life is severely hampered by judgment. Because of the fear of guilt, shame, and condemnation, we are no longer free to be ourselves and own our experience. We deny who we are and hide behind the fig leaf. We will talk more about this in the chapters on acceptance and guilt (chapters 8 and 9 respectively), but suffice it to say here that judgment makes us hide our experience and the truth of what is really going on with us.

Likewise, we can no longer fully experience each other. When we judge one another, we miss knowing the other. This is what was happening with Rich and Stephanie. In the beginning of their relationship, Rich and Stephanie were open and honest with each other and were both deeply touched by the acceptance they experienced. They freely shared their life wounds and failures with each other. The grace and deep knowing of each other was a part of their falling in love.

But now they were so into judging each other in a godlike way that they could no longer experience themselves or each other. And Rich was so caught up in judging his behavior and unable to really share what was going on inside himself with her. The judgment/act out cycle was keeping him stuck, unable to experience his true feelings and to share them with her.

As in any relationship, there is a big difference between accepting a person's failures in outside life versus accepting this person's failures against us. That is, we can accept another person's failures when they don't involve our relationship more readily than when they do involve it. Stephanie could accept Rich's "pre-marriage" foibles, but as time went on, she more and more judged his failures in the marriage. Whereas grace had been bountiful in the early days of their relationship, eventually judgment crowded it out as they failed each other.

When Rich, in his "big picture" style, would forget details important to her, Stephanie would judge him with the full wrath of a god. She would do all three things we mentioned above. She would talk down to him as if she were above this kind of failure herself; she would condemn him and subject him to wrath, shame, and guilt; and she would make up standards that were not even in the Bible. Her own expectations became the standard by which she judged Rich.

As she operated this way, she experienced less and less of who he really was, and he experienced less and less of himself as well. She saw his failures and not his heart. She saw his imperfections and lost out on knowing his fears, vulnerabilities, and passions. And as she judged him, he hid more and more behind a variety of fig leaves. He slowly lost the ability to experience himself with her. He no longer felt his need for her, his love for her, and his own vulnerabilities. He was too busy warding off judgment and condemnation from her to be aware of his own experience and share it with her, which is the key component of intimacy.

Personally, he was also losing more and more of his experience of himself as he judged himself for his sexual sin and other failures. Guilt and condemnation were so strong that he could not experience and know what was going on in his heart. He could not open up to finding out what was driving the behavior, because he felt so "bad" about it. A key component of growth is grace—enough grace to open up and bring things into the light to be healed. Because of shame and hiding, Rich was keeping his feelings, weaknesses, failures, and other problems in the darkness and his slavery was increasing. Judgment was keeping him from knowing himself and being able to bring all of who he was into relationship. The judgment was playing the role of the law in his life, and whenever someone is under the law, sin increases (Rom. 5:20).

Rich was also judging Stephanie—a key component to his acting out sexually as well. He would see her as a "nag" and as less than a supportive wife. When she failed him in ways important to him, he was not a healing, evaluative husband but rather a condemning god. And then when he judged her according to his own standards and condemned her, he felt justified to seek relational and sexual satisfaction elsewhere. He felt entitled to it because Stephanie was such a "bad" partner. He withdrew from her more and more, and knew her less and less.

Playing God the Judge was killing their relationship and also destroying them personally. Healing came when judgment left.

I confronted this aspect of their relationship harder than any, and they both came around.

For example, one day when Stephanie was getting controlling toward Rich and he was reacting to her control, I intervened. "What are you doing?" I asked him. "You sound so judgmental."

"What do you mean? I am just confronting her being so reactive. That's fair."

"It may be fair, but it is fair like a judge in a courtroom sending someone to prison. If you want to be helpful, how about having some grace for her and trying to see past her behavior?"

"What do you mean?"

"Well, stop judging her as the controlling wife—even though she is—and see her as being afraid. Then do what God does when she acts out. He does not condemn her; he connects with her heart."

Rich had to give up judging Stephanie when she was not the all-loving, supportive wife he longed for. (In reality, his expectations were rooted in a lot of dependency and childish needs.) He learned to see her unloving reactions to him as a cry of panic and vulnerability. He found out that she reacted in nonsupportive ways when she feared chaos. Even though she sounded powerful and judgmental, she was really vulnerable and afraid. When he was able to see that, he moved toward her instead of away in judgment.

When Stephanie learned to stop judging Rich for his failures, she began to express her vulnerability and fear. When she did this, he comforted her and actually became more dependable. It is a powerful dynamic when a person gets out from under the control of another. This freedom leads to autonomous functioning and self-control, an essential ingredient of responsibility.

God as Rule Maker, People as Rule Keepers

Rich and Stephanie did not lead godless lives, blatantly redesigning life according to their own rules. They did not go through the Bible rewriting it according to their own wishes as Adam and Eve did at the suggestion of the serpent. But Rich and Stephanie also did not see their violation of God's principles as the way into the mess they were in, nor did they see obeying his principles as the way out. Adam and Eve overtly doubted God's rules and believed the serpent's temptation of "Did God really say that?" or "Surely you will not die" (see Gen. 3:1, 4). Rich and Stephanie did not do that out loud. Their doubting, like ours, was much more subtle and unconscious. But it was deadly nevertheless.

For example, when God said, "Be kind and compassionate to one another, forgiving each other, just as in Christ God forgave you" (Eph. 4:32), Rich and Stephanie did not say that God really didn't say that or that it wasn't really true. Instead they did two things. They ignored the reality that if they disobeyed it, their relationship would die. And when their relationship was dying, they did not seek God's rules and principles as the way to revive their marriage. They did not ask, "Where is our marriage suffering because we are not living in deep obedience to God's ways?"

God has designed life to work in a certain way, and he has designed growth and healing to work in a certain way with very specific precepts. When life is not working, it often means some of his ways are being violated, either willfully by us or by sin done to us. More often than not, we find that we have to discover and align ourselves to God's ways to get out of our suffering.

With regard to many of God's precepts for relationship and for healing, Rich and Stephanie were living as if to say, "Did God really say that?" or "Surely we won't die." For example, they were not bringing their pain, needs, and hurts into the light and into relationship with God and others. They were not showing kindness, acceptance, and empathy to each other. They were ignoring many of God's precepts.

To get well, they had to rediscover the idea that God's design and ways were given to make life work. As Moses said, "The LORD commanded us to obey all these decrees and to fear the LORD our God, so that we might always prosper and be kept alive, as is the case today. And if we are careful to obey all this law before the LORD our God, as he has commanded us, that will be our righteousness" (Deut. 6:24–25).

Initially, Rich had to align himself with the Bible's teaching on returning to weakness. "Blessed are the poor in spirit" became an entirely new way of life for him. He regained his ownership of the power of powerlessness and weakness, and he learned what Paul meant when he said he would see weakness as strength (2 Cor. 12:9–10).

TIPS FOR GROWERS:

- Make the connections between Rich and Stephanie's story and your own life. Figure out, with the help of others, where the "big picture" has broken down and needs to be restored. Look at all the areas mentioned earlier, now that you have a picture of how these areas affect the dynamics of life and relationships.
- See if you are truly seeing God as the source of returning you to life.
- See if your system and practice of growth has relationship as primary. Determine if it sees real relationship with God and others as primary instead of just religious service and/or principles. Figure out if community and relationship is being the delivery system for what God provides.
- Ask yourself and others what role God is playing as the boss, or master, of your life. Find the cracks in your submission to his role as Lord.
- Take a close look at how well you are playing the roles of a human and not a god:
  —Being dependent
  —Having self-control and not being controlling of others and life
  —Experiencing life and others instead of judging yourself and others
  —Obeying the rules instead of writing them

TIPS FOR FACILITATORS:

- Think about how you will create ways to both understand the big picture and connect it with the specific details of the growth issues in people's lives. Teaching theology is important, but relating it to real life is the focus of this book and of the sanctification process.
- Spend time and energy in coming up with ways to have people look at the issues of dependency on God and others, self-control, giving up judging, and obedience to God's life. Make it practical and experiential. Find ways to have people face these issues of real life and make the connection to God and spiritual growth.

When he reclaimed his weakness and saw it as God's design, he felt totally different about being a struggler, and he was able to reach out for help. This was one of the keys to conquering his addictions.

When Stephanie discovered again that God had said that judgment belongs to him (Matt. 1:7) and that she was not to play the judge in

Rich's life, she found a whole new way of being with him. She was able to know him and actually become a source of healing to him. In return, she got the husband she had wanted.

Not many serious Christians overtly say to God that his ways are not to be taken seriously. But when we live more according to our own design than God's, we suffer. We have our own ways of coping with life and its hurts instead of searching for God's principles that will lead us into the light. When Rich and Stephanie dug deeper into God's design for relationship and healing, they found the life they were looking for.

MOVING PAST THE BEGINNING

IN HEBREWS 6:1–3 we find the following statements:

> Therefore let us leave the elementary teachings about Christ and go on to maturity, not laying again the foundation of repentance from acts that lead to death, and of faith in God, instruction about baptisms, the laying on of hands, the resurrection of the dead, and eternal judgment. And God permitting, we will do so.

The writer has gone to a lot of trouble to explain the elementary teachings about Christ, and he wants people to go on from there to maturity, or "completeness" (which is the meaning of maturity in the Greek text). Life works when we are being completed, but completion cannot take place without building on the foundational things.

These verses say that the elementary things are repentance, faith, beginning doctrinal teachings, eternal life, and judgment. The "first things" we have been talking about are, in part, these "elementary principles" of the spiritual life. (This is why we began our discussion of making life work with the simple picture of life the way God designed it and of redemption of that life through faith, repentance, and obedience.)

But to make life work and to help others grow toward a life that works, we must remember two things. First, there are foundational principles without which nothing else works. If we do not live according to the foundations of the faith, we will have nothing secure to build upon. If we do not order *our* growth and the growth of *the ones we minister to* according to these foundational things, we are building on quicksand.

Second, the foundational things are not all there is to growth. There is a process that takes us from the "foundation" to "maturity," or completeness. We must learn and do more than just the elementary principles of the faith. So often we either learn the elementary things and over time forget them (as Rich and Stephanie did) or try to make the elementary things the entire picture of growth.

We contend that in order for "growth that makes life work" to truly happen and for people to come to "completeness," both things must occur. We must order growth according to a firm foundation, and we must also build on the foundation with the rest of God's provision. We must have the basics in place and then go beyond the basics.

It is our strong belief and experience that God has answered our need to grow with a complete system. It has rudimentary elements as well as advanced processes. When taken altogether, when all the different ingredients are used, people do grow. And they grow in profound ways. Lives can be transformed, and the creation can be reconciled.

In the following chapters we will both show God's foundation and how to use it and also "go on to maturity" by looking at the rest of the story beyond the foundation. Join us now as we begin that journey.

PART II

THE MASTER
GARDENER:
THE GOD OF
GROWTH

4

THE GOD
OF GRACE

People must discover that God is for *them and not* against *them.*

It was the spring of my sophomore year at Southern Methodist University, and I (Henry) remember that Sunday afternoon as if it were yesterday. I was at the end of myself.

I had been recruited to play NCAA golf, and I was pursuing my life-long dream of competitive play. With a great deal of hope and excitement I anticipated a college career of playing golf and then making it a profession. Since I had had significant success as a teenage amateur, the future looked bright. But in my freshman year I began to have severe on-again, off-again pain in the tendons of my left hand. I went to many doctors to find out what was causing the pain, but they were stumped.

The next two years I played through the pain, but my game never was the same. It was frustrating to play with half my ability, but I persevered as long as I could with periods of hopeful performance followed by periods of diminished performance. I could see that unless my tendons healed, I was not going to be able to continue. Finally, after two years of hampered play, I decided to quit.

I found myself in one of those times of life when a door has been slammed shut, and I did not see another one to open. I wondered what I was going to do next. I looked at various interests and majors, only to arrive at a deep emptiness and sense of darkness regarding the future.

I had many friends, but a few failed dating relationships had left me wondering if I would ever be able to make a relationship work. *How did one find the right relationship? What did it look like? Was I even the kind of person who could pull that off?* My relational future did not look any more hopeful than my vocational one.

It was in this state of mind and circumstance that I found myself that Sunday afternoon in my room. Thoughts about all the aspects of life that were not working went through my head like a whirlwind. *What will I do? Who will I end up with? How will I find my way in my career and in my relationships? How can I change into a person who is not so depressed and unable to figure all this out?* I didn't have any answers.

As I sat on my bed thinking, I looked up at my bookshelf and noticed a Bible. I had not read the Bible since I had left for college. Although I had read it a lot before then and had had a strong childhood faith, this faith had never been tested in the crucible of despair. Nevertheless, something drew me to that Book, and I picked it off the shelf and randomly opened it. A verse jumped off the page as if it were up in neon lights:

> "But seek first his kingdom and his righteousness, and all these things will be given to you as well" (Matt. 6:33).

This verse indeed hit me like a light. "All these things" was exactly what I was worried about. And I then noticed a verse above that one:

> "Therefore I tell you, do not worry about your life, what you will eat or drink; or about your body, what you will wear. Is not life more important than food, and the body more important than clothes?" (v. 25).

And then the kicker:

> "Therefore do not worry about tomorrow, for tomorrow will worry about itself. Each day has enough trouble of its own" (v. 34).

I was hit hard by a reality that I did not at that moment even understand—by one that has taken years to grasp. But I knew that these words spoke to me. Was it true that all of these things would be given to me if I sought God? What did that mean? I did not even know God provided things for people; I thought he was just someone to talk to and to try to keep happy enough so that he did not hate me. But I was hit hard enough to want to give it a try. After all, I had already tried everything that I knew to do.

So I took a walk. I thought about what I had just read, and I made a decision. I would seek God's righteousness and see if it worked. I would "seek God." But I really didn't know how, so I did the only thing I could think of—I walked into a church. I found the Highland Park Chapel on the SMU campus empty, and I went to the front and said a simple prayer:

"God, I don't even know if you are there. But if you are and you can do this, then show me, and I will do whatever you tell me to do."

Nothing happened. The silence was deafening. Yet I knew that I had come to a crossroads and that if God did not answer, I did not know where I would go from there. I went back to my room, wondering if anything would come of my having reached out to God.

Later the phone rang. It was a fraternity brother. What he said stunned me: "I don't know why I thought of you, but we are starting a Bible study at my apartment, and I wanted to see if you would like to come."

Without explaining why, I simply said, "I'll be there."

I could not believe that my fraternity brother had called, but I could only hope that it was an answer to my prayer. It was the first inkling I had ever had that God might actively meet a person's need. I did not let myself believe it completely, and it was some time before I would—but I do remember seeing a ray of hope. Maybe God really had heard me and was going to help.

I went to that Bible study. It lasted a while. And there I found out that there really is a God who can and will help and that what I had read that day in the Bible had been more true than I ever could have imagined: The answers to life and all of its issues are found in seeking God *and* his righteousness. What I did not know was that both the seeking and the righteousness would be a long process. Nevertheless, he really is there, and he really is the answer.

In this chapter we take a look at how a relationship with God "grows life." We will look at concepts that might seem elementary to some—but ones that we need to be continually reminded of—and at how those concepts help us grow. We hope you will use these realities to take an inventory of the kind of growth you are pursuing for yourself and providing for others. If they are present, we believe that growth cannot help but occur.

A True View of God

ONE OF THE BIGGEST obstacles to growth is our view of God. If we are going to grow in relation to God, then we must know who God is and what he is really like. I have been amazed—in my own life as well as in the lives of others—at how unnatural it is for us to see God as he really is. In fact, one of Jesus' main emphases was to show people how their concept of God was way out of whack. It is probably what led him in part to respond as he did to his disciple Philip's request:

> Philip said, "Lord, show us the Father and that will be enough for us."
> Jesus answered: "Don't you know me, Philip, even after I have been among you such a long time? Anyone who has seen me has seen the Father. How can you say, 'Show us the Father'?" (John 14:8–9).

Jesus had been on a mission to show people what God was really like. "Immanuel"—one of the names given to Jesus—means "God with us." And when Jesus walked the earth, he showed us a very different God from the one we might expect.

People do not grow until they shift from a natural human view of God to a real, biblical view of God. *The first aspect of that shift has to be the shift from a God of law to the God of grace. People must discover that God is for them and not against them.* This is what it means to have a God of grace.

Many Christians misunderstand grace, even those who are helping people grow. Usually people think that grace means forgiveness or the absence of condemnation. And the God of grace is the one who forgives. But while forgiveness is an expression of the grace of God, grace is much bigger than just forgiveness. Theologically, grace is *unmerited favor*. This definition has two important implications:

1. As I have said, favor means that God is for us and not against us. He is on our side and desires good for us and not evil.
2. His favor cannot be earned, and even if it could be, we do not have the means with which to earn it. We cannot merit it. Therefore he will freely give us things we cannot provide for ourselves.

Practically, these two implications of grace undergird the entire growth process. To grow, we need things that we do not have and cannot provide, and we need to have a source of those things who looks favorably upon us and who does things for us for our own good.

The Bible teaches that if we have faith in God, we are in an entire life situation of grace. This contrasts with being in a life situation of law. This is heavy theology for those of us who help people grow in practical ways, such as healing a marriage or helping a depressed college student, but bear with me for a moment, and let's see how the theology of grace intersects life.

Paul contrasts the phrase "under the law" with being "under grace" (see Rom. 6:14–15; Gal. 4:4–5; 5:18). Instead of having a God who is for us and giving us what we need, the law is against us and says we have to earn, through our own performance, what we need. What this means is that life is basically a place where we get what we deserve and we have to be afraid of God (Col. 1:21; Rom. 6:23). To get anywhere, we have to make it all happen ourselves. Law means God is ticked off and says, "Do it yourself." Grace means God is for us and says, "I will help you do it." Grace reverses the law.

When we are under the law—in our natural state—we feel that God is the enemy and that we get what we deserve. We naturally try to "earn" life. We try to do whatever we think will get God to like us or whatever we think will solve our day-to-day problems. Thus, we are trying to "save ourselves" (see Matt. 16:25). We try to get God to not be mad, and we try by our own efforts to grow and resolve our issues. Yet Paul says that this way of living is the exact opposite of living according to faith and grace and that if we choose that law, we end up living out the law in real life (Gal. 3:12). This is not just theology; it is exactly how people end up living out their real-life problems until they grasp the reality of grace. And the result is failure. Watch how it works in a real example.

I recently talked with a minister-friend who was trying to help another friend lose weight. His friend, whom we'll call Dirk, needed to lose about a hundred pounds. Dirk had decided that he needed to make a commitment to God and to his friend to lose the weight, and he was going to go on a diet to that end. Dirk was to be accountable to my friend to check in every few months to see how he was doing with his plan. When Dirk checked in, his weight had gone, not down, but up.

When my friend confronted him about the seriousness of the situation, Dirk responded as someone living under the law: "I know. I've failed. I know this is sin and that is all it is. I know that God is displeased with me, and I feel terrible. I'm such a sinner. This is really bad. I'm such a sinner. I'll ask God for forgiveness, and I'll do better. I'll really commit this time, not only to sticking to a diet, but also to exercising. I know I've done wrong and failed God and you, and I promise to do better."

I told my friend that I could guarantee that Dirk was headed for another failure until he revised his whole belief system. He was still under the law and not in grace. First, he felt that God was angry at him for his failure, and therefore he wallowed in guilt. The last thing that he suspected was that God was for him and ready to give him undeserved favor. He was expecting quite the opposite. Second, he still thought that he could earn his way out of his problem by "trying harder." He was going to, in Jesus' words, "save himself." He was going to try to lose weight by making a deeper commitment.

What would have been a grace response? First, Dirk would see that God was not at all angry with him for his failure and was really more interested in his getting healthy than he was. He would not feel condemned, and he would not wallow in guilt. He would see a God that he could turn to for help in his time of need. As Hebrews 4:16 says, "Let us then approach the throne of grace with confidence, so that we may receive mercy and find grace to help us in our time of need." Grace teaches that God is inclined to help us in our failure and that he sees our inability as a part of reality and he is not mad at our weakness. In fact, he calls it a "blessed" state, our being unable to do what we need to do (Matt. 5:3; 2 Cor. 12:9–10).

Second, Dirk would see that he is unable to lose weight by his own efforts and that he would have come to the end of himself. If he had done this, he would have realized that help was going to have to come from the outside.

I described to my friend what this unmerited favor would look like in losing weight. Dirk would have to reach out. The support, healing, and structure he needed to lose weight would have to be provided from outside himself, not from his own effort. He needed support and encouragement, so he had to agree to submit to a group or a person who could offer that support to the degree he needed it—daily, if necessary. He needed to deal with the pain and stress driving his need to eat compulsively, so he needed a place to process this pain. He needed limits and control on his eating, so he needed a structured program in which he could call several people and ask for help at times of temptation. He could not lose the weight on his own.

When we first look at having a view of God that affects growth, we must begin with grace. But it has to be grace that is more than "forgiveness." This "grace" is God's provision of various resources and tools to help us grow. We do not grow because of "willpower" or "self-effort," but because of God's provision. God offers the help we need (that's grace), and then we have to respond to that provision.

PRACTICAL THEOLOGY

UNDERSTANDING GRACE IS NOT just a theological exercise; it is essential to constructing a system of growth. If you lead a small group in your church, for example, do you wrongly see grace as just the forgiveness and acceptance your groups provide? Some small-group leaders do. They establish accountability groups that do three things: They ask someone if she is living up to the standard, they forgive her if she is not, and then they encourage her to go out and do better. This common evangelical mode of operation is a good picture of the law at work. Give the standard, offer forgiveness for falling short, and then ask for a deeper commitment to do better by trying harder.

Or, do you have a small-group ministry that sees someone as having a "standing in grace," where she is not condemned, even in failure, and where she knows she is unable to stop the behavior just by trying harder? This kind of ministry directs her to places where she can be given what she cannot provide for herself, like support, structure, healing, and help with the appetites driving the behavior, with depending on God's Spirit, and so on.

So, first, make sure that your ministry is one of letting people know over and over again and in a thousand different ways that God is not their enemy, but one who wants to help. This means teaching "no condemnation" (Rom. 8:1), even when someone fails (see chapter 9 on guilt), and teaching what it means to have a "standing in grace" (see Rom. 5:1). It also means understanding God as the source of life, not of rules.

Too often Christians who fail think of God as being mad at them and view him as someone they need to avoid instead of being the One they need to turn to. They are still "under the law" at a deep emotional level. Christians who fail also avoid other Christians, especially when they are feeling bad and guilty in the midst of failure. It is sad to see this dynamic of the law happen in the church and then see the opposite happen in Twelve Step groups. In these recovery groups, people are taught that the very first thing to do when you fail is to call someone in the group and get to a meeting. They are taught to "run to grace," as it were, to turn immediately to their higher power and their support system. The sad part is that this theology is more biblical than what is practiced in many Christian environments, where people in failure run *from* instead of *to* God and the people they need.

Second, make sure that favor is really being shown in ways that help people see they are getting "favors that they don't earn." Make sure they are not subtly providing their own help. Make sure they are doing the kinds of things we suggested earlier for Dirk. He had to find the favors, the grace, and the resources from outside. He could not earn them or create them. What was given was unmerited favors.

Two things must happen in any ministry designed for growth. First, emphasis on the law must be eliminated. The law will make things worse, not better (Rom. 5:20; 7:10). It must be died to (Rom. 7:4; Gal. 2:19). Whenever you see it, you must do everything you can to get people to "die" to it. It destroys any growth God has begun in someone's life. Just as trying to be justified with God by the law alienates people from Christ and makes them fall from grace (Gal. 5:4), trying to grow by being under the law's ways of wrath, condemnation, and trying harder does the same thing. Second, we must help people realize their need for grace.

GETTING TO THE NEED FOR GRACE

GRACE IS ONLY EFFECTIVE when there is a need for it. When we contrasted the law with grace above, we were not saying the law is without value. But we need to make sure we do not confuse the value of the law with the value of grace. The law cannot change people or make them grow. It is "powerless" to do that, as Paul says (Rom. 8:3). But the law does provide awareness of "spiritual death," which people need in order to find the God who seeks them. The law makes us conscious of our need for God (Rom. 3:20; Gal. 3:24). It shows us that we are hopeless to help ourselves.

Likewise, in growth as well as in salvation, to get people to a place of grace, they must experience a need. They must be aware of death. In the example at the beginning of this chapter, I experienced the death of all my dreams and of my ability to find a life that worked. By realizing my inability to live up to the laws of life, I had reached the end of myself. I was a candidate for grace, for unmerited favor. I was a candidate for God to be for me and to give me things that I did not have on my own. I realized that I was "poor in spirit" and in need of God.

Sometimes we must help people get to a "death experience" for grace to take effect and growth to begin. We must let them (and sometimes help them) reach the end of themselves and find out that things are really bad. This is contrary to what many counselors, groups, and teachers do. We live in an age of people wanting to feel good and avoid pain, and sometimes we construct ministries geared to making people feel good about themselves.

John and I once felt very understood and validated when a man told us, "I think I get it. The ministry I used to go to was into winning, and you guys are into losing!" We knew what he was getting at. We had been talking to him about facing the fact that all of his attempts at success and building "self-esteem" were taking him farther away from the answer to his problems. He had to get to a place where he faced how bad things really were; things were not going to get better until he saw that reality. This is what addicts call "hitting bottom." It is the realization that one has come to the end of himself. Some have called it "ego death."

This is the place to which I was trying to bring Rich and Stephanie when I told them to stop fooling themselves by thinking that they had enough love in their marriage to save it. They had to realize that their love had died and that they were powerless to revive that love. They did not have it in them. I needed them to get to this death experience to see that their only hope was to turn to God. When they realized that, they were ready for God's grace. They were ready to turn to God and receive the things he had to offer—things they had never seen or known about before.

In your work with people, you have to be a funeral director, showing them that they need to die not only to the law, but also to themselves. All of their efforts have not worked, and they need to die to trying. To get people to give up is very hard, but it must be done so that they can try God instead.

HELPING OTHERS GET TO THE NEED FOR GRACE

Confrontation

As we continue to think theologically for a moment, remember our saying that although the law is useless as a change agent, it does have value. Its value is to show us our need for grace (Rom. 3:20; Gal. 3:24). For this reason it *is* important that the helping process include law. Do not include law as a way to get better, but *as a way to help people know their need.*

In other words, those who do not know their need must be confronted with their denial. Dirk was in denial of his need for "grace." He still thought he could lose weight on his own. He had not been brought to the end of himself and his ability. I told my friend that he was going to have to "lay down the law" for Dirk. By that, I did not mean he should say, "Go and lose weight."

What I did mean was that he should say, "You are failing in your attempts to change, and you had better realize that you will not lose weight by trying harder. You need help." This would cut through Dirk's denial and get him to the end of himself.

Confrontation is an important tool to get someone to see his inability to change and to see his need for help. Many people are too soft-hearted; they give *encouragement* to someone who needs *discouragement* instead. To encourage a powerless person to try harder is one of the worst things you could possibly do. The best thing you can do is to discourage him from believing that he can do it on his own.

Another use of the law is to show a person that she is not living up to a standard. We will talk about the role of the truth and confrontation in chapter 17, but it is important to understand in this context that people will never get to the end of themselves if they do not see themselves as failing.

One night at a dinner with a group of people, a single friend of mine was telling us about her dating life and how God was not providing her with a mate. Since I knew this young woman, I thought her singleness had much more to do with the way she interacted with people than God's lack of provision for her. When I heard her blame it on God, I had to intervene, at least to defend God's name!

"Why do you think God is keeping you single?" I asked.

"Well, he has not chosen to bring someone to me yet. And he has not given me the feelings necessary to marry the ones he has brought."

I almost lost it on that one. "What do you mean 'given you the feelings'? Whose feelings are they, yours or God's?"

"What do you mean?"

"Well, they are your feelings, not God's. Why don't you say that 'you have not had the feelings' instead of blaming the lack of feelings on God? Maybe you have not allowed yourself to have them, or something else in you gets in the way of having them. Or the men who have come into your life are not your 'type' or something. But don't blame your feelings on God."

"I believe God has control of my life," she replied. "If he wanted me to have the feelings for them, I would."

"I believe that God is trying to help you gain control of your life, that your feelings about men are out of control, and that God would love to help you change them if you would stop blaming him and see yourself as having something to do with the problem."

"What are you saying?" she asked indignantly. The other six people at the table listened to our exchange with a combination of discomfort and attention.

"I am saying that I think you have growth issues to deal with and that those have a lot more to do with why you are not dating or married than with God's keeping you stuck. In fact, I think that I know what some of those issues are and that I could get you dating seriously in one year."

She looked at me as if I were crazy. "What do you mean?"

"What I mean is that if you will do whatever I tell you to do, I will have you dating in one year. Guaranteed. But you have to do whatever I tell you. I demand total obedience. If you don't do what I say, I will quit. I won't ask you to do anything illegal, unethical, or immoral. But you have to do whatever I say."

She was not about to be beaten in a challenge in front of her friends, so she said, "Okay, Smarty Pants. Let's do it!"

The ending of the story is that in six months—not one year—she was in a significant relationship after not having had a date in three years.

What had to happen for her to grow was threefold, and all three things had to do with the law. First, I had to get her to admit she was failing. She did not see herself as not meeting a standard, but she saw God as the one failing her. In her mind, he was not providing a significant relationship for her. But in reality, she was not relating in ways that would produce significant relationships. I had to show her the patterns of relating in which she was failing. So, first, to get her to start to grow, I had to get her to see that she had a problem, not God. She was "missing the mark." I got her to keep a log of how many times a month she was even in a place where she could meet someone new as opposed to seeing the same people over and over again. The answer was zero.

Later, as we worked on her relationships and I got her to be active in meeting men, she found that she was a lot worse off than she had thought. She found that she had many dependency fears she had been warding off by blaming God. As she got closer to some men, she discovered she had huge fears of rejection that had led her into her protective "spiritual" state and taken her out of the dating game. The more we worked, the more standards she found she had failed. This "law," or set of standards, I was judging her by was helping her see that *she* had failed, not God. This bad news was the best news she could have heard, for it led her to some issues that she could take steps to resolve, like her passivity in the social arena.

Second, she had to see that she did not know how to make it better. As we talked about it, and she saw that blaming God was not the answer, she also saw that she didn't have a clue what her issues were, much less how to resolve them. She needed outside help. When she stopped blaming God, she was left with the state of her dating life. And when she saw that, she went into despair. She had little hope in herself; she did not know what to do. She realized that she needed help from outside herself. She realized that she needed "grace." This is one of the most important things the law can do for us. When we are convicted and sentenced to our own realities, then we realize that we need to be rescued.

Third, she had to find out what to do from there. What was she missing? What truths did she need to learn and follow? What principles of relationship were going to help her "prosper"? (Deut. 6:24). One of the important roles of the law is to show us the truth. She needed God's truths and the knowledge of how to put them into practice. Although the Bible has few specific verses on dating, it has many principles that ultimately led to her growing out of her stagnant dating situation.

Reality Consequences and Discipline

Allowing people to suffer logical consequences is another way of getting them to realize their need for grace. Ideally, we can do that by confronting them as I did my friend above. When I confronted her, she had to face the reality of her dating life. But sometimes people cannot (or do not) hear the truth of confrontation, and they remain stuck. At those times we often have to allow reality to touch their lives.

The Bible reveals this consistent pattern. God would try to help the Israelites, talk to them, and give them resources and promises in the hope that they would turn to him. When they did not, he would send prophets with severe warnings. If this confrontation did the trick, things would be better. But sometimes the Israelites would not listen to the prophets, and then it was time for consequences. To discipline Israel, God would send a flood or a plague or, often, an army from a neighboring country. He used many methods to persuade them to see the reality of their ways and its consequences.

Too often in the church, we protect people from the harsh realities of logical consequences that would force them to see their need for grace and what it can provide. Either we feel sorry for them and bail them out, or we fear them and kowtow to them. The Bible warns against both: "'Do not pervert justice; do not show partiality to the poor or favoritism to the great, but judge your neighbor fairly" (Lev. 19:15). No matter what the person's plight, we must help him face the truth. And sometimes that means letting him deal with harsh realities.

This chapter's main topic is not discipline and correction; we cover these issues in greater detail in chapter 13. But in this chapter on the God of grace, it is important to see that sometimes our "helping" may keep people from experiencing the tough realities that will ultimately lead them to the grace they need. It is the old idea of letting people "hit bottom." It may mean letting them lose a job, or lose a relationship, or lose membership in a group or a fellowship. God uses reality consequences in our lives to get us to see our need for him and what he has to offer us. Those of us in positions of helping others grow must have the courage to allow people to experience those consequences, or else we may be keeping them from grace (see chapter 11).

The story of the prodigal son in Luke 15 is an example. The son asked his father for his share of the estate. Certainly the father could have nagged, made offers, or become angry to persuade his younger son to change his mind. Who knows—maybe he did, but we are not given that information. What we do know is that the father allowed his son to choose and then to experience the consequences. The son, after receiving his share of the estate, set off for a distant country, where he squandered his wealth in wild living. After his money was gone, he was forced to feed pigs for a living.

These consequences of the son's own choices turned him around, helped him see his need, and put him in a position where he could receive the things his father had to offer. This shows that the consequences that lead to grace are an act of grace in themselves (Heb. 12:4–11; James 1:2–4). The pigsty was a correcting experience, thus a gift of grace.

TIPS FOR GROWERS:

- Examine your view of God. Do you see him as for you or against you? In what ways might you see him as both?
- See where are you gaining "unmerited favor" or, if you are not, where you are going to get it.
- Determine what favor you need God to provide for you.
- Take a look at what standards could lead you to the reality of your situation and your need for God and growth. Be open to them as you see them.
- Find the confrontation you need and the people who will give you reality consequences. Take an inventory of the reality consequences you already face.

TIPS FOR FACILITATORS:

- Put forth grace in everything you do. Communicate that God is for your people and not against them. Teach them what it means to need favor and not law.
- Teach that it is a good thing to get to the end of oneself. Then God has an opportunity to work. Teach that no one can earn, merit, or provide for oneself what one needs to grow.
- Figure out what favor is appropriate for the kind of growth experiences you are providing and make sure that it is in place. Remember that the role of a shepherd or facilitator is not necessarily to provide all the favor, but to see that it is provided. Use the Body.
- Decide what standards, confrontation, and reality are appropriate for the various settings you are facilitating, and make sure they are provided. Make sure they are communicated with grace. Remember that community is not helpful if it shields people from the realities of life and the standards they should be living up to. The trick is to bring those standards to them in ways that lead them to grace, not take them farther away from it.

So, in thinking about growth, leave room for people to fail. Sometimes you may even have to be the agent of failure, as in kicking someone out of a group or firing a staff member. Reality consequences are not all bad. They are part of God's plan.

Putting Grace and Truth Together

In summary, we have seen how a relationship with God affects growth. First, for growth that makes life work to occur, we have to seek God. We heard Jesus' words to seek first the kingdom of God and his righteousness so that life could be added to us. Spiritual growth is the foundation of any kind of "life building."

Second, we need to realize that God is the God of grace. In desiring to find God, we often do not have a true view of him. We sometimes see him as a religious standard that we must live up to, and we fail to see his true acceptance of us for where we are. Or, more commonly in the evangelical world, although we see God as a God of grace, the view of grace that guides us is basically one of forgiveness. Grace that leads to true life transformation is one of unmerited favor—the understanding that God is truly for us and that he will provide what we cannot provide for ourselves. Grace means that we receive the gifts we need for growth to occur. We don't "willpower" our way there.

Third, grace does not come easily, and we do not naturally recognize it. It only comes in the classroom of God's law. We encounter the law of God either through realizing our failure to attain his standard and thus our need for his grace, or through experiencing the consequences of having our lives fall short of the standard. Either way, we die to self. We must realize that we have failed and that we have no hope of reaching the life we desire in and of ourselves. After that, the law of God guides us, empowered by grace, to structure life as it was created to be. His principles are a "lamp unto our feet."

5

JESUS:
OUR EXAMPLE
FOR LIVING

Jesus' life and death provide important keys to the spiritual growth process.

For the longest time in my life, I (John) didn't know where to put Jesus. As a child I can remember seeing God the Father as someone who could help me. I would ask him for help with things such as having good grades, getting me out of trouble with my parents, and having my team win in baseball. I would pray "in Jesus' name," as I had been taught. And that was about it for Jesus and me.

In college I grew a great deal in my faith, especially faith in God's grace and providence for me. I learned about the Holy Spirit's ongoing ministry in my heart, and I studied Christ's sacrifice for my sins, giving me a righteous standing before God. But though I saw the Father and Spirit's roles in my ongoing spiritual growth, I didn't realize what the Son did beyond salvation. I did learn about abiding in Christ (John 14–15), which helped me see I needed an ongoing relationship with Jesus; however, that was about it.

Some people told me how profoundly meaningful their walk with Jesus was, others talked about his power, and still others mentioned having deep spiritual cleansings done in their lives "in Jesus' name." I wanted to delve more into my relationship with Jesus as these people had, but conceptually there was little they attributed to Jesus I couldn't ascribe to the Father and Spirit.

What I didn't want, however, was to make up stuff. I didn't want to manufacture something about Jesus' work in my life so that I would feel more whole. I felt strongly that if I did, I would never recognize him when he did show up in my life. So Jesus stayed somewhat unknown for me.

Then, during my graduate studies in theology and psychology, I looked at the unique role Jesus plays in the spiritual growth process. As I did, I realized I could not imagine genuine spiritual maturity without the contributions of Jesus. That is the subject of this chapter. We will look at several specific areas in which Jesus helps people grow.

THE ONGOING RELATIONSHIP

FIRST, JESUS IS "WITH" us. Jesus has gone to be with the Father, but he also lives in the heart of each believer: "And surely I am with you always, to the very end of the age" (Matt. 28:20). By faith, he lives inside us: "so that Christ may dwell in your hearts through faith" (Eph. 3:17). This means we have an ongoing, sustaining relationship with him. In some mysterious way, Jesus and the Holy Spirit indwell us. (In the next chapter we look deeper at the Spirit's presence within us.)

In the Old Testament, God resided in the temple. Now *people* are the temple (1 Cor. 3:16). With Jesus we have a personal, living connection with God. This is a tremendous source of good things people need for spiritual growth. Here is a brief list:

- Life (John 15:4)
- Good fruit (John 15:5)
- Answers to prayer (John 15:7)
- Power (2 Cor. 12:9)
- Peace (Col. 3:15)

People need two sorts of relationships to grow: the divine and the human. If you are helping people grow, make sure you look for how connected they are to the indwelling Christ. No matter what the issue or struggle, relatedness must come first. It is as important as checking the gas gauge before you leave on a car trip.

Much of this process involves learning to become aware of Jesus. Our natural bent is to use only our five senses to experience this world and its realities. However, the Bible teaches that the spiritual reality is much more than a concept or idea; it is just as real as the physical world. Your growers need to know that being aware, responsive, and dependent on Jesus is a daily part of life. For example, as over the years I have become more "rooted and built up in him" (Col. 2:7), I have found myself often asking Jesus for help or wisdom in some situation. The response is varied. Sometimes I will get an inner urging to do or stop doing something. Sometimes a passage from the Gospels will come to mind that reflects Jesus' teaching on the issue I'm dealing with.

If you are a growth facilitator, you will often find that people who have been hurt in relationships may have difficulty trusting God or anyone else. Others may have become emotionally detached to the point they have become self-sufficient and insular. For them, an indwelling Presence may be meaningless. They are glad Jesus is there, but don't know what to do with him. Still others may even see him as dangerous, because they view all relationships that way.

Help growers see that God is good, that Jesus lives in the believer's heart, and that trusting relationship brings good things.

IDENTIFICATION

ANOTHER WAY JESUS IS essential to spiritual growth is called *identification*. He serves as a model that can teach and comfort us in many growth situations. Biblical principles tell us how people grow; Jesus shows us. He gives us a personal and human example we can see and internalize within our hearts. We have a living, breathing picture of how God wants us to live. The bulk of this chapter will show those aspects of identification with Jesus that apply to people's growth.

RESPONSE TO SUFFERING

ONE OF THE MOST important tasks of spiritual growth is to understand how to suffer. Although suffering is negative, it is part of life—especially the growth part of life. No one grows to maturity who does not understand suffering. (We say more about suffering in chapter 11.) For example, dealing with our hurts, sins, and failures involves pain, both within us and in our relationships with others.

Many times people see Jesus' example as a way to avoid suffering. They focus on his power, glory, and majesty in his role as King of kings (Rev. 19:16). They identify with his victory over sin and darkness.

At the same time, even though we are "in Christ" and we know that everything will ultimately be okay, here on earth today things aren't yet okay. Remember that Israel was given the Promised Land, but they had to wait forty years to possess it. In the same way, we have much work to do before we celebrate the final victory.

NORMALIZE SUFFERING. Jesus shows us much about how to respond to suffering. Most important is that he did not avoid suffering, but saw it as part of the growth path: "Although he was a son, he learned obedience from what he suffered" (Heb. 5:8).

We naturally wish to avoid pain and discomfort. Yet, if you are a growth facilitator, you will need to require people to normalize the suffering aspects of the process. For example, when a woman who has never looked at her past hurts explores her character roots, she may find a lot of pain there. Remembering injurious relationships and experiences and bringing these to the light of vulnerable relationships brings up the pain again, often intensely. She may want to change the subject, or minimize what has happened to her. It may be helpful for her to see how Jesus resolutely moved toward the pain ahead for him (Luke 9:51).

Jesus turns our natural bents upside down. In the world's view, the path to glory is being "on top of it" or "having it all together." In Jesus' way, the path to glory is experiencing pain and suffering: "Now if we are children, then we are heirs—heirs of God and co-heirs with Christ, if indeed we share in his sufferings in order that we may also share in his glory" (Rom. 8:17).

CHOOSE GODLY SUFFERING. Sometimes people have difficulty understanding when they should suffer and when they should avoid it. A person in a difficult relationship may endure abuse, thinking that this is part of the path of suffering when actually this suffering can injure her soul and also help her abuser stay immature. Some suffering needs to be avoided (Prov. 22:3; also see chapter 8 in *Hiding from Love*).

Conversely, some people will avoid good pain. The woman mentioned above may keep herself from confronting the hurtful person in her life because she is afraid of conflict or abandonment. In a sense, her fears may cause her to choose the wide gate instead of the narrow one (Matt. 7:13–14). For example, she might avoid the person rather than calling her and asking if they can meet to discuss the problem they are having. Avoidance of conflict or compliance with others are often less difficult than working through issues.

Jesus is a wonderful example of embracing needful suffering and rejecting that which was not. He understood that pain must have a purpose. He chose the path of the Cross because of the fruit it would bear for all of us. Yet he refused to enter suffering that would be inappropriate to his purposes. He escaped, for example, the grasp of those who opposed his teaching, for he knew it was not yet his time (John 10:39).

BE HUMBLE. Not only do growers need to learn from their pain directly and learn how to distinguish godly from ungodly suffering, but they also need to learn how to bear suffering themselves. One way to bear necessary pain is to be humble. If we are humble, we will be willing to allow something uncomfortable to happen to us *if* it is the right thing to do. This is because part of being humble means not perceiving ourselves to have rights or privileges that we do not possess. We certainly do not have to pretend to enjoy the pain, and we should bring others into our experience so they can comfort us in it. But humility is a necessary character trait for bearing pain.

The opposite of humility is grandiosity, a defense mechanism that prevents us from suffering rightly. There are several types of grandiosity. Some people deny their experience, trying to be strong and saying, "This doesn't hurt me." Others insist their righteousness should prevent their suffering, saying, "Why me? I've been good." Still others attempt to avoid suffering altogether, saying, "Because this is uncomfortable, I will not experience it"; they thwart suffering's growth benefits.

Jesus' example is so instructive here. He could have rightfully claimed his divinity and avoided all he went through. Yet he "did not consider equality with God something to be grasped, but made himself nothing, taking the very nature of a servant, being made in human likeness" (Phil. 2:6–7). Ultimately, he humbled himself and underwent pain he didn't bring on himself. This is a wonderful example for people in your growth groups. It will help them see the value of humility in suffering rightly.

DEPEND ON GOD AND PEOPLE. While we must endure the work of growth, we can't bear it alone. To be comforted, understood, and strengthened, we need God and people with us. Jesus was dependent on God and people. He taught us to be like him and ask God for our daily bread (Matt. 6:11). Yet he also asked his closest friends to be present with him in his dark hours (Matt. 26:38). We can't bear life on our own, nor were we created to. Jesus did not model independence, but dependence.

A woman I know who had major overeating problems finally came to terms with her inability to stop eating. One of the things that helped her most was the covenant she made with several people she trusted; she had permission to call them whenever she felt the urge to eat after a bad day at work, a fight with her husband, or a conflict with her kids. Whatever the cause and whatever the time of day or night, she could contact one of these people. For several months she phoned these faithful people several times a day, sometimes on short calls, sometimes on long ones. They stuck with her, listening, encouraging, and connecting. Finally, she had internalized enough protection and restoration that her urges to overeat became much more manageable. This is one way she identified with Christ's stance on dependency.

RESPONSE TO BEING SINNED AGAINST

A SPECIFIC TYPE OF suffering growers must endure is suffering caused by being sinned against. We bring a great deal of pain to our lives by our own transgressions (sins by us); at the same time, others inflict much injury on us (sins against us). If you have spent time helping others grow spiritually, you are well aware of how the sins of others greatly impact the grower's life. It is an important part of the growth process and one for which Jesus' life is a helpful example.

We have natural responses to being hurt that are part of our fallenness. We do not always respond righteously to stresses in our lives, in the same way that Adam did not, both in succumbing to temptation, then in attempting to avoid responsibility for it (Gen. 3:9–12). These responses come easily to us, but do not help us grow; however, God provides a better way in Jesus, the last Adam, whose life gives us life: "So it is written: 'The first man Adam became a living being'; the last Adam, a life-giving spirit" (1 Cor. 15:45). Jesus, as the New Adam, provides a better way to look at injury that helps us grow closer to God and also grow in character. Here are some tools for the suffering caused by others.

1. ACKNOWLEDGE THE WOUND, DON'T DENY IT. When we are hurt emotionally, we tend to deny it. For example, an unloving wife may wound a husband's heart, but he may not want to appear weak or vulnerable. Or he may think he is being overly sensitive. Or he may think that admitting his hurt is being disloyal or mean to his wife. So he shrugs off the wound. However, he is living a lie. Just saying something doesn't hurt us doesn't make it go away, and the wounded heart stays injured.

Jesus modeled a different way. He never pretended hurtful things didn't hurt. In fact, he spoke to his disciples about his future suffering, which upset them greatly. They were horrified he was being so "negative" (Matt. 16:21–22)! Yet he knew they needed to understand the suffering he was to go through. If he had denied his pain, they (and we) would not have understood the cost of his sacrifice.

Jesus promises his followers an inheritance with him if we don't deny suffering, but share it with him: "Now if we are children, then we are heirs—heirs of God and co-heirs with Christ, if indeed we share in his sufferings in order that we may also share in his glory" (Rom. 8:17). Growth facilitators need to help people open up about the realities of their past and present hurts. Jesus didn't pretend everything was okay when it wasn't.

2. STAY CONNECTED, DON'T ISOLATE. We tend to withdraw from relationship when we are hurt. Some people are afraid of their dependencies on others. Others feel guilty about burdening friends with their

problems. Still others try to be self-sufficient. None of these responses helps a person heal and grow.

Jesus stayed connected when he was hurt. In the garden of Gethsemane, during one of his darkest hours of preparing for the ultimate injury, he asked for support from his friends: "Then he said to them, 'My soul is overwhelmed with sorrow to the point of death. Stay here and keep watch with me'" (Matt. 26:38). Teach his example to those you are helping grow. Help them see that Jesus' way is not the way of detachment, but of emotional dependency on God and others.

3. LOVE AND FORGIVE, DON'T RETALIATE. People also "naturally" lash back when they are hurt, and they desire revenge on the one who hurt them. Like little kids, they will harbor murderous intentions and attempt to retaliate. For example, a woman who has been betrayed by a man she is dating may then do the same to him. Perhaps they had agreed to an exclusive relationship, deepening their commitment and trust. Then she found that he was seeing someone else. She might in turn date another person also, thinking, *That will show him how it feels.* The problem with this rationalization is that while he certainly needs to know how he hurts others, retaliation is more likely to help him justify even more his own bad behavior.

We are by nature a people who have the Law of Retaliation in our hearts: an eye for eye and a tooth for tooth (Ex. 21:24). But Jesus taught and lived a greater principle: "I tell you, Do not resist an evil person. If someone strikes you on the right cheek, turn to him the other also" (Matt. 5:39). His first response was not to extract revenge, but to give the other person a chance. This is quite "unnatural"; in fact, it is a work of God in someone's life to not retaliate against one who has wounded him or her.

Jesus' teaching on this subject confuses many people. They wonder if he is saying we should never protect ourselves from hurt. It is an important question. However, remember these two facts: (1) Jesus' words are true. We are called not to take revenge, but to make peace, which is a higher calling; and (2) the passage needs to be understood in the light of all of Scripture, not by itself. Other passages teach us to protect ourselves also (Prov. 22:3). Thus we need to look at each situation individually and work out how much to protect ourselves without vengeance.

4. PRACTICE SELF-CONTROL, DON'T BE CONTROLLED. Our initial response to being hurt is that we lose self-control. Our getting hurt in a relationship is proof of how little control we have over others in the first place. Many times we transfer power onto the person who has hurt us, which makes things worse.

For example, a man may realize his parents have been emotionally unresponsive to him all his life. He may see how this unresponsiveness has made his relational life difficult, as he has not been connected enough to his inner self to connect to others. As he understands this, he may then become obsessed with trying to get his parents to see what they did to him, or to get them to apologize, or even to get them to re-parent him and provide for him what they did not when he was a boy.

Good relationships do involve confronting, forgiving, and reconciling. However, some people make the injured person the focus of their lives, letting the other person control them. In this way they put their hearts under the power of the very ones who injured them.

Jesus handled this in a different way. When others hurt him, he did not allow it to change his values or direction in life. This trait is called self-control. Jesus didn't give control of his life to those who injured him. He completed the tasks the Father had given him, and the last words he uttered before he died from his suffering were "It is finished" (John 19:30). He was in charge of his life to the end.

If you are a growth facilitator, help your people to develop self-control even as they work on injuries by others. While they need to confess and process pain, they also need to take back ownership of their lives. One of the most important tasks they will have is to repair their injuries. Some, like the man above, may need to learn to receive emotional warmth from others. Others may need to learn how to be separate. Still others may need to learn how to give up self-critical and perfectionistic ways. These are all forms of self-control rather than staying stuck and being controlled by the hurts of others.

AUTHORITY OVER EVIL

OUR OWN EVIL TENDENCIES, those of others, and the influence of the Devil himself can be major stumbling blocks to the growth process.

However, we can identify with Jesus in his authority over evil. God has placed all things under Jesus' feet (Eph. 1:22), and that includes authority over sin and evil. In fact, Jesus even delegated authority to his disciples to drive out evil spirits (Matt. 10:1). In the same way, growers can take the delegated authority Jesus gives over evil and apply it to their own lives and growth paths. Here are some of the aspects of his authority.

ZERO TOLERANCE. Jesus did not deny evil's existence. He knew about sin. Yet he did not approve of sin; he acted against it. Growers can take the same strong stance against evil: "How shall we who died to sin still live in it?" (Rom. 6:2 NASB) This zero tolerance position can take place in many forms. For example, I know a man who did not see his drinking as a problem. He thought his problem was a controlling and perfectionistic wife. However, as he honestly looked at the life of Jesus in the Gospels, he realized he had crossed the line into evil with his drinking. He took a zero tolerance stance toward his habit and entered the process of growth and healing.

SPIRITUAL WARFARE. Evil exists in the form of a personal Devil. Jesus has overcome Satan's power by his death, and he has destroyed the Devil's work (1 John 3:8). Yet the Devil continues his attacks against people for now. There truly is a spiritual battle going on (Eph. 6:12). It can be in the form of the presence of evil in our lives, as in the above two examples, or it can be in the form of direct demonic oppression.

Recognize the power of the Devil as well as the authority of Jesus over that power. The question of the Devil's part in a grower's struggle has at times become a controversial issue in the church. For example, is depression caused by brain chemistry, hurtful experiences, our own badness, or the Devil? All are possible. The Devil is certainly behind any sort of injury that is designed to separate people from God, others, and growth. The best approach is to look at all the possibilities with people who have balanced experience in these areas, that is, those who understand spiritual warfare yet have sound theology, understand psychological issues, and give credence to medical problems also. However, don't look for a demon behind every problem until you have thoroughly looked at all other aspects of a person's life.

DEALING WITH TEMPTATION

THE GROWTH PATH IS not straight. There are many temptations along the way. People who want more of God and want to mature in their character often find that their temptations don't decrease, but the temptations change according to what they are working on. Jesus' stance toward temptation is instructive, especially as revealed in his own temptation (Matt. 4:1–11).

The Devil tried several strategies in tempting Christ. First, he approached Jesus in a weakened state, after he had fasted many days (v. 2). Growers understand this dilemma, as people are often tempted, not when they are strong and stable, but when they are weak. We are not alone in this problem.

Satan told Jesus to command the stones to become bread, so that he might eat. At a deeper level, this was a temptation to Jesus to get his needs met in ways other than God's. An example of this might be a person who tries to meet his loneliness needs through sexual sins. The dependency is good, but the way he chooses to meet those needs is not.

Jesus responded by going back to Scripture and confronting Satan with the reality that he would get his needs met God's way. Likewise, the man in the above example might go to relational sources of love and comfort for the lonely places in his heart instead of acting out.

The Devil then told Jesus to test God by throwing himself off a temple (vv. 5–6). This was a temptation to control God rather than to trust him and his ways. Jesus confronted that strategy also. For us, the same dynamic exists when we attempt to live life our way and not God's. A good example is a woman with a relational pattern of rescuing dependent and immature men. She would take men on as projects, comfort them, give them money, and provide answers and advice for them. All the time she thought God would reward her by having a man fall in love with her and marry her. After many painful failed attempts, she realized she was trying to leverage God by rescuing these men instead of requiring that the men in her life be mature (or maturing) adults. This was hard to give up, as the rescuing made her feel in control of herself and ultimately God. However, as she related to men

God's way, he eventually brought her a mature man, and they are now happily married.

Finally, Satan offered Jesus all the kingdoms of the world for his worship (vv. 8–9). Had Jesus accepted, he would have not had to die on the cross. Yet he strongly rebuked the Devil. This was a temptation to avoid suffering. Growth involves suffering, as we explain in chapter 11. And Jesus' response to this temptation is a living invitation for us to see that when we follow his path, we may suffer. However, that suffering is a very small price to pay for the spiritual growth that results.

JESUS' IDENTIFICATION WITH OUR SUFFERING

THERE IS ANOTHER TYPE of identification that deeply assists our growth. It is identification in the opposite direction. Jesus knows about our suffering through his own experience:

> Because he himself suffered when he was tempted, he is able to help those who are being tempted (Heb. 2:18).
> For we do not have a high priest who is unable to sympathize with our weaknesses, but we have one who has been tempted in every way, just as we are—yet was without sin (Heb. 4:15).

Jesus put himself in a unique position by his suffering. If anyone can say about our situation, "I've been there," it is he. There are two key terms here: "help" (2:18) and "sympathize" (4:15). They point out that Jesus both assists us and feels compassion for us. His loving nature sympathizes and understands, and his active nature does things to help us grow. If you have ever had a friend who wanted to help you but didn't understand you, or one who understood you but had no help for you, you see why it is so good that Jesus has both capacities in his identification with us. Here are some of the benefits.

COMPLETING THE ROLE OF HIGH PRIEST. The first way has to do with the fulfillment of Jesus' high priestly role for us, a very important task he undertook: "For this reason he had to be made like his brothers in every way, in order that he might become a merciful and faithful high priest in service to God, and that he might make atonement for the sins of the people" (Heb. 2:17). As the one who is our advocate and representative before a righteous God, he had to be able to identify with those he represented.

In some way that we don't truly understand, Jesus used his experience of being with us to fully know his people. The Greek word for "sympathize" means "commiserate." It indicates that Jesus "knows" our suffering at much more than an intellectual level, at a very personal one. Experience is the only gate through which he could have gained that knowledge of us, and he did it at a terrible cost. Thus, he fulfilled one of his tasks of becoming the complete high priest for all the ages, being able to feel our frailties with us.

I was once asked by a large church to treat a pastor who was caught in a sexual sin that threatened to destroy his marriage and ministry. He worked very hard in the process for a long time, and he developed good fruit in his life. The church wanted to be involved in his restoration, and he wanted them involved, so I would periodically consult with a small group of leaders about this man. They cared deeply about him and were concerned about knowing when he would be ready to reenter the ministry.

As we worked together, I also came to care about the man. As we looked at his life and character, I saw many reasons why he had entered this disastrous path. And I also saw how much he simply wanted to love and serve God and his family at the same time. Although I knew he and he alone was responsible for his sins and problems, I found myself identifying with his frailty. I knew what it felt like to be tempted as he was.

During a meeting with his leader group, one of the men asked me, "Can you guarantee me that he'll never do this sin again?" I remember that a feeling of protectiveness came up inside me. I said, "I can't guarantee that you nor I will ever do this, on the basis of God's Word." We talked about the problem of sin and weakness described in Romans 7 and how dependent we all are on God's grace. The discussion worked out well. Yet I think that that sense of protectiveness was based on my identification with the pastor's weakness.

Without justifying what he had done, I knew enough from my own experience to have compassion for him. And it helped me to know what to say in order to represent him accurately to the group. I think this is a little like how Jesus is able to represent us to the Father, because he has truly "been there."

RECEIVING EMPATHY. One of the most important aspects to growth in our suffering is that we need to know that we are understood. This is what empathy provides for us. We cannot grow if we are all alone emotionally. Life is too difficult. But if we know that someone truly understands, we know we are not alone with our feelings and thoughts, and we gain encouragement to persevere in our growth. We need to know that we are "heard"—on a human level from each other, and on a divine level from God: "You hear, O LORD, the desire of the afflicted; you encourage them, and you listen to their cry" (Ps. 10:17). This is what Jesus' identification provides. When we realize that he "gets it" because of his own suffering, we are buoyed up and can continue down the path.

TIPS FOR GROWERS:

- Examine your assumptions about the role of Jesus in your growth. Look at any tendencies to see him only in his Savior role and not involved today.
- Explore the suffering Jesus experienced that you can identify with in your own life. In addition, look at his attitude toward suffering.
- Develop an awareness of how to make suffering normal, be humble when experiencing it, and not retaliate when you are hurt.
- Look at the ways Jesus can identify with your own suffering so that you gain comfort and perspective from him.

TIPS FOR FACILITATORS:

- Help your growers see the importance of a continual, sustaining relationship with Jesus. Focus on any tendency to segment him into the "Savior only" role, and help them see all the benefits that come from their identifying with him and his identification with them.
- Work with them on understanding Jesus' stance toward suffering, particularly in the balance between humble submission and being a righteous person who doesn't tolerate evil.
- Investigate with them any areas of their lives in which they do not see Jesus as a high priest who indeed sympathizes with their weaknesses, and help them work through those issues.

When I graduated from college, I was lost, in terms of career direction. I tried several things, and none of them worked out. After a couple of years I moved back home with my parents for a while as I tried to figure life out. My folks were very gracious about it, but it was a real low point for me. While all my buddies were either well into their careers or in graduate school, I was back living with Mom and Dad, doing odd jobs around the town in which I had grown up.

I was fortunate to have some good friends who were believers. We would meet, talk about our lives, study the Bible, and pray for each other. Yet their lives were moving along much better than mine. Although they really cared about me, I didn't feel as if I fit in. I remember reading one of the passages that begins this section—Hebrews 4:15, the one that talks about Jesus' ability to sympathize with our weaknesses. That verse meant so much to me, because I knew Jesus truly understood whatever I was going through, even though I certainly didn't understand it. I received much comfort and strength from this realization. Things did finally work out, and I got on a path that made sense to me. But I never forgot God's empathic identification back then.

CONFRONTING DISTANCE FROM GOD. Another benefit of Jesus' identification with us is that it leaves us without excuse when we want to turn from God in our pain. We have a natural tendency to think that no one understands the uniqueness of our particular situation. This tendency is based on our bent toward blaming and externalizing our problems, thereby avoiding the hard work of taking ownership and working through them. If we can say, no one truly understands my life, it helps us feel justified to stay out of the growth path. Jesus' suffering breaks through that obstacle and helps us repent of turning away from him and his healing ways.

God the Father and Jesus the Son both powerfully guide how people grow. In the next chapter, find out how the Holy Spirit is just as important in the process.

6

THE HOLY SPIRIT

*The Spirit begins the process of growth by wooing us to
Jesus, and he is working to finish the task.*

What if Jesus came to your house today for a visit, and you told him you wanted to grow. What would you expect him to do? Heal you? Teach you? Challenge you? Give you new talents? Think about it. I can come up with many things I would want him to do, and I can think of a number of things I might expect him to do, but in all of my thoughts one of the last things I would expect him to say is, "Oh, you want to grow? Well, if that is what you want, I will have to leave. See you later." And I would never expect him to walk away. Wouldn't this be a strange way for him to produce growth in us? I surely think so.

But this is exactly what Jesus did:

> "I tell you the truth: It is for your good that I am going away.
> Unless I go away, the Counselor will not come to you; but if I go,
> I will send him to you. . . . But when he, the Spirit of truth, comes,

he will guide you into all truth. He will not speak on his own; he will speak only what he hears, and he will tell you what is yet to come. He will bring glory to me by taking from what is mine and making it known to you. All that belongs to the Father is mine. That is why I said the Spirit will take from what is mine and make it known to you" (John 16:7, 13–15).

For reasons we do not fully understand, Jesus decided to go to heaven and work on us from there, and he sent the Holy Spirit to be with us and produce the growth and change we seek. And he said that this is better than his being here himself. Therefore all I can think is that it must be incredible to have the Holy Spirit in our lives.

So what are we to do with the Holy Spirit? There is certainly no shortage of answers in the Christian world about the life of the Spirit and all that it entails. But this is not a book about all the Holy Spirit does in the life of the believer or in the church or in the world at large. It is a book about growth and how it occurs, so we want to take a look at the ways the Holy Spirit is involved in that process.

THE INITIATOR AND THE COMPLETER

WHEN I (HENRY) FIRST began my path of growth, I wondered one day if God wanted to have anything to do with me anymore, or if I were someone he didn't want. I prayed, and God did not seem to answer me; my hurts and pains were not quickly going away. I thought God had left me.

In the midst of these thoughts I remember a pastor telling me, "If God were through with you, you would not be worried about it or wanting to have anything to do with him. The desire you feel for him and for growth can only come from him and his Spirit. If you are moving toward God, it's because he's moving toward you. Rest in this fact. If you want him, he is looking for you." Then he showed me a verse to prove his point: "No one can come to me unless the Father who sent me draws him" (John 6:44). I found out there is no such thing as "wanting God" and not being able to have him. If we want him, he is looking for us.

God not only begins a process in us, wooing us to him, but also pushes our growth to completion. As Paul said, "He who began a good work in you will carry it on to completion until the day of Christ Jesus" (Phil. 1:6). If we feel some desire toward completion, God has not given up on us. He is still working, wooing, revealing light, and working to make us whole. Knowing his Spirit is at work on you and in you is a very good place to begin working on any issue in life. So the first point of how the Holy Spirit operates in our lives is this: *The Spirit begins the process of growth by wooing us to Jesus, and he is working to finish the task.*

One of the first things you should teach people is that they can trust the growth process, no matter how they feel in the midst of it. It is not going to be only up to them to "make it." The Holy Spirit is always going to be there, drawing them to God and to greater and greater growth. I was greatly comforted by this fact, and I have seen it bring great comfort to others, especially when things were not going smoothly.

Security

In chapter 4 we talked about the importance of knowing that God is for us and not against us. In any relationship, to grow and change we have to first know we are secure. Our relationship with God is no different. How can we know we belong to him? How can we be sure we are secure?

The Holy Spirit gives us this security. After bringing us to a relationship with God, he locks the door behind us. Just as Noah locked the door of the ark to save a remnant of life from the flood, the Holy Spirit locks the door of our saving "ship," our relationship with Jesus. Listen to what happens: "And you also were included in Christ when you heard the word of truth, the gospel of your salvation. Having believed, you were marked in him with a seal, the promised Holy Spirit" (Eph. 1:13). "And do not grieve the Holy Spirit of God, with whom you were sealed for the day of redemption" (Eph. 4:30).

When we put our trust in Jesus, we enter the boat, so to speak, and the door is sealed behind us. Through the sealing work of the Holy Spirit, God himself protects us to be always his. This has wonderful implications for the growth process. We cannot work on the real issues of our lives if we are insecure in our relationship with God. Because of the work of the Holy Spirit sealing us in him, we can stop worrying about whether or not this relationship is secure and we can get on with the path and the work of growth.

One way to help someone know that this has happened in her life is to ask her what she believes about Jesus. If she believes he is the Christ and she trusts him for forgiveness, then this is proof she has been sealed with the Holy Spirit. The Bible says we can only believe if we are born of the Spirit, if he is inside us. As John puts it: "This is how you can recognize the Spirit of God: Every spirit that acknowledges that Jesus Christ has come in the flesh is from God" (1 John 4:2).

If someone believes in Jesus, she has the testimony of the Spirit in her heart and she belongs to God (1 John 5:10). So if anyone has doubts, these verses can be very reassuring. Growth must begin in a secure relationship, and that security comes from the work of the Holy Spirit. Growth must be undergirded by this foundation.

The Partnership

Beyond the security and assurance the Spirit provides, what does the work of the Spirit look like day to day? What does he do? How do we work with him? As Jesus said, one way to think about the Holy Spirit is as the "Counselor." He is someone who comes alongside us and helps us. And the ways he helps are numerous. It is very helpful to know what those are, so that in the growth process, as we shall see, we can ask for them. Although it would take an entire book to talk about all the ways he helps us, here is a partial list of what we can expect to happen in the Christian life as we ask for and work with the Spirit:

- He will always be with us, no matter where we are or what we are doing. He never leaves us (Ps. 139:7).
- He will search our hearts and show us what it is we need to change (Ps. 7:9; Prov. 20:27; Rom. 8:27; 1 Cor. 2:10).
- He will give us the abilities to do things we need to do, even gifts for work, or wisdom, or words to say when we don't know what to say (Ex. 31:3; Deut. 34:9; Judg. 14:6; 2 Sam. 23:2; Mark 13:11).
- He will lead us and guide us in life (1 Kings 18:12; 1 Chron. 28:12; Neh. 9:20; Ps. 143:10; John 16:13; Acts 13:4; 16:6).

- He will show us truth and teach us (John 14:26; 15:26; 16:13; 1 Cor. 2:13; 1 John 2:27).
- He will counsel us and help us (John 14:26; 15:26; 16:13).
- He will help us to live the life we need (Rom. 7:6; 8:2, 4–6, 9, 11, 13, 26).
- He will fill us and control us (Rom. 8:6; Eph. 5:18).
- He will correct us and convict us (Ps. 139:23–24; John 16:8; Rom. 9:1; 1 Cor. 4:4; Phil. 3:15).
- He will change us (2 Cor. 3:18; Gal. 3:3; 5:16–25).
- He will give us gifts to help each other and put the Body of Christ together (1 Cor. 12:7–12).

This is a lot to expect, but God promises that all these things are available.

The problem becomes the "how." *How* does he do it? How can we get him to do it?

A Mystery

I wish I had a formula to give you about how the Holy Spirit works. It feels as if I have read everything ever written by those who say they do, and I've tried most everything I've read about. All I can say is that in my experience, the formulas have failed me. The Holy Spirit cannot be controlled.

But when we think about it, this makes perfect sense and also fits with what the Bible says, for the Holy Spirit is a Person, not a thing. We cannot reduce all of the work of the Holy Spirit to a formula. What we can do is what the Bible tells us to do: Ask for him to be in our lives and to help us. God promises us that if we ask him for the Spirit, he will come:

> "So I say to you: Ask and it will be given to you; seek and you will find; knock and the door will be opened to you. For everyone who asks receives; he who seeks finds; and to him who knocks, the door will be opened.
>
> "Which of you fathers, if your son asks for a fish, will give him a snake instead? Or if he asks for an egg, will give him a scorpion?

If you then, though you are evil, know how to give good gifts to your children, how much more will your Father in heaven give the Holy Spirit to those who ask him!" (Luke 11:9–13).

Basically, if there is a formula to how the Spirit works in our lives, this is it. It is to seek him, ask for him, and then follow him. Most of the problems people have in understanding the Holy Spirit come when they are asking for a particular experience of him, or a particular gift (or they are not asking for him at all). If we could get rid of our preconceptions of how or what he is going to do, and ask him to come for the need we have, much of the confusion would go away.

The best way to think about the Holy Spirit and growth is to think about a moment-by-moment relationship of dependency on him. We depend on him to guide us, lead us, talk to us, reveal truth to us, empower us to do what we can't do, give us gifts to be able to give to others what they need, and many other things. But all this happens in an "abiding" sort of way. We yield to him and follow. We open up our hearts and beings to be "filled" with him. We ask him to invade all that we are and to work in us. In a sense, we give ourselves to him as we live out the life of growth.

Therefore, in light of the growth processes we encounter, life in the Spirit means that we do not "do growth" without him. It also means that he does not do growth "without us." The miracle of the Holy Spirit's invasion of our lives is that he is at work within us to change us and to lead us and guide us, but there is still an "us." Paul said, "I have been crucified with Christ and I no longer live, but Christ lives in me. The life I live in the body, I live by faith in the Son of God, who loved me and gave himself for me" (Gal. 2:20).

The old way of trying to "do it right" by ourselves is over (vv. 16, 19). Now we live a life of faith with him inside us. *But we are still the ones who have to live this life and be accountable for it.* As Paul said, the "life that I live in the body, I live by faith." So, as I go through the process of growth, each step I take is a faith step, depending on the Spirit to live it out with me. I live this life as he lives in me. It is mystery. I live this life with him living in me.

PRACTICAL SPIRIT-FILLED LIVING

JUST BECAUSE SPIRIT-FILLED LIVING is a mystery doesn't mean we can't do it. Nothing is more practical in the growth process than to need help and empowerment in taking very difficult steps of growth. Take Julie, for example.

Julie had been struggling with eating for several months as her life had gotten more and more stressful. She had prayed about it and confessed her overeating again and again. She felt bad about herself and was getting discouraged. Then she read a piece on how the Holy Spirit could empower her to do what was difficult. So she decided to put that to the test.

Julie's two most difficult tasks were turning from food and bringing people into her struggle. She had been reading about how breaking patterns of behavior had to do with confessing to God and to others and also finding out the root causes driving the behavior. One night she found herself at home alone and wanting to eat ice cream that she knew she did not need. She had just finished a healthy dinner an hour or so before.

She remembered what her growth partners had told her. When you feel tempted, ask God to empower you through his Spirit to do two things: *to turn from what is destructive* and *to turn to what is good, the things he says to do.* So, in her craving she stopped and prayed. She asked the Holy Spirit to help her. She prayed for his strength. She sat there with him, and then she asked him to show her what she was feeling. When she did not eat, her feelings of loneliness and stress became clearer to her; then she asked him to help her open up to someone. The name of a friend came to mind. She called the friend, who helped her move past the struggle.

This was a whole new world for Julie. For the first time she didn't have to fight the battle alone. She learned to depend on the Spirit's strength to do what she needed to do, and she yielded to the answers he provided. Before that, she had been alone in fighting temptation and not depending on him and his strength. She also depended on him for help through the support he provided in her friend. *She was both dependent and active.* He helped, she yielded to his help, and she took steps to follow him by reaching out to the person he made available.

Just the other day I talked to Ted, who had for years been fighting sexual addiction with sheer willpower. He had hit bottom, and for the first time he decided to bring God and his Spirit into the battle. One night he and his wife had an argument, and he was tempted to act out his feelings of betrayal and powerlessness. He felt justified. But this time he asked for God's Spirit to help.

Unexpectedly Ted "bumped into" a friend he had not seen in years, but who knew about his problem. His friend asked how he was doing with his addiction, and he said, "Horrible!" He opened up to the friend, who then told him he was on his way to a sexual addiction group, and he took Ted with him. The Holy Spirit had provided the help he needed and a whole new support system for his problem. When I talked to Ted, he had been clean for a few months.

Let me give you a more personal example. I was once in a difficult business relationship with a particularly strong-willed businesswoman. Discussing even the smallest issues with her proved to be very taxing. Sometimes I dreaded visiting her company because I knew I was going to have to work on an issue with her and I knew I was not going to be understood or listened to.

One day we got into a particularly heated argument and were getting nowhere. The more we tried to work it out, the worse it got. I was losing my temper and finding myself having attitudes and feeling moods I had not had or felt since my pre-spiritual teenage years. I did not know what to do, so inside myself I asked God's Spirit to work in me and in the situation. I asked him to find an answer and a way out of the impasse. I prayed, "Please help me to see what to do. Please give me the words to say. Please show me how to fix this." The words I prayed were not as important as my feelings of absolute dependency on the Spirit.

What happened surprised me. It was not that this business associate finally heard me or that I found the right words to communicate to her to be understood. What happened is that I heard the Holy Spirit. He showed me that it was I who had to listen to her and accept what she was saying to me. I had to hear her and understand her position. I also had to see where I had been wrong in the situation and apologize. His answer was as clear as a bell.

So I asked the Spirit to help me do that. I asked him to help me find the right words. I don't remember exactly how it happened, but we got past the problem. The Spirit showed me other ways I had been wrong. When I acknowledged them, everything changed, and we worked it all out. She did not change, and I don't know if she will ever see her side of the conflict, but the Spirit made it clear to me that the answer I needed did not involve her doing anything, but involved my confessing and repenting. I needed his help both to show me what to do and to help me carry it out. It reminded me of Jesus' words: "But when he, the Spirit of truth, comes, he will guide you into all truth" (John 16:13). God's Spirit has promised to always be there to lead us into the truth we need to know.

Let's look at one final example.

Robbie did not like confrontation, especially when the other person might become angry or upset with him. He tended to feel "bad" and then give in to the person, or he avoided difficult conversations altogether. Over the years this behavior had significantly affected his business life, and he knew he needed to change. He was forever getting the worst ends of lots of deals, and he was putting up with nonperformance and unfairness.

He recognized this about himself and wanted to be different. But it was not happening. Then Robbie realized God could help him in difficult confrontations, and he took a step of faith. He made a tough phone call and depended on God's Spirit to empower him. After he did it once and learned that stepping out in faith worked, other confrontations became easier. Finding out that character change could happen as he depended on the Spirit to help gave him a whole new arena for growth.

I have seen the same thing happen with other steps of growth people have had to take. Confession of pain, bringing things into the light from the darkness of their souls, opening up about feelings, taking risks in love and relationships, and asking God to empower with gifts and talents in career moves are all part of the scope of life in the Spirit. We are made to grow, to stretch ourselves into new arenas. But we are not made to do that without help. The Spirit will give us power to do what we could not do before, or at least to take the step to learn how.

The important thing to remember is this: The Spirit-filled life is a supernatural life that surpasses our strengths and abilities. We can depend on that. The Spirit has promised it. But this does not mean that we do not have to do anything. We still have to step out in faith. We have to risk. We have to love, open up, confess, reach out, repent, obey, and do all the other things we are commanded to do. Our part is to live the life. But we do not have to do it alone or in our own power. We are partners with the Spirit. Listen to how Paul taught that we work and the Spirit works at the same time:

> Since we live by the Spirit, let *us keep in step* with the Spirit (Gal. 5:25).
>
> I pray that out of his glorious riches *he may strengthen* you with power through his Spirit in your inner being, so that Christ may dwell in your hearts through faith (Eph. 3:16–17).
>
> The one who sows to please his sinful nature, from that nature will reap destruction; the *one who sows to please the Spirit*, from the Spirit will reap eternal life (Gal. 6:8).
>
> Now to him who is able to do immeasurably more than all we ask or imagine, according to *his power that is at work within us* (Eph. 3:20).

The Bible teaches we are to do our part by faith and the Spirit will do his part by his power.

For Julie, this meant, "The struggle I have with eating I must do with faith in him to help me turn from food, pray, and call a friend to find out what is hurting me. So, God, help me do that right at this moment when I feel like snacking."

For Ted, this meant, "The battle I have with this addiction I have to fight by faith in him. Help me, God, to resist and to reach out."

For me, this meant, "The conflict I have to resolve with this woman I have to resolve by faith in him. Help me to see what to say, God."

For Robbie, this meant, "The fear I have of confrontation I must face with faith in him to help me step out and say the tough thing. Help me, God, through your Spirit to make that call and give me the words."

It is a real life and a practical life. It is not the life of summoning up willpower and strength we do not possess. Instead, it is a life of summoning up faith that will be given to us and stepping out on that faith in a very real God who has given us his Spirit to help us in every situation and for every need.

If there is a formula, the closest thing I have found to one is that old hymn, "Trust and obey, for there's no other way to be happy in Jesus but to trust and obey." Life in the Spirit is one of faith and action. We believe that he will empower and lead us into truth, and then we yield, trust, and step out. We "sow to please the Spirit," and he promises us the reaping of life.

YIELDING

OFTEN IN THE GROWTH process we do not know what to do, or we do not want to do what we know we should do. This is where the "control" of the Spirit comes into play, and we must yield. We must submit to what the Spirit is telling us to do and allow him to have the reins of control moment by moment. Paul tells us: "Do not get drunk on wine, which leads to debauchery. Instead, be filled with the Spirit" (Eph. 5:18). "You, however, are controlled not by the sinful nature but by the Spirit, if the Spirit of God lives in you. And if anyone does not have the Spirit of Christ, he does not belong to Christ" (Rom. 8:9).

The moment-by-moment task is not only one of asking, but of being filled with his power and of yielding to his control. The Holy Spirit talks to us, brings to mind things God has said, shows us a way out, gives us answers, gives us things to say, and pushes us to take a risk. But when he nudges or reminds, *our job is to yield to him and allow him to have control. We are to submit and yield our will.* In that way, he takes us where we need to go, and we have taken another step of change.

Sometimes we might not even know what that next step is. That's when we can ask God to show us.

"SHOW ME"

"BUT I DON'T KNOW why I feel this way. It just happened. There is no reason for it," David replied when I asked him what had triggered his depression.

"I believe that you don't know why you feel depressed or what happened to trigger your feelings. But I can promise you that there *is* a reason for it. God made you in such a way that you don't feel so bad for no reason."

"Well, I don't have any idea what it would be. It just hit me. I don't have a clue."

"Let's think about it," I said, knowing that when we talk honestly, more truth usually emerges. We talked, but nothing emerged. We talked more. Nothing. Then I felt that urge to pray that I have learned to trust over the years as being from the Spirit. So I said, "Let's ask God to show us through his Spirit what was happening." And we did.

As we began to talk again, David's expression changed. His face quivered, and he began to shake. Some powerful emotions came to the surface as he realized what had triggered his depression. The day before he had had a conversation with someone who had attended a funeral. This conversation had put him in touch with his feelings over the loss of his mother at a young age. His depression made total, rational sense. We, in our limited awareness and knowledge, could not find the reason, but the Holy Spirit could. As Jesus said, he leads us into all truth.

One of the main ministries of the Holy Spirit is that he leads us to truth—the truth of God and Jesus, the illuminating truth of God's Word, the truth about people through supernatural knowledge, and the truth of situations through wisdom and prophecy. This is what he does. In fact, he is called "the Spirit of truth" (John 14:17; 16:13).

The Spirit also knows the truth of our own lives and souls, and he knows what needs to change and be revealed. I suggest that you ask the Holy Spirit specifically to show you what he wants to reveal to you about your growth, your soul, issues in your life, and so on.

Ask the Spirit to show you the truth about you as a person, and also about his answers and God's ways. Truth is healing, and we need as much of it from him as he will give. And that is usually as much as we are ready, able, or strong enough to receive.

WHERE HE LEADS, FOLLOW

IT HAS BEEN SAID that spiritual and emotional growth is a path further and further into reality. I always try to remind people that as painful as it may be, *truth is always your friend.* No matter how difficult it is to swallow, truth is reality and that is where ultimate safety, growth, and God are. We need to know the truth.

Sometimes the truth leads us to what is hurting us, as with my client David above. Sometimes it leads us to what we need to change. At other times it leads us to what we need to do next in a relationship. At still other times it leads us to what our weaknesses or limitations are, such as what we are *not* ready to deal with. But whatever the truth is, it is our friend. It is also where God lives.

So one of the most important things God does in the process of growth is to send us his Spirit of truth. He is always showing us the truth about ourselves, about life, about relationships, about God and his Word, and about our path. The Spirit convicts us when we are wrong, teaches us when we need it, guides us when we need to see the path, and shows us how to get there.

The flip side to the Spirit's work in this area is that we must follow his lead and do what he shows us to do. This is part of the "sowing to please the Spirit" Paul refers to. As he says in Galatians, "Since we live by the Spirit, let us keep in step with the Spirit" (Gal. 5:25). When the Spirit leads us to truth, we need to follow.

Sometimes the Spirit's calling is internal; for example, he calls us to pray. The last few days or so, my parents were on my mind a lot. I thought about them and prayed for them, but the thought of them did not go away. God was telling me something about a need they had. I knew I needed to call, and I intended to do so the first break I got. But something happened yesterday.

My sister called from across the country and told me that my dad had not been feeling well for a few days and that yesterday he had had a stroke. By the time they called me, everything was fine and he was doing well. There seems to be no serious damage, and he will go home from the hospital in a few days, so I stayed in California. Yet now I know why my parents were on my mind and heart more strongly than usual. I think that the Spirit was leading me into some truth I did not have access to by myself: that my parents needed prayer and support. Even though everything turned out okay, I wish now I had followed his leading earlier.

I have seen this in business, where I was led to call someone. I have seen it in ministry, when I was led to reach out to someone. I have seen it in my own personal growth, when I was led to face an issue or a sin in my heart. I am slowly learning to recognize the Spirit's leading; the hunches I feel are often his whispering to me to do something. I am slowly learning to hear and then to follow.

The Holy Spirit talks to us all in different ways, as everyone's relationship with God is personal. But even though he does it differently with everyone, he does it. He talks to us about our lives and about things we need to change. For me it usually happens in a few ways.

The most common way is when something stays in my mind without my trying to think about it. I have recognized the difference between my own obsessive worry about things and the Spirit's gently "camping out" in my brain. He just sits there constantly with an issue until I deal with it.

Another way is that the Spirit will bring up an issue from the outside. I will hear the same issue talked about in fifteen different contexts, from a sermon to a passage of Scripture, a friend telling me, a book, a radio or TV show, and so on. He will find many different ways to show me the same thing to the point where I cannot deny he is talking to me.

Then there is the one-time, immediate quickening of my own spirit when I hear or read or see something. The other day I was reading some contracts for one of my business deals, and I read something and felt my spirit jump inside. (And, for my interests, it jumped in the wrong direction!) I was convicted that the way this relationship was structured was not fair; it was too much in my favor. I think the Spirit was possibly telling me to give more to the other side. I had been wrong. It is not something I would have come up with, as I had negotiated for my position. But when I read the material I was reading, I felt he was speaking to me. It was immediate, and it was strong.

I don't know how you hear the Spirit. Probably you hear him in some similar ways that I do and some different ways as well. If you are a parent, you communicate differently with each of your children, because they hear and learn differently. We talk to our various friends differently. But our message should always be one of truth. And this is how I think the Holy Spirit operates. He talks to us all in different ways, but always with the truth we need to hear for the moment. Even though it may seem to be "bad news" at the time, it is always good news for the long haul. So listen for how he speaks to you.

One thing is sure: The Holy Spirit can't lead past where he is leading if we don't take that first step of following him into the truth he is showing us. If he shows me an issue to deal with, I have to take the steps to deal with it. If he shows me a sin, I have to deal with it. And so on. He leads, we follow. That is "keeping in step with the Spirit." It is a relationship we follow step by step.

The best illustration I know of this step-by-step relationship is one I told a man the other day who was thinking of going into the ministry. He was feeling as if God was leading him to drop out of business and attend Bible school. God's leading was very clear. But the man wanted to talk to me, since I am in the ministry myself, to "know how you know what you are going to do." He knew God was leading him to Bible school, but he did not know what God wanted him to do later, so he did not know what courses to take.

I told him, basically, "Welcome to following God." That is how he usually works. All God tells us is the next step. Take that one, and the one after that will appear, but not before. It is like wearing one of those miners' hats with the light on it, I said. You look down and only see enough light to take the very next step. As you take that one, the next one becomes clear, and so on. God rarely shows us the whole picture at once.

It is like that in a career move or in growth or in learning about him. He leads us one step at a time, but we have to "keep in step" with an active following. I told my friend that when God told me to go into the field of Christian counseling and study psychology and theology, I had no idea I would be doing the things I do now, like writing and teaching. For all I knew, God could have led me into research. He just told me to go into the field. He only shows the next step. And it is our job to be obedient and follow the little truth he gives us.

Jesus said God is looking for people to worship him in Spirit and in truth. He is looking for a real relationship with us from the depths of who we really are. In our limited capacities to know ourselves and to see external reality, we must be dependent on the Spirit of truth to show us those realities. In that way, in the path of truth that he provides, growth happens. We become more of who we truly are and begin doing what we are truly made to do, seeing him as he truly is as well. The Spirit is ultimate reality.

MISCONCEPTIONS

OVER THE YEARS WE have found many misconceptions about Spirit-filled living in the Christian world of growth. While we can't go into these in great detail here, we want to list a few for you to watch out for.

1. IF YOU ARE "FILLED WITH THE SPIRIT," YOU WILL ALWAYS BE HAPPY AND HAVE NO PAIN OR STRUGGLE. This common misconception is nowhere close to the experience of any human who has ever lived, even Jesus. We know that Jesus was always connected and yielded to God. We know his power came from the Spirit of God. Yet, he felt pain, and he struggled enormously. In the garden of Gethsemane he had immeasurable distress and agony. Certainly no one would say that he had "lost his victory" or "lost his walk." Yet, sometimes struggling people are told that if they are hurting, they are not letting the Holy Spirit control them.

The truth is that yielding to the Spirit and being filled by him is something that we do *in* the pain and struggle, not *instead of* the pain and struggle. Jesus, the apostle Paul, and others all knew pain and struggle. This was not the issue. The issue was what they did in that pain and struggle. They took their pain and struggle to God and leaned on his Spirit, the Helper, for strength. Struggling does not denote failure of the Spirit-filled life.

2. IF YOU ARE FILLED WITH THE SPIRIT, YOU WILL NOT SIN. This idea is similar to the first, but has to do with sin, not pain. The truth is that everyone sins, and if anyone says that he does not, he is "a liar" (1 John 1:8, 10). No one is ever without sin, for even if our behavior is okay for the moment, unconscious, sinful, dark parts of the soul are not yet cleansed. The Spirit-filled life is a progressive one of "cleaning up the inside of the cup" as well as the outside. No one has that totally finished. Sinless perfection is an ideal to strive for, but an unreality for any

human except Jesus. The Bible says, "There is not a *righteous* man on earth who does what is right and never sins" (Eccl. 7:20). But we do all know righteous men who walk in the Spirit. So walking and perfection do not mean the same thing.

3. IF YOU ARE WALKING IN THE SPIRIT, YOU WILL HAVE THE FRUITS OF THE SPIRIT INSTANTLY. Remember, sanctification is a process. Paul said he didn't have it yet (Phil. 3:12–13). Peter said the qualities of good character are built over time in increasing measure (2 Peter 1:8). Fruit is the result of walking in the Spirit, as we sow to please the Spirit (Gal. 6:8–9). Growth takes time, and it takes time to sow to please the Spirit and to grow in the spiritual life. It is not just a switch that someone pulls—off with the old immature me and on with the new totally mature me. As we see in other chapters, the Bible says that all things have become "new," but not "complete" (2 Cor. 5:17). It says that maturity is something we have to move toward (Heb. 6:1) and that we are "being made holy" (Heb. 10:14). This takes time.

So do not let anyone discourage you by making you feel that if you do not have it all together, you are not "in the Spirit." If you are leaning on him to the best of your ability, asking him for all the help you know how to ask for, facing all that you know how to face, and obeying all that you know to do, just keep on trusting. The fruit will come.

A WARNING

ON THE ONE HAND, just because a person is not perfect does not mean that the Spirit is not in his life. On the other hand, if a person's life has zero evidence of light, faith, change of direction, repentance, and love, then she must ask herself if the Spirit is in her life. Either he is being quenched and not followed, or he is not even there. As Peter says,

> If you possess these qualities in increasing measure, they will keep you from being ineffective and unproductive in your knowledge of our Lord Jesus Christ. But if anyone does not have them, he is nearsighted and blind, and has forgotten that he has been cleansed from his past sins. Therefore, my brothers, be all the more eager to make your calling and election sure (2 Peter 1:8–10).

Or as Paul warns, not walking with the Spirit and following sin results in bad fruit:

> The acts of the sinful nature are obvious: sexual immorality, impurity and debauchery; idolatry and witchcraft; hatred, discord, jealousy, fits of rage, selfish ambition, dissensions, factions and envy; drunkenness, orgies, and the like. I warn you, as I did before, that those who live like this will not inherit the kingdom of God.
>
> But the fruit of the Spirit is love, joy, peace, patience, kindness, goodness, faithfulness, gentleness and self-control. Against such things there is no law. Those who belong to Christ Jesus have crucified the sinful nature with its passions and desires. Since we live by the Spirit, let us keep in step with the Spirit (Gal. 5:19–25).

So, while you need not worry if you do not have it all together, you should be concerned if you are not showing any fruit of the presence of the Holy Spirit in your life. The good news is that, as we saw in the beginning of the chapter, if this concerns you and you want his help, this is a sign that he is with you already. No one should ever be concerned if she wishes for his help and forgiveness, as that wish itself is a fruit of the Spirit. But showing no fruit and no concern is a different story.

It's Not Just "Let Go and Let God"

WHEN YOU PREACH THE work of the Holy Spirit in people's lives, there is a danger. Some want to bail out of their responsibility, and they want to "let go and let God." I was doing a training workshop with some people who were in the ministry. As I talked about all the things we need to do to grow, such as face fears, take risks, and join a support group, one man asked, "Isn't this just another way of saying you set your goals and just do them? That sounds like any other system of psychology and self-help."

I told him that I very much disagreed and that what I had been saying all along was the exact opposite: We *cannot* do the things we need to do on our own. We are *unable to make choices* on our own. We have to face our inability and depend on God. We have to depend on others. We have to reach out and be empowered. I emphasized we could not do it on our own. There is no "self-help."

TIPS FOR GROWERS:

- Seek and understand your security in God and how he is seeking you through his Spirit.
- Learn how he is to work and what he promises so you can expect and find it. Learn the list of things the Holy Spirit will do.
- Seek him as a person in a relationship. Depend on him as a person moment by moment for all that you need.
- Ask for help in every situation.
- Follow him.
- Yield to him.
- Ask him to show you and reveal to you what you do not know about everything in life.
- Follow him in whatever he reveals to you, one step at a time.
- Don't confuse pain and suffering with a lack of his presence. Ask him to be with you in the pain and suffering and do all of the above in the midst of it.
- Examine yourself always to make sure you are in the faith and his life is in you.
- Pray for his supernatural healing and deliverance when needed.
- Remain in the paradox of both you and God living your life.

TIPS FOR FACILITATORS:

- Clear up any misconceptions about the Holy Spirit.
- Teach people how the Spirit works and what the Bible promises about what he will do.
- Make sure you focus always on the moment by moment dependency and relationship with him.
- Provide ways and contexts of seeking the Spirit and asking for him from God.
- Give encouragement to depend on him, and don't judge struggle as a lack of his presence in someone's life.
- Give the warnings that the Bible gives regarding a lack of the fruit of the Spirit.
- Provide teaching and experiences and contexts for the supernatural healing and deliverance the Spirit offers.

I thought we were on the same page, but then he showed me we were not by saying: "Oh, I see. We can't do it so we just depend on the Holy Spirit to do it. We give it all to him."

"No," I said. "We don't just give it all to him. We can't do it, and we don't just give it all to him. We must 'work out our salvation,' but we also have to be asking him to help us to do all of it. *It is both, not one or the other.*"

Humans tend to be unable to hold opposite ideas in dynamic tension. But this is a tension we will always need to hold: God has a part, and we have a part. Beware of dichotomizing between your tasks and God's.

Supernatural Healing

In addition to the moment-by-moment work and dependency on the Holy Spirit, we can ask him to heal. I strongly believe we can ask God to heal our own souls and can ask him to break other kinds of bondage in people's souls, such as deliverance from demonic influence or possession. This is not a treatise on how to do that, so we will not go into it here. There are many good books on healing and deliverance. But since this is a chapter on the Holy Spirit, I would like to remind us all that he does heal and deliver.

Throughout the Bible, God is spoken of as healer and deliverer. And I have seen him heal and deliver. Sometimes he heals instantly and miraculously. But in the emotional arena with issues like depression, anxiety, and overeating, when people are prayed for, we often see that God begins to heal them by helping them work out their issues. The depressed person, for example, finds the strength and courage to come out of isolation. Just because a healing was not instantaneous does not mean that the prayer was ineffectual. God did answer it, but he answered it in a deeper way by helping the person to change. Prayer changes things, either instantly or through time, as shown in both Scripture and real life.

I have also observed a lot of deliverance from demonic oppression. Sometimes that needs to be done by a skilled person who has done it before and knows the difference between spiritual strongholds and emotional and psychiatric problems. If you are dealing with someone who has this sort of demonic issue, make sure you get him to a person with good diagnostic backgrounds. There is a lot of strange stuff floating around the church.

But the bottom line is that we are to pray for people's healing. I love it when anyone I am working with has a regular prayer group or team praying specifically for the healing of the issues we are dealing with.

Ask God to give you the gifts you need for the moment when you are praying for someone. He may give you supernatural wisdom or knowledge, for example. He may visit you with a gift or manifestation of his Spirit for that person. He may show the person or you what issue should be addressed. Or he may just work a direct miracle—we never know. What we do know is that the "prayer of a righteous man [and woman] is powerful and effective" (James 5:16). It is as important a part of all of growth as anything else.

So whether you are growing yourself or are in the process of helping others, make prayer a part of what is happening. Send your growers to a prayer group. Or start one. Or suggest that they get a prayer partner to pray together for the issues they are dealing with. However it is done, prayer must be in the picture for you to have a complete picture of growth that includes God and his Holy Spirit.

NEVER TOO LATE TO BEGIN

I HAVE TALKED TO many people who have been Christians for a long time and have adhered to God's principles and taught others, but have had no real life "in the Holy Spirit." For them, Christianity is in some ways not supernatural. If this is you, don't be dismayed, for it is never too late to begin. And the "formula" is a simple one: Just ask.

As Paul told us, "Just as you received Christ Jesus as Lord, continue to live in him" (Col. 2:6). We receive Jesus by faith, and we walk the same way. Just ask the Holy Spirit to do all the things we talked about here, or whatever else you need him to do. As Jesus promised, God will give him to you (Luke 11:13). You received him in the beginning by trusting and asking. Now, in the arena of growth for yourself and others, do the same thing. Ask and trust. He will show up, just as he promised.

PART III

FINDING THE
BEST CLIMATE

7

GOD'S PLAN A: PEOPLE

To be truly biblical, as well as truly effective, the growth process must include the Body of Christ.

During my own "hitting bottom" experience, I (Henry) went to dinner with a Christian friend. I told him how depressed I had been and how much I felt God had let me down. I had asked God to help me, and I wasn't feeling any better. I had thought that if you prayed, God would make you feel better. I still felt lousy. I had concluded God was not doing much.

My friend listened supportively and said he really didn't know a lot about that, but knew someone who did. He gave me Bill's phone number. It was good to talk to my friend, but I was bummed out that the only Christian I knew very well didn't know how to get God to make me feel better. I wondered, *Does God really make people feel better?*

I called the number my friend gave me. It turned out that Bill was a student at a seminary. He and his wife, Julie, had a lot of experience ministering to college students.

I went to meet them, and we hit it off. It felt different to be around them. They talked to me about God. They wanted to know all about me and my newfound "faith." I told them all about my hand injury, my struggles with trying to play golf in pain for two years, and my decision to give it all up. Then I talked to them about how I had looked around for what I wanted to do and really hadn't gotten anywhere.

"I just don't think I should be feeling this way," I said. "Something feels wrong."

To tell you all that happened would be a long story. The short version is that this couple literally took me in. They decided they wanted to "disciple" me—a concept I had never heard of. They thought I needed to learn more about God, and since I had nothing else on the horizon, I thought, *Why not?* I decided to take a semester off from school, think about life, live with Bill and Julie, and "get discipled."

I learned a lot about God. Bill was a great teacher. He gave me access to all of his books and took me to his classes. He showed me where the seminary library was, and I fell in love with studying theology. He taught me about doctrine and how to interpret the Bible, and he tried to answer whatever questions I had.

As time went on, I could feel something changing in me. I don't know how to put it into words, but it was as if God was coming into view. A structure for understanding God began to take shape as I studied the Bible. An experience of God took shape as I learned about spending time in prayer (sometimes hours) both by myself and with Bill and Julie. At times I could actually feel God in the room.

While Bill taught me about God, Julie talked to me about my life. As I opened up, I found there was a lot inside of me I had never ever thought about. The emptiness I had been feeling was not emptiness at all, but sadness and hurt. I knew I was sad about the loss of my dream to play professional golf, but I got in touch with other losses and hurts as well. Julie had been going through counseling materials that walked one through an "inventory" of the soul, and we worked through those materials together. As we did, I learned I had a lot to work through. I found I had not only hurts, but forgiveness issues, both for myself and for others I held things against. Great loads were lifted off my shoulders as I went through this process.

At the same time, Bill and Julie encouraged me to join a small group that examined my life. I learned things about myself and how I related to people. The members of this group taught me that I was "emotionally detached" and did not let people get close to me. They showed me I knew very little about love and most of my life had been based on performance and accomplishment, not "abiding intimacy." They challenged all of my relational patterns.

When I was wrong, they confronted me. At first I felt bad and guilt-ridden when confronted, but later I learned the freedom that comes with being confronted in love. I found out people could discipline me and at the same time be for me and not against me.

Another thing happened in this same community. Bill and Julie and others saw something in me I had not seen. They said I had a particular gift for understanding the Bible as it relates to counseling issues and I had the gift of insight into those matters. For my part, I was feeling an increasing desire to study the Bible and counseling. These two paths, the external one and the internal one, merged, and before long I knew God was calling me to go into the field of Christian counseling.

GOD USES PEOPLE TOO

ONE DAY, SOMETIME LATER and after going into counseling myself, I realized my depression and my feelings of emptiness were gone. I actually felt good about life and about me. As I examined my feelings, I discovered I was both happy and disappointed. God had changed my life. My life had taken a 180-degree turn. But God had not healed me when I had sought healing. He had not supernaturally "zapped" me. God's supernatural zapping seemed like Plan A to me. As I talked about this disappointment, people told me the same thing over and over again: "But God uses people too."

I hated hearing that phrase. I had wanted God to touch my depression instantaneously and heal me. Instead, he used people to help me. I came to call this God's Plan B. I thought that when God supernaturally intervened and healed, it was Plan A. And this was true spiritual healing. When God used people to heal, it was the "inferior," although effective, Plan B. I accepted that I was one of those people who got Plan

B. So there I was, grateful and somewhat disappointed at my grade B healing. It was good, but felt more like sitting in the bleachers than in the box seats.

Then, one day I made a discovery in Scripture that changed my way of viewing Plan B: "From him the whole body, joined and held together by every supporting ligament, *grows and builds itself up in love, as each part does its work*" (Eph. 4:16).

I could not believe it. I read the verse again. Not only was it true that "God uses people too," but this was not Plan B or second rate at all! In fact, people helping people was Plan A! The Bible said so. Not only that, but it was not *just people doing it. It was God himself!* God was working directly through people when they were helping me. So Plan B was the original Plan A after all.

I had wanted God to heal me, but thought I had to "settle" for his getting people to do it. But it *was* God doing it, in and through people. This might seem like a nuance, but for me the idea was life-changing. It helped me realize that God was not far off and uninvolved, just delegating things to people. God did not *delegate* the process to people at all. He *wore* people as his uniforms. He came to live inside people and then lived out his wishes and will through them in a mystery called the Body of Christ. Jesus was with me all along by being *in* all of those who were helping me. God was using people as his Plan A:

> Each one should use whatever gift he has received to serve others, *faithfully administering God's grace in its various forms.* If anyone speaks, he should do it as one *speaking the very words of God.* If anyone serves, he should do it with the *strength God provides*, so that in all things God may be praised through Jesus Christ. To him be the glory and the power for ever and ever. Amen (1 Peter 4:10–11, italics added).

I was waiting for God to give me his grace through supernatural zapping; he was giving it to me through his people. I was waiting for him to speak to me directly; he was speaking to me through his people. I was waiting for him to give me direction in life; he was the strength behind the direction people were giving me. I was waiting for him to heal my depression; he sent special people to comfort me.

I could see that God himself was healing my depression through my friends Bill and Julie and others. I no longer felt as if I had gotten Plan B. I had received God himself and the healing he had always planned to give me through his people. I learned what Paul had experienced in his own depression when he said, *"But God, who comforts the depressed, comforted us by the coming of Titus"* (2 Cor. 7:6 NASB, italics added).

When I went to graduate school and studied theology, I discovered that this is the doctrine of the church. This doctrine holds that the church, with its indwelling Spirit, is the real physical presence of Christ on earth today. It is true that where two or more are gathered together, he is present (Matt. 18:20). It is true that he is inside each believer. It is true that the Body is the temple of God (1 Cor. 3:16). In the Old Testament, God lived in the temple and in the Holy of Holies. Today he lives in temples of human flesh. He lives in us, and wherever we are, he is. What an incredible reality!

This discovery at that point in my life was intensely personal. It led to great thanksgiving and a real feeling of God's looking out for me and being active in my life. But I had no idea of the significance it would play later in my professional life.

THE ROLE THE BODY PLAYS IN GROWTH

SEVERAL YEARS LATER, THIS reality has become much more than a personal testimony to how God heals. It has become one of the foundational understandings of everything we do as professionals. If you are going to help people grow, you *must* understand the necessity of relationship for growth. Often people in the church who are teaching others how to grow eliminate the role of the Body. In fact, sometimes these people teach that their students don't need people at all, that Christ alone is sufficient or that his Word or prayer is enough. They actively and directly lead others to not depend on people at all. They think that is wrong.

But the Bible teaches that *all* these things are part of the process, including other people. So, as we talk about all the different aspects of how people grow, we want to emphasize loudly the role of the Body. Years of research and experience back up this biblical reality: *You must have relationship to grow.*

As we said in chapter 2, relationship with others is part of the created order. Independence from relationship is independence from God himself, for he is present in his Body; it is also independence from the way he designed for us to grow. As Paul told the Ephesians, to "grow up in him" includes the Body doing its work with each other (Eph. 4:15–16).

If you are helping others grow and you become aware of an area of life in which a person needs something from God, think of other people as part of the solution. Look at the Body resources available to that person to get his or her needs met and to grow.

Let's take a look at the role the Body of Christ plays in how people grow. I want to make clear that this is not meant to be a complete theology of the church or to describe all that the church does for individuals. A book on doctrine can do that. What we want to do is highlight the more salient processes that occur within the Body as people enter into the growth process. Here is our main emphasis:

> *Biblical growth is designed to include other people as God's instruments. To be truly biblical as well as truly effective, the growth process must include the Body of Christ. Without the Body, the process is neither totally biblical nor orthodox.*

So let's look briefly at some of the roles the Body plays. (We discuss some of these roles in greater depth in other chapters.)

Connection

People's most basic need in life is relationship. People connected to other people thrive and grow, and those not connected wither and die. It is a medical fact, for example, that from infancy to old age, health depends on the amount of social connection people have. Infants and older people die from a lack of relationship, and those in the middle suffer and fail to recover from illness.

At the emotional level, connection is the sustaining factor for the psyche, the heart, and the spirit. Virtually every emotional and psychological problem, from addictions to depression, has alienation or emotional isolation at its core or close to it. Recovery from these problems always involves helping people to get more connected to each other at deeper and healthier levels than they are.

Ironically, one problem we often see in the Christian community is that people get more into religion and less into the connectedness the Bible prescribes, with the result that they get sicker. For the same reason, many people feel disconnected from God because they have not been connected to his Body. Paul describes the problem this way: "He has lost connection with the Head, from whom the whole body, supported and held together by its ligaments and sinews, grows as God causes it to grow" (Col. 2:19).

The clear teaching of the New Testament is that the Body of Christ is to be people deeply connected to each other, supporting each other and filling each other's hearts. Virtually every day we receive calls or letters from people who tell their stories of victory over some area of life as a result of getting plugged into a group somewhere and working on their issues. Since we work mostly with individual Christians and Christian organizations, the victory stories are often from believers who have been trying for years to conquer some problem "with God alone."

As letter-writer Sandy said, "For years I have struggled with depression and an inability to make relationships work. I prayed, read my Bible, and tried all the things I thought I was supposed to do. Then my church started this group that was going through your book. I could not believe what happened in my life as I began to share openly with other people. I felt connected, and things are so different now. I cannot describe how significant that group was. I feel like I am connected to God again."

What she found was that, although she had been seeking spiritual growth and healing for some time, not all of the elements of growth were working until she experienced being "held together by [the Body's] ligaments and sinews," where she could grow "as God causes it to grow." Through the small group she joined, the Body was doing its work in her life.

This connection also impacts people who are in recovery from addiction or compulsive behavior. Hardly anyone completely recovers from an addiction without connection to a support system. Some stop their addictive or compulsive behaviors, but their relational patterns do not change, and most times they relapse if they do not do group work.

The reason is complex, but part of it is the alienation driving the addiction itself. Paul calls it the "continual lust for more" caused by being "separated from the life of God" (Eph. 4:18–19).

As people are cut off from others and their souls are starved for connectedness, the need for love turns into an insatiable hunger for something. It can be a substance, sex, food, shopping, or gambling, but these never satisfy, because the real need is for connectedness to God and others, and to God through others. When people receive that, the power of addiction is broken. This is why many people in the ministry find relief from addictions only after getting into a recovery group. Before that, they had become isolated in the ministry, feeling as if they had to hide because of their position.

So, if you are in the growth process yourself or responsible for the growth of others, see connectedness as the foundation of how people grow. They grow first through their connection with God, but also through their connection with other people in his Body. And as we have seen, if they don't have the latter, they don't have all of the former. They are cut off from aspects of what God gives.

Discipline and Structure

"I just need more self-discipline," Jerry told me. "I know I have all of this potential to reach my goals, but it seems as if I just can't make myself get around to doing it all."

"Where are you going to get this 'self-discipline'?" I asked.

"What do you mean, 'Where am I going to get it'?"

"Well, just what I said. You don't have any self-discipline. If you had it, you would have done the things you haven't done. So I agree with you. You need 'self-discipline.' I just want to know where you are going to get it, because you obviously don't have it. And if you don't have it to give yourself, I want to know where you are going to get it."

"By disciplining myself."

"You're not 'getting' it," I said. "If you could discipline yourself, you wouldn't need self-discipline. You would have it. But you don't. So, again, where are you going to get it?"

He looked at me with one of those looks that is a cross between insight and a deer caught in the headlights. I could see that he "got" it.

His chances of disciplining himself were nil. To delude himself one more day would have been to set himself up for more failure.

"I don't guess I know. Where *can* I get it?" he asked sheepishly.

"Well, it's not that hard to figure out. Everyone gets it the same way. Self-discipline is always a fruit of 'other-discipline.' Some people get disciplined by other people early in life and then internalize it into their character; then they possess it themselves. Other people don't get disciplined early in life, and they don't ever have self-discipline until they get it from others and internalize it for themselves. It's not rocket science; it's the way God designed us to grow. Others discipline us, and then we can do it for ourselves. Kind of like everything else in life— we get it by receiving it from others (as it says in 1 Corinthians 4:7)."

"How? How do I get disciplined by others?"

"Now you've asked the sixty-four-thousand-dollar question, and if you understand the answer and do it, you'll have the discipline you seek."

We went from this conversation to looking at precisely how this process takes place. Jerry had to find an accountability partner, join a group that would give him specific assignments, get correction and feedback on his assignments, get consequences when he did not perform, submit to the structure of the group meetings no matter what the cost, call his accountability partner when he was tempted to slide, and get the support he would need to motivate him, work through his fears and resistances, and heal the pain that drove the irresponsibility, and so on.

Through the structure of his assignments, the group meetings, his submission to the structure, his accountability partner, and the feedback provided by all of that, Jerry began to internalize what he had never possessed in his own soul: discipline. Finally he had it for himself—but he got it from others. As Hebrews 12:11 says, "No discipline seems pleasant at the time, but painful. Later on, however, it produces a harvest of righteousness and peace for those who have been trained by it." He had to get "trained by it," not do it himself. And the Body of Christ was the disciplinary agent.

Jesus further explained the disciplinary role of the Body in Matthew 18, where he said, "If your brother sins against you, go and show him his fault, just between the two of you. If he listens to you, you have won your brother over. But if he will not listen, take one or two others along, so that 'every matter may be established by the testimony of two or three witnesses.' If he refuses to listen to them, tell it to the church; and if he refuses to listen even to the church, treat him as you would a pagan or a tax collector" (vv. 15–17).

God's Plan A, his "being there," operates when his Body comes together to help someone achieve control over his or her life. This is the role of the Body in discipline—to help people regain the freedom (or the "harvest of righteousness and peace") that comes from self-control. Many times in the Bible (as in Matthew 18:15–16; Galatians 6:1–2; Titus 3:10) we are told that we get discipline, structure, and correction from other people whom God gives us, and we are in trouble if we do not: "A mocker resents correction; he will not consult the wise" (Prov. 15:12).

So, as you try to grow in self-control over some area of life, consider the constant role of discipline. And if you are helping others grow, make sure that the role of "other discipline" is somewhere in the mix, or growth will stagnate. Whether individually or in groups, we need the discipline, structure, and correction others provide.

Accountability

We have already mentioned accountability, but we need to offer one caution here. There has been a big movement in recent years toward accountability groups and accountability partners, especially when someone acts out or lacks discipline in some area of life. We see this, for example, with men in regard to moral purity.

Accountability is very important, and the Bible tells us over and over again to build it into our lives. But here is the caution: *Accountability is not a cure for lack of self-control.* Often when a man encounters a problem, he is required to join an accountability group. There he is asked a list of questions about how he is doing in various areas to see if he has slipped. If he has, he confesses, he is forgiven, and he commits to doing better. All of this is very important.

The problem with accountability is that all it does is "count." It is like the temperature gauge on a car; it can tell you the engine has problems, but it can't fix it. Accountability can expose a problem, but it can't fix it. Just as a car must go to a mechanic to get fixed, so the person must get further help past the diagnosis from the accountability group. A person with a problem has to enter the process of discipline and structure mentioned above as well as find healing for what is driving his behavior. Accountability is only a monitoring system to tell him when he needs more.

When a problem surfaces, the role of an accountability group changes. It is now a group not only to see how a person is doing, but also to see if the person is doing the other things he is supposed to be doing to solve his problem, as in the example of Rich or Jerry.

I have been part of the disciplinary process for many spiritual leaders, and I always require them to have an accountability partner or group, *not as the agent of change,* but to make sure they are going to the agents of change. If it is an addiction, are they going to their meetings? Are they going to counseling? Are they doing the spiritual disciplines? The key here is that there is more to the process than accountability. It is necessary but not sufficient.

Grace and Forgiveness

By definition, grace is something we can't give ourselves. It comes from outside of us, as unmerited favor; we can't do anything to obtain grace. And, as we see in this chapter, part of the "outside" God uses to dispense his grace is other people. As people use their gifts, they are "faithfully administering God's grace in its various forms" (1 Peter 4:10). God made us stewards over the administration of his grace.

Many ministers have heard their parishioners say, "I know in my head that God forgives me and accepts me, but I can't feel it in my heart." They have memorized verses on forgiveness, God's love and acceptance, their position of grace, and all the related doctrines. They "know" the information in their heads, but they are far from "knowing" it in their hearts. They commonly think this "head" knowledge is somehow going to "sink in" to their hearts. This is not the way things work.

The head and the heart work in different ways. The head works by gaining, assimilating, and accommodating new information. We take in data, compare these data to what we already know, and then form an understanding of the new information as we grow in "knowing."

While the head works with "information gathering," the heart works with "experience gathering." It is similar to how a doctor comes to "know" surgery. She must study the books, but she must also get into the operating room and experience surgery firsthand to "know" how to operate. In like fashion, we may know what the books say about God's grace, but until we have experienced it, our "knowing" is only in our head.

To experience God's grace, however, our hearts have to be connected to it. We can certainly connect to God "vertically" through prayer, but to feel his grace completely we have to open our hearts to the full expression of it "horizontally" through other people. To connect fully with the grace of God, we have to go to where it is, and he has chosen to put it into other people. So those who only study the "facts" of the grace of God and do not experience other people loving them, as Peter directs us, will fall short in their realization of that grace.

To connect with God's love, however, we not only need people, but also need our hearts to be available to those people. We have to be open and vulnerable for the grace and acceptance to do any good. Many people "fellowship" with others, but they share so little as they fellowship that nothing happens at the heart level. As Paul told the Corinthians, "We have spoken freely to you, Corinthians, and opened wide our hearts to you. We are not withholding our affection from you, but you are withholding yours from us. As a fair exchange—I speak as to my children—*open wide your hearts also*" (2 Cor. 6:11–13). So for growth to occur, it must include *experiences* where hearts are open with each other. Otherwise, it is just known in someone's head and never experienced at the levels God has designed.

This is one of the meanings behind James 5:16, which says, "Therefore confess your sins to each other and pray for each other so that you may be healed." Many Christians do the vertical confession of 1 John 1:9, where they confess to God, but not to others. So they "know" they are forgiven and loved in their head, they just don't "know" it in their heart. We are made to experience both, and it is one of the reasons that Jesus commands us to love one another.

Years ago we treated a pastor for a sexual addiction. For years Joe had struggled and labored under the fear and guilt that go with this problem. He had confessed and prayed to God over and over again, but he had not been able to get out of his addictive cycle. Finally his sense of failure and depression was so great that he checked himself into our hospital and joined a group I was leading.

One morning I arrived for a group session, and a nurse told me that Joe was not going to attend that day. He said he didn't feel like it. What was really happening, however, was that the night before Joe had had a "slipup." He felt so guilty he did not want to come to the group.

I went to his room and talked him into coming.

As members in the group began sharing, someone asked Joe if he was okay. He said yes, but we didn't believe him. During the entire time he had been a member of the group, he had mostly helped others, as he had in his professional life, and he had not shared much of his pain. But this particular morning, I did not let him off the hook. I prodded him to share with the group. He finally agreed.

As he told his story, he looked at the floor. He recounted years of sexual acting out and his fears, when he was preaching, that someone would recognize him from the night before. His life was a duplicitous nightmare. He told about how depressed and alienated he felt and, most of all, about his inability to stop. He painted a horrible picture.

Then something happened. As Joe was looking down, telling his story, I looked around the room and noticed something. All the members of the group had tears in their eyes. They ached for him. I could feel the compassion and grace in the room. But I could also see that Joe was not at all connected to the grace available to him.

"Joe," I said, "I want you to look up at the group."

"No," he said. "I can't."

"Yes, you can," I said. "Look up."

He resisted some more, but I would not give up. Finally, with a struggle, he looked up at the other members. As he looked around the room, he saw the same teary, compassionate eyes I had seen. He saw the gentle smiles. He saw the acceptance. In short, for the first time he saw grace. He broke. It was like a reed snapping. He fell forward and sobbed like a little child. At that moment his addiction was broken. Of course, he had additional work to do, but the power of his addiction had been broken as he experienced grace in the depths of his soul.

Until then, his experience of grace had only been propositional. He had not experienced grace "in the flesh," as the New Testament talks about it. But when the Body did its work, "administering God's grace in its various forms," healing occurred.

The point here is that grace can be available to us, but we might not be available to grace. We can be around a lot of acceptance and grace, but until the hurt and guilty places of our hearts are exposed, we do not *experience* grace, and the gap between our head and our heart continues.

So, with Paul, make sure that you are helping others to "open wide" their hearts also. Provide vulnerable experiences with each other from the depths of the heart so that the Body's work of grace can be done. Grace must be experienced to be known. Many Christians have experience with the Body on Sunday morning in a pew, but not in a private setting where they can share the pain and the vulnerable places of their hearts. Yet, this is where healing takes place. Fellowship on Sunday or at a potluck or a Bible study is great, but fellowship with the depths of the heart is what heals.

Support and Strengthening

In the book *Boundaries with Kids* I told a story about my own mother during a tough period in our family's life. When I was four years old, I came down with a leg disease that left me bedridden, then in a wheelchair, and then in braces and on crutches for two years. I went overnight from a very active child to one with a serious disability. My doctor told my parents it was imperative they make me do things for myself and not spoil my character by doing everything for me.

I remember an incident at church when my parents were making me go up a long flight of stairs on my crutches. I was struggling and taking a long time, but they were prodding me on. I stumbled, got redirected, and continued on one slow step after another. I'm sure it was painful to watch.

Suddenly, from behind us I heard a woman say to her husband, "Can you believe those parents are making that child do that?"

I don't remember what my parents said, but years later I wondered how my mother did it. One of the most caring people I know, she is also one of the most caretaking, the kind who has difficulty making the dog go outside in the rain. I can only imagine what it was like for her to let a crippled child struggle through things she could have helped with. So, years later, I asked her.

"You are one of the most codependent people I know," I said. "How in the world did you let me suffer through what I had to suffer through without rescuing me?"

"Emmett," she said.

"Emmett?" I asked.

"Yes, Emmett. Every day, when I had to do something I just could not face doing, I would call Emmett, cry my eyes out, and listen to her tell me I had to do it. She would help me through it each time. It was awful."

Emmett was my mother's best friend, a wonderful Christian woman. What my mother had discovered was that by herself she could not do what was required of her. But with support she could. She was being "built up" (see 1 Thess. 5:11) .

When we support something, we hold it up. Support is required throughout the growth process. We will face tasks and realities past our strength and abilities, so we need others to support us. As Paul says, "We urge you, brothers, warn those who are idle, encourage the timid, help the weak, be patient with everyone" (1 Thess. 5:14). And in another place, "Carry each other's burdens, and in this way you will ful-fill the law of Christ" (Gal. 6:2). Support enables people to go through grief, trials, growth, and a whole host of other difficult times.

Recently I was having lunch with a friend I had not seen for years. She was doing wonderfully in her work as a lay leader with a church. I asked her about her children, and she proudly told me all about them, and then said, "We lost one."

"What happened?" I asked.

"Well, our four-month-old died of SIDS [sudden infant death syn-drome]. He just did not wake up one day."

My breath was taken away, and my heart sank. My own daughter was about that age at the time. I could not imagine how a parent could go through something like that. But here she was, a few years down the road, and doing well. My friend was talking about all God was doing in her life and how blessed and grateful she felt. I was really touched by her heart and where she was, so I asked her the obvious.

"How?" I asked. "How did you make it through?"

Her answer came immediately and with deep conviction: "The Body," she said. She paused, and then repeated it. "The Body."

She went on to tell me how their friends and the church community had come around them and had been there for them through the experience, holding them up when they were unable to hold themselves up and unable to take the next step.

This was the answer to what I had been wondering. How could a parent go through the death of a child and come out as she did? How was that possible? Only through the Body. For this is what the physical body does when one cell suffers. It sends healing to the injured part of the body. If you have a wounded arm, for example, the body sends antibodies, healing agents, fresh oxygenated blood, white cells, information, anti-inflammatory agents, and so on to that limb. And they do their healing work. That was what had happened with my friend and her husband. There *is* no way to go through that alone. But, as Jesus said, hell can throw whatever it wants toward us, even death, but his church, the Body, can withstand it all (Matt. 16:18). There is nothing that can prevail against his church.

Many people, however, find themselves cut off from the church and the healing and protective functions it provides. In their isolation—or at least the isolated growth plan they are using—they are easy prey for the gates of hell to overpower them. This is analogous to Jesus' story about the shepherd and his sheep (Luke 15:3–7). Wolves do not attack an entire herd. They attack the one lamb that has wandered off the path. This is the one who is in danger. As Jesus said, he would leave the ninety-nine to fetch and return the wandering one.

When people try to grow spiritually and emotionally without the organic and metabolic functions of the Body, they are essentially off the path and subject to all the forces of death. And hell does have its way with them until they are returned to the connectedness and healing of the Body. Consider these verses in this light:

He has lost connection with the Head, from whom the whole body, supported and held together by its ligaments and sinews, grows as God causes it to grow (Col. 2:19).

From him the whole body, joined and held together by every supporting ligament, grows and builds itself up in love, as each part does its work (Eph. 4:16).

This Body of Christ heals itself just as a physical body does. Each part has a function in that healing just as a physical body does. The antibodies against infection come in the form of discipline and structure as individuals who confront in love help the person stand against the "infections" of sin in her life. They put boundaries and limits up against the evil that has overtaken the person, either from within or from others. They help her stand.

Others, with grace and love, bring healing anti-inflammatory agents to the wound. They "mourn with those who mourn" (Rom. 12:15) and flush out the sickness. They bring teaching and truth to the wound and help it to rebuild stronger cellular structure through teaching gifts. And on and on. The Body has a myriad of gifts, and as a person is exposed to all the ingredients of growth in that Body, the infection is healed. This is the way God designed it. This is Plan A.

This is also why we see very sincere, spiritual people often struggle for years with problems they are trying to overcome by Bible study and prayer. While those are necessary, they are not all that the Bible tells us to bring to the situation. It tells us to bring the rest of the Body with all of its healing agents. Then the limb can be restored to health. As my friend said, "The Body." I don't know if she fully understood the depth of theology she communicated in that one answer to how she made it through. But the Bible does understand it. It commands it.

MENTORING THE WHOLE PERSON

IN THE MID–1980S JOHN and I started a psychiatric hospital that grew into a chain of clinics in more than thirty-five cities in the Western United States. Since we partnered with public companies and hospitals, insurance companies, and the like, we had to know a lot not only about our field, but also about health-care delivery systems and the whole world of business to make it work. These clinics ended up having an impact in ministry for a long time, but we could never have done it if something had not happened first.

A Christian mentor God had placed in my life helped prepare me for this task. He took me under his wing right after I got out of graduate school and challenged me to do something with my degree in Christian counseling past seeing people one on one. He pushed me, taught me, and coached me on how to put deals together with hospitals, radio networks, and insurance companies.

This is when I discovered that God wants us to develop *all* of our gifts and talents, not just our "spiritual" ones. We often see spiritual growth as affecting only those parts of life that relate to God, like prayer, Bible study, and worship. We do not see growth in our work and career as spiritual growth. Yet, in reality, all of life belongs to God, and the Bible speaks to all of it.

Many passages talk about the importance of work and using one's gifts fruitfully in life (Prov. 27:23–26, for example). So why don't we include spiritual oversight of people's careers in our discipleship of them? How people are doing in their work and career development is an important part of their spiritual growth process. Character issues such as diligence, perseverance, honesty, responsibility, facing failure, and taking risks are all spiritually developed traits that relate to success in life. These should all be included in our models of spiritual growth.

The process of career growth usually entails mentoring. In fact, I go so far as to say that no one has ever become successful without mentoring. When someone succeeds in life, many others have taken him "under their wing" to help him along and develop him in his chosen field, whether or not they realize it. But we mostly leave this up to a person's boss or colleagues.

Mentoring, in our opinion, however, is best done within the context of the "church" for two reasons. First, it makes the character issues, which drastically affect a person's work life, grist for the mill, and, second, it helps to integrate a person's life by eliminating the all-too-common split between work and spiritual life. It is a good thing for a person to be mentored by someone who can see what is happening in his or her overall walk of faith and growth in Christ.

I am so grateful that my professional development came in the context of the church, from people who shared my values and vision. This important role of the Body helps people grow. We think it is a travesty to leave career development outside of the purview of spiritual development and to delegate it to people's companies and other entities. That is like leaving all of the parenting of kids up to the school system. For sure, they have a role. But discipleship is not just about how to pray, witness, and have a relationship with God. It is also about how to "know the condition of your flocks, give careful attention to your herds" (Prov. 27:23). We should provide mentoring in all aspects of life as part of spiritual growth in the Body, and then we would not only see people achieve more success, but also see them resolve the split between their spiritual and professional lives.

Recently a friend who is starting a new business told me he had decided not to buy the house he was on the verge of buying. A wise, older Christian businessman, who was mentoring him as he started his company, showed him a verse in Proverbs that applied to his decision: "Finish your outdoor work and get your fields ready; after that, build your house" (Prov. 24:27). Because of this scriptural guidance, my friend said he had decided to put his money into his business and grow it first.

This was good business wisdom, but it came in the context of spiritual mentoring and as part of the spiritual life. I wish that the Body would do more of this for people, for it certainly is its role. As a business consultant, I see much business training that is not only weak, but also antithetical to the way God wants us to conduct our talents and productivity.

GRIEVING

ONE OF THE MOST important processes in life is grief. God has designed grief to help us get over things. When bad things happen in life, we have to work through them. Working through bad things is a little like digesting food. In life, we basically digest experience; we walk through it, take it in, use what is useful, and eliminate the waste.

When someone dies or when there is another kind of loss or injury in life, we have to be able to work through that experience and move on, leaving our hearts available for new experiences and relationships. We get rid of the hurt and pain by grieving and then keep the learning experiences that come with it.

Through tragedy we learn about God's faithfulness and how the love and support of others brings us through. We learn that when bad things happen, we can get through them, and then we have hope for the next time. We learn about untrustworthy people so we can avoid them the next time. This is what happens in a good divorce recovery program in a church, which is much better than someone going out on the rebound and getting into another bad relationship.

We talk elsewhere about how grief works and how it promotes growth. But here, as we talk about the Body, we would like to emphasize that *grief can only be accomplished in the context of relationship*. We need others to hold us as we go through the process of letting down and letting go. In addition, we must have something good in hand to be able to let go of something bad. It is a little like being a trapeze artist: You can only let go of one trapeze if another is in view.

If people do not have a support system to attach to, they cannot grieve a good relationship that is lost or a bad one that they need to let go of. People also need the feedback and observations of others to learn from an experience and to contain all of their distortions and emotions. Feedback and containment, as we will see, are essential to the grief process. As people grieve, they can get well. Solomon said, "Sorrow is better than laughter; for by the sadness of the countenance the heart is made better" (Eccl. 7:3 KJV).*

Grief is God's way of getting us through and past things. And we need others to help us do that. Therefore the Bible says to "mourn with those who mourn" (Rom. 12:15). If we do that, people find out that it really is true what Jesus said: "Blessed are those who mourn, for they will be comforted" (Matt. 5:4).

---

*The *New Living Translation* of the Bible draws out even greater insight with its rendering of this verse: "Sorrow is better than laughter, for sadness has a refining influence on us."

Since grief is absolutely necessary for successfully moving through life, and since it is an essential part of the growth process, we have to make sure it happens well when helping people grow. The only way it can happen well is in relationship—the way God designed it to work. It is the reason tear ducts are in the corner of the eyes. Someone's grief should be evident as he or she looks into the eyes of another person. It is a relational process. Get people grieving correctly—*with other people*—and they can get on with life.

HEALING

WE DEAL WITH THE specifics of healing the brokenhearted in chapter 14, but here we have to mention that it occurs within the Body. Relationships provide care, support, structure, and the balm of love to heal hurts.

"He heals the brokenhearted and binds up their wounds" (Ps. 147:3). We know from all the commandments in the New Testament that Christ's Body is supposed to be carrying out that work with him.

Healing is part of the grief process, but it is also a different process. Hurts of rejection, abuse, and abandonment are deep wounds inside people's souls. These hurts must be lanced, held, medicated, and protected, and other processes applied, as we see in chapter 11. Again, that process takes place in the Body.

If hurts are deeply healed, people do not repeat these hurts in other relationships, nor do they try to medicate their wounds in sinful ways, such as with drugs, alcohol, gambling, illicit sex, or other lusts. If the Body is there to be the medicine—the medicine that heals, not just dulls the pain—then the destructive cycle of sin is broken.

CONFRONTING, CONTAINING SIN, ADMINISTERING TRUTH

IT WAS GOING TO be a difficult conversation, but one we knew was inevitable. Michael was a good friend's son, and my other friends and I knew him well. We had watched him grow up, and now we were watching him sink further and further into addiction. We were concerned for his health.

We were also concerned about his family's involvement. At age twenty-four Michael was supposed to be an adult, but he was still too dependent on his family and too much under their control. In fact, we suspected this was part of his problem.

As we found out more about the destructiveness of Michael's behavior, we thought he needed help, but we also thought we should help him as friends and leave his parents out of it. In our view, they had been in denial of the situation for a while, and he needed to face his problems squarely as an adult with adult friends. So we arranged for an intervention.

My friends and I called Michael over to one of our houses for dinner. At the end of dinner we told him we wanted to talk to him. It was tense, and he knew something was up.

We began by affirming our love for him and telling him that, because we loved him, we wanted to talk to him. We told him we knew about his addiction and considered him in danger. We wanted to know what he planned to do about it. We told him that if he wouldn't do anything about it, we were prepared to do whatever we could to get him to face it. But we wanted to start with him before going to his family, his employer, or his community.

At first Michael balked. He denied he had a problem. We gave him instances of what we knew, and we did not budge. We held him to the truth.

We also told him about times in our own lives when we had needed help. We did not see him as any different from us, even though he had different problems. We did not see ourselves as above him at all; in fact, we identified with his problem of being stuck and not knowing how to get better.

Then Michael broke down and cried. He opened up about how difficult it was—particularly with regard to his family. We told him we understood and would help him get help. We hooked him up with a good counselor, and we promised to hold him accountable for staying in the recovery process.

The result was twofold. First, Michael got into counseling and recovery and did very well. His life was turned around, and he grew instead of remaining in denial. Within a couple of years he had ended a string of bad relationships, and he had met and married a wonderful young woman. She was the first of all the women he had dated who was emotionally healthy. We could tell by his choices he was truly getting better.

Second, his parents were very angry with us. They felt that we had gone behind their back and meddled in a family problem. I understood their perspective, and they were right. We had gone behind their backs. But we had done it intentionally. I explained to the father that we thought his son's problem, in part, was that he was too dependent on his family and that this was one of the reasons he was not facing adulthood responsibly. Therefore, to bring parents into the problem would be for us to continue to address him as if he were a child. We considered him an adult and thought the Body of Christ around him had a responsibility to him as an individual, not as someone's son. Thus, we told the father that we were happy with our decision and sorry that he felt betrayed.

Our intervention made waves in our relationship for a while, but it also made the family face issues about their relationship to their son. It also underscored a point. We were acting responsibly as the Body of Christ to Michael as a brother. And this is what was most important to us, not to please his family. It was important for the Body to do its work.

So part of the role of the Body is to step in and contain the effects of sin in someone's life. The Body is sometimes an "antibody"; its role is to fight infection. In Matthew 18:18 we see that two or more together can stop the destructive sin process through Body discipline. As Paul puts it, "Brothers, if someone is caught in a sin, you who are spiritual should restore him gently" (Gal. 6:1). It is the role of the Body to intervene and save people from the destruction they find themselves in.

But the key is how it is done. Remember, this is the Body of Christ. The way Jesus would do it is, as the verse says, in a spirit of gentleness. He, a high priest who can sympathize with our weaknesses (Heb. 4:15), was never judgmental or condemning toward those in need or in sin. He gently restored them and never lorded it over them. He said to the woman caught in adultery, "I do not condemn you, either. Go. From now on sin no more" (John 8:11 NASB). If it is truly an act of the Body, then it will be as if Jesus were there in the flesh, for that is what the Body is. So, when you confront, make sure you are doing it his way, speaking the very words of God (1 Peter 4:11).

MODELING

ONE DAY, IN A group I was leading, a woman confronted another woman about something the other woman had done. When she spoke of the problem, speaking the truth in love, the other woman responded, owned her behavior, and they reconciled.

As I was listening, I noticed something interesting. A new member of the group was staring at them with a dumbfounded look on her face. Finally I interrupted them and asked the new member what was going on.

"I was just watching them," she said. "I have never seen that before."

"Seen what?" I asked.

"Well, she was mad at her and told her. And then they didn't get into a big fight. They just talked about it and now it is okay. I have never seen that."

The new member explained that it was the first time she had ever seen anyone bring up a problem with someone else and not seen a nasty outcome. It had been different from both sides. The way the first woman had brought up the problem was different from anything she had ever seen, and the way the second woman responded nondefensively was just as different. The new member also talked about feeling a strange sense of hope—hope that her own relationships in the future did not have to be the way they had been in the past. All she had known was what she had seen, what had been modeled to her through the years.

We cannot do what we have never seen done. We need models to show us how. Both Paul and John talked about the dynamic of modeling. As Paul says, "You became imitators of us and of the Lord; in spite of severe suffering, you welcomed the message with the joy given by the Holy Spirit. And so you became a model to all the believers in Macedonia and Achaia" (1 Thess. 1:6–7). Or as John tells us, we are to walk as Jesus did, following his example (1 John 2:6). God designed humans with a need to see others first do what they need to learn, and then to internalize that modeling and be able to repeat it.

The modeling we experience has a lasting effect upon us, for good or for ill. This is one reason why the Bible emphasizes the confession of not only the sins of the people, but also the sins of the fathers (Neh. 9:2).

We have to see the wrong modeling we are following in order to renounce it. The goal is to replace the poor modeling with the modeling of people who "imitate Christ," the ones in his Body who show us how he would do it; then we can do it the same way. As Paul said, we imitate those who imitate him. His Body carries on his walk upon the earth, and others learn it.

UNIVERSALITY OF IMPERFECTION AND SUFFERING

I LED A PASTORS' retreat in a secluded setting for a few days. Eight pastors from all over the country had gathered together to support each other and go through the material I was presenting. The first night I had them all talk about where they were in their lives and ministries and what they desired to get from our few days together.

We went around the circle, and each story was different. The first pastor had gone through an ugly church split. The second one was having significant marriage problems. The third was dealing with the betrayal of a life-long ministry partner. The fourth was doing very well and asking how to deal with success. The fifth was burned out. And then the sixth said something I will never forget.

He was the youngest of the bunch, an up-and-comer in his denomination. The other members of the group were older and further along the path, some with very significant ministries. In his mind, they were the models of what he was supposed to be like.

When it was his turn, I asked him what he would like to share.

"Well," he said, "I just have to say I feel a lot better already. You guys are as screwed up as I am!"

The group burst out in laughter, for they knew exactly what he was saying. Being the youngest one in the group, he had come with idealistic expectations of what these older sages were like. He thought they had it all together. They were all successful in their careers and in the things they desired to do. At the same time, they all had some significant struggles. This had surprised him.

It did more than that. It had comforted him. This young man had discovered that he was not so unusual after all. He had thought what most of us think until we get together with others who are honest enough to say where they really are. He thought he was the only one who struggled. To find out that others did—even successful people—was a big help to him. It reduced his shame, fear, and guilt and gave him hope and models of how to cope. He discovered you don't have to have it all together to be a follower of Christ. Listen to what the apostle Paul told his "group":

> Not that I have already obtained all this, or have already been made perfect, but I press on to take hold of that for which Christ Jesus took hold of me. Brothers, I do not consider myself yet to have taken hold of it. But one thing I do: Forgetting what is behind and straining toward what is ahead, I press on toward the goal to win the prize for which God has called me heavenward in Christ Jesus (Phil. 3:12–14).
>
> We do not want you to be uninformed, brothers, about the hardships we suffered in the province of Asia. We were under great pressure, far beyond our ability to endure, so that we despaired even of life (2 Cor. 1:8).

Paul was honest about letting others see he too could hurt, despair of life, and not have it all together. This is such a lost art in many Christian circles. When people find out others struggle too, wonderful things happen.

First, they feel less guilty, ashamed, and afraid something is wrong with them.

Second, they obtain a more accurate view of the standard they are trying to live up to. Many times the standard is superhuman. By seeing others, the standard gets modified to a real person who grows, struggles, does not have it all together, but is dealing with all of it.

Third, they gain hope and problem-solving skills. They find through the struggles and testimonies of others that people do get better and that they do resolve very difficult problems in life. They see how these imperfect strugglers accomplish all of that. This gives them a model for getting past what they are dealing with at that moment.

In other words, they find out that we are all on the same path. While we all have different struggles, one thing is certain: We all struggle. And this is one of the best things that the Body can give to one another, the knowledge that we are not alone on our path of struggle. No one is exempt. Therefore no one needs to be ashamed for not having it all together. Struggle is universal.

DISCIPLESHIP

IN MY STORY OF healing at the beginning of this chapter, I referred to the discipleship process. Many people know the value of being taken under someone's wing and having the basics of the faith imparted to them one on one.

The Bible has many examples of people investing their time in others; its value can't be overestimated. It is one thing to sit in a church and receive teaching about the faith, but it is another thing to be taught the things of God in a one-on-one relationship with a spiritual director, or a discipler. In this context, doctrine can be passed on in a personal way as it relates to real life. Questions can be asked. Sin can be confessed, and accountability offered. Encouragement can be integrated into the spiritual learning process. In short, faith development becomes a relational process where personal development and faith intertwine in an organic way.

In many circles of self-help spirituality, discipleship is a lost art. It is seen as too rigorous, rigid, or religious. This view may arise in part from the way discipleship was done a few decades ago in some evangelical circles, leaving a bad taste in some current Christian leaders' mouths. In a sense, these leaders are trying to keep others from the bad experiences they had. But many times they are also keeping people from good experiences.

Take a look at disciple making in your life—whether as discipled or discipler—and ask yourself if it could have more of a role. We encourage this as a function of the Body for everyone, in two directions. One is to be "under" a spiritual mentor or director's care and to be accountable to that process. The other is to be offering that to someone else who is a little younger or less mature in the faith. Both are important, and both are a developmental role that the Body should play in every life. How beautiful it would be if everyone could experience what Paul said of his work with others, and then could pass that on to others as

TIPS FOR GROWERS:

- Examine your feelings about Plan A. See if you are okay with God's using people to accomplish what he wants to do in your life or what you want him to do. See if you have a bias against his plan for people's involvement in your life.
- See if you are cut off from Plan A. Find out if you have amputated yourself from his provision for you.
- Take an inventory in your life of the elements the Body provides: connection, discipline and structure, accountability, grace and forgiveness, support and strengthening, mentoring, grieving, modeling, healing, confronting.
- Determine whether you experience the universality of suffering and imperfection by close relatedness to others.
- Figure out whether you have ever been personally discipled or need to be.
- Get an orientation toward seeing spiritual growth as a total makeover and growing up again in a new family, the family of God. Find a community that will provide those elements.

TIPS FOR FACILITATORS:

- Examine your own theology and see how much of a part the Body plays in your teaching or delivery of the good things God has for people. Correct and repent of any views you might have that do not give the Body of Christ the high position Scripture gives it.
- Teach people to realize the importance of being connected to the Body.
- Provide experiences and contexts for that connection to be realized.
- Take an inventory of these elements to see if they are all present in your own ministry or group: connection, discipline and structure, accountability, grace and forgiveness, support and strengthening, mentoring, grieving, modeling, healing, confronting. Add the ones that are not present.
- Make suffering and imperfection part of the culture and experience of the Body life you are promoting. See perfectionism and "total victory all the time" as impediments to people's being honest and real with God and each other. Confront them the way the Bible does.
- Provide contexts for discipleship if appropriate.
- Teach an orientation toward (1) the new birth as being a beginning, and (2) the process of sanctification as being one of growing up all over again in a new family.

well: "For you know that we dealt with each of you as a father deals with his own children, encouraging, comforting and urging you to live lives worthy of God, who calls you into his kingdom and glory" (1 Thess. 2:11–12).

A COMPLETE MAKEOVER

ENTIRE CHAPTERS IN THIS book talk of how these processes work. In fact, throughout this book you will notice the role of the Body threaded through every task. The Bible teaches that growth happens in the Body of Christ as he imparts his gifts to each member.

The metaphor of the developing child (one that the New Testament uses often) is a good way to remember the overall concept. The theology of redemption is not one of rehabilitation. It is not as if God comes to us and says, "You look like a good candidate for a 'fixer-upper.' Let's take you where you are and clean you up a little, improve you here and there, and then you will be ready for my kingdom and for life." This is not what the Bible teaches at all.

The theology of redemption is one of total destruction, of starting all over again, at *birth*. We are not to be "improved"; we are to be crucified and *born again*. As Paul says, the old has been crucified, and all things have become new (2 Cor. 5:17; Gal. 2:20). (Remember, he says "new," not "complete," as some would teach.) So we need to enter an entire developmental process. John speaks of us as "children" who are learning, whether young or old (1 John 2:12–14). Peter uses the term "newborn babes" (1 Peter 2:2). Hebrews refers to "infants" (Heb. 5:13). The spiritual developmental path is one of reconciling the creation to the way it was supposed to be.

We were to be born into the human race to grow up to be perfect or "complete" people. But the human race fell, and none of us has made it to adulthood "complete," for we all came from a dysfunctional family: *the human race*. We all "missed the mark," which is the Bible's term for sin. So God wiped out the old and started over. We have to go through a rebirth and a re-growing up, this time in a new family. This family is his family, the Body of Christ. In that family we are to get all the things we missed out on the first time. Nurturance, modeling, truth, love, accountability, development of talents, and more are all to be present in this family to give the babies what they need to grow up to maturity and completeness. It is all about character development, the process of sanctification. And sanctification always happens in a family setting.

So, in this new family, the family of God, his Body, the developmental process takes place the same way the Bible describes the physical process occurring. Proverbs 13:20 says, "He who walks with the wise grows wise, but a companion of fools suffers harm." As people are walking and spending time with good people, they are growing into good people. God's pattern has always been about life giving life. As he breathed life into mankind, and as that life is passed on by mankind from one person to another, so is spiritual and personal growth. It is produced in one and passed on to another. That happens in the Body.

Hebrews 10:24 tells us, "Let us consider how we may spur one another on toward love and good deeds." Make sure you are in a Body that is growing you up, and make sure you are designing those experiences for the ones you shepherd. If you do that, you are growing people in the way God designed. You are doing it according to Plan A.

8

OPEN SPACES: THE POWER OF ACCEPTANCE

When we finally understand that God isn't mad at us anymore, we become free to concentrate on love and growth instead of trying to appease him.

One night at my (John's) small-group meeting, in which we were scheduled to talk about a Bible passage and our own lives, Gary asked if he could speak first.

"I don't know how to do this," he began, and then he wept uncontrollably. None of us knew what was wrong, so we sat with him, offering comfort, until he could speak again. "I need to confess something to you. After I tell you though, I want to ask you a favor. Would you tell me what you feel toward me? I'd like to know, even if it's not positive."

We all nodded, and Gary began. He told us a story about how he, a single man, had recently ended an affair with a married woman. He had been having the relationship while he was in the group and had been afraid to bring it up. Two of the reasons he had terminated the affair were his spiritual torment and the barriers he experienced in not being able to be open with us, his spiritual family.

Gary finished his confession. We were quiet for a while, each lost in our own thoughts and feelings. Then, one by one, people told him how they felt about him.

—"I feel closer to you now than before you talked."

—"I know that must have been really hard for you. You're okay with me."

—"Tell us how we can help."

—"I have had a similar struggle."

—"How could we have made it safer for you to talk about it?"

Gary was overwhelmed by the acceptance. He was so ready for people to say anything from at best, "I am so hurt that you didn't come to us sooner," to at worst, "I can't be in the group with you anymore."

This night was not the end of the conversation. Over time, Gary dealt with factors that led up to the affair, such as his own family background and his isolation and perfectionism. We discussed the fears that kept him from telling us sooner. The group helped him stay accountable to the restoration and healing he needed.

Several years have passed, and Gary and I have kept in touch. He is married with kids, and he has a fruitful ministry in his church. Gary still regards that night as one of the milestones on his spiritual journey.

This event affected more than Gary, however. It shifted the entire nature of our group. Things got deeper with everyone, and we discussed life and God in more vulnerable and open ways. Gary's confession helped make it safe for the rest of us to bring more of ourselves to the group. Not that it was a bad group to begin with. It was made up of some spiritual, caring honest people who wanted to study the Word and grow together. But we had all been playing it safe with what we divulged about our problems and struggles—until that night.

Sometimes I reflect on the Bible's words about a divinely appointed time for everything: "a time to tear and a time to mend" (Eccl. 3:7). It was the right time for us. Gary's openness tore down our fears of being vulnerable and mended deep places within all of us. Being a member of that group was one of the most growth-producing experiences in my life. I learned much about the good things that happen in our hearts when we feel accepted.

IT STARTS WITH GOD

WHAT IS ACCEPTANCE, AND why is it necessary in order for people to grow? The Bible teaches that acceptance begins with God: "Accept one another, then, just as Christ accepted you, in order to bring praise to God" (Rom. 15:7). Christ's acceptance of us is the model for how we are to accept each other.

The word *acceptance* means "taking to oneself." It is an invitation. Briefly defined, acceptance is the state of receiving someone into relationship. To be accepted is to have all of your parts, good and bad, received by another without condemnation. It applies to all our relationships: with God, others, and ourselves. It is closely related to grace, undeserved merit. Acceptance is the result of the working of grace. Because of God's grace, we are accepted into relationship. It is both a fact and something we are to take into our subjective experience, our hearts.

God originally designed acceptance as a way of life. As humans, we were to relate to him and to each other with no thought of condemnation, judgment, or criticism. We were connected with each other. In the beginning, Adam and Eve "were both naked, and they felt no shame" (Gen. 2:25). They were vulnerable and not disconnected.

However, when we sinned and fell from grace, acceptance posed a problem for God. His holy nature could not accept our sinfulness; yet his love kept him caring about us. So God provided a costly solution: his Son Jesus—fully God, fully man, and without sin—died to atone for our sins (1 Peter 3:18). This sacrifice appeased the requirements of God's holiness and restored us to acceptance.

God's acceptance of us in no way negates or minimizes our badness. In fact, he is able to receive us now, not because we are innocent, but because our debt of guilt has been fully paid, once and for all. So when we are afraid that he will not accept us because we have done something wrong, it is we who, at some level, are negating and minimizing what he has done for us. There is truly now no condemnation for those who belong to Jesus (Rom. 8:1).

WHAT ACCEPTANCE DOES IN GROWTH

ACCEPTANCE PLAYS MANY ROLES in how people grow. It is central to the process.

ACCEPTANCE FREES FROM BONDAGE TO THE LAW. First, acceptance breaks our bondage to the impossible demands of the law. The law has not been done away with; rather, in Jesus, it has been fulfilled (Matt. 5:17). So when we break the law now, we do not lose our relationship. We are forever in a state of acceptance.

This truth is so important to spiritual growth. We tend to work very hard to make ourselves good enough for God. This is the law working within us. It helps some very sick parts of us—such as our self-righteousness, our pride, and our fear of being dependent—feel safe, in control, and less vulnerable and needy. Acceptance does away with the need to prove ourselves worthy and replaces it with an appeal to living on the basis of relationship rather than by performance and good works.

When we live under the law, we are forever trying to appease God so he won't be mad at us. We can't do this for very long without getting angry ourselves, either toward God for being so strict, or toward ourselves for failing (Rom. 4:15). When we finally understand that *God isn't mad at us anymore,* we become free to concentrate on love and growth instead of trying to appease him. It is one of the most liberating truths in the Bible.

The law operates in spiritual growth circles, as, for example, when someone encounters a problem, such as a teenaged son who is drinking. The desperate mother may be afraid to let others know how this problem is breaking her heart for fear of being judged. She may try to reason with her son, nag him, force him not to drink, or hope that the issue will go away if she keeps a peaceable relationship with him. She is trying to deal with the problem by herself, without the grace and acceptance she needs.

ACCEPTANCE BUILDS TRUST AND RELATIONSHIP. Acceptance is a bridge to developing safe and growth-producing relationships, both with God and with people. We can't grow unless we are sure that we are both known and loved. Some people like us because they don't know us; some know us, and therefore don't like us. Relationship can't occur unless both knowledge and love are present.

Acceptance bridges this gap between being known and being loved. It is freeing to understand that being known doesn't ruin a relationship but in fact strengthens it. When people are in an accepting environment, they can stop pretending to be someone they aren't. They can rest in the relationship. This is what trust is about. An Old Testament definition of *trust* is "to be careless." In a sense, accepting relationships provide "carelessness." You don't have to edit every word and step on eggshells to stay connected. You can be careless in how you talk about yourself; you can be who you are.

ACCEPTANCE PROVIDES HEALING AND GROWTH IN AND OF ITSELF. Relationships in which we are accepted go a long way in helping us grow. The warmth and permission to be ourselves allow us to be more honest and vulnerable and allow us to bring to light parts of ourselves that need to be connected to relationship. This connection to relationship itself fuels growth in us.

When I think back over my dearest relationships, I do remember the wisdom and advice I received. But I remember more profoundly the acceptance I experienced. Knowing I could bring my inner swamp to some sane people who wouldn't leave me has forever changed me for the better.

This principle is the underlying reason why you hear so much in growth circles about the value of "being there" for someone versus giving advice. Nothing is wrong with advice in its proper place; however, many people simply need to be accepted to gain security, stability, and strength to solve their problems. Become an accepting person, and you will have a long line of people at your door!

ACCEPTANCE CREATES SAFETY TO BE AND EXPERIENCE OURSELVES. Many people are stuck in their spiritual growth because they can't be completely themselves. They may be able to be real about their opinions, happy times, humor, or care for others; however, they think that their depression, sad times, addictions, or neediness are unacceptable to God or people, so they live their lives as though these parts didn't exist. We need to experience all of our souls, whether good, bad, or broken; otherwise, what is not brought into the light of God's love and relationship cannot be matured, healed, and integrated into the rest of our character.

One woman who had always been the "giver" in her relationships found that she had been forever terrified that if she had a need, people would leave her because she was so selfish and such a burden. So she lived as though she had no needs. If you asked her how she was, she would either automatically say, "Fine, how are you?" or, if she were in a pensive mood, she would think about it and not be able to come up with anything. She had not been able to experience her own dependency and neediness. Nor, as a result, could she experience the joy of having someone care about her in deep ways.

When she experienced acceptance in her Bible study group, this woman felt safe enough to feel things like loneliness, needs for comfort, and dependency. These new emotions at first were not pleasant for her. However, as she, God, and the group persevered, she experienced her need for relationship as a good thing and as something that brought her closer to people she cared about. Acceptance made it safe enough for her to be and experience herself, especially parts of herself that had been in darkness for a long time.

Here are some of the parts of our soul that acceptance can bring to light:

- **Needs.** Like the example of the "giver" above, we need to need (Eccl. 4:9–12). Acceptance makes it acceptable to feel our incompleteness and spiritual poverty, without shame or guilt.
- **Sins.** By our very nature, we hide our sins even from ourselves. The law makes us fear that we will incur wrath if our sins are exposed. But when we experience acceptance, we not only tolerate looking at our transgressions, but look even deeper into ourselves for other dark places in which sin resides (Ps. 139:23–24).
- **Judged parts.** Certain feelings and aspects of our souls may not be intrinsically sinful; however, they may be parts that we don't like or accept. Often we judge ourselves the way we have been judged. For example, someone who has encountered a lot of criticism in life for being angry may beat himself up when he gets mad, whether or not the anger is legitimate (Eph. 4:26). He may think of himself as bad and wrong for being angry. Thus, he may find himself in dangerous situations and

not be able to use his anger to protect himself. For example, the man who feels that his anger toward his wife's financial irresponsibility is bad may avoid dealing with the problem until they are deep in debt.

- **Hiding styles.** We also wear "fig leaves" over parts of ourselves to avoid experiencing negative things. For example, some people intellectualize to stay away from emotions that trouble or frighten them. They live in their heads to avoid their hearts. (*Hiding from Love: How to Change the Withdrawal Patterns That Isolate and Imprison You* deals in detail with these hiding styles, also called defenses.) Sometimes people condemn themselves for the very styles they are using to avoid other condemned aspects of themselves. For example, the intellectualizer may hate herself for seeming so distant or disconnected from her friends.

- **Brokenness and weakness.** All of us have weaknesses that need to be accepted by God and others to be restored. Many times these frailties aren't sins, but merely inabilities. For example, some individuals may be emotionally unable to trust and reach out; others may struggle with standing up to controlling people; still others may be easily wounded by criticism because of some unresolved need for approval. The healing begins when acceptance makes it safe enough to admit these realities to ourselves.

I read in the newspaper recently about a major professional athlete who has had severe problems with addictions. He has tried unsuccessfully many times to kick his habits. However, this last time he has encountered better results. He attributes much of this to his finally admitting he has a serious problem rather than thinking nothing is deeply broken inside him.

ACCEPTANCE CREATES SAFETY TO CONFESS AND HEAL. To experience and "be" our sinful or broken selves is only one step in spiritual growth, however. Another necessary step is to bring those feelings and parts into relationship with God and others (James 5:16). The Bible calls this step "confession," meaning "to agree with the truth." Confessing involves taking a risk with a negative part of ourselves, letting someone else know about it. As we experience comfort, identification, and truth without judgment, we begin to heal. God created us to be confessors. We were not designed to sequester parts of our lives from others, but to involve others in the connection. This is what it means to "live in the light" (see Eph. 5:8–14).

ACCEPTANCE INCREASES INITIATIVE AND RISK IN GROWTH. Acceptance often starts "movement" in someone's spiritual growth. In an environment of no condemnation, people are honest about issues they haven't felt safe to reveal before. When they find that it's okay to confess one problem, they fire up the backhoe and they dig deeper into the dark parts of their souls. As acceptance increases, so does confession, and with confession come intimacy and growth.

For example, Judy, one of the members of a group I was leading, had never in her life disagreed with anyone who had a strong personality. She had always been compliant, easily controlled, and intimidated. Her fear of disapproval kept her a people pleaser instead of a God-pleaser (Gal. 1:10), and she hated it. So she joined the group.

Judy needed a lot of acceptance. She thought she was selfish for having opinions. She knew that she was passive and that she had waited too long to work on her passivity. She didn't have enough love and structure inside to stand up against others with the truth. In the group, she received acceptance for all of these legitimate needs.

Finally, one day Judy approached Linda, the most controlling, dominating person in the group. "I would like to have a relationship with you," Judy said, "but when you interrupt and negate people's feelings and try to control things, it keeps me apart from you. I would like for us to address this together."

More fainthearted group members almost fainted, waiting for Linda to explode. But instead, she said, "Thanks! You are right. I do all those things you said, and I'm ruining my marriage and children. I would love to work on this with you."

They both went to work, and both grew a great deal.

Judy risked being truthful for one of the first times in her life. She exercised a spiritual "muscle" she had never before developed. Much of the credit went to the acceptance and encouragement she had received from others in the group.

When you know that risking won't bring judgment, you can try new things. This assurance is the cure for fears of failure. The Bible teaches that "solid food is for the mature, who because of practice have their senses trained to discern good and evil" (Heb. 5:14 NASB). As we mature, we grow by practicing and trying out new things. The only penalty, when we are accepted, is failing and learning. There is no condemnation.

As acceptance increases, so does our awareness of other broken parts of ourselves. This runs counter to much emotional-growth thinking that says that the answer to life is finding out how good we are. This thinking states that our problems rest in feeling better about ourselves. The reality is that we are indeed loved, but finding our goodness by itself is never the solution. In fact, a quest for goodness can lead to missing the mark of our need and missing God's grace. Truly healthy people know they have good parts, but they also know their bad parts. However, they have the acceptance and grace to deal with them in God's process of growth.

ACCEPTING ACCEPTANCE: FOR THE GROWER

IF YOU ARE GROWING, several things can help you find greater acceptance from God and others. Often we don't know what to do with acceptance, or we are afraid of it. The following steps will help you in your path to maturity.

BE AWARE OF YOUR NEED. Whether you are seeking spiritual growth because of a desire to know God better or to deal with a problem disrupting your life, it is important to identify the need or needs that drive you to growth. Acceptance is meaningless if there is nothing that needs to be accepted. Take the humble step of confessing your lacks and needs to God and others. Enter into your spiritual poverty (see chapter 14).

GIVE UP THE LAW AS A MEANS TO ACCEPTANCE. We are born legalists. In other words, we want to earn love and acceptance. It is less risky than receiving it gratis; it helps us think we are in control and can keep us disconnected from relationship. Ask God to shine his light on your tendencies to work for acceptance from him or others. Question your motives for working hard in life: Is it because you are already accepted, or because you want acceptance?

DEAL WITH TENDENCIES TO NEGATE ACCEPTANCE. Many of us are afraid of acceptance because we try to earn it and we can't, or because we don't want to be vulnerable or dependent on someone. Explore the various ways you might be pushing away the acceptance of God or others. You might reject someone's love because of your fears, or you might have a severely punitive conscience, which makes your badness seem too big to be accepted. Recognize that badness isn't the problem. Rather, see the problem as the harsh voices inside you, and replace them with the feedback of loving, balanced people.

USE ACCEPTANCE TO GROW. Being received by God and others is not an end in itself. It is the beginning of the safety and grace you need to grow personally, relationally, and emotionally. It gives you the courage to accept who and what you are, and to take steps to deal with who you are.

Some people, especially those who have been hurt by harsh criticism and rejection, will center their growth on acceptance alone, in a form of "let go and let God" thinking. They will evaluate their friends and spiritual growth partners by how accepting or nonaccepting they are. If you ask them why they haven't addressed some particular struggle in their lives, they may say, "It will all work out as I receive more grace and acceptance." This attitude misses one of the main purposes of acceptance, which is to create an environment in which we can actively face, own, and transform realities about ourselves.

REQUEST, DON'T DEMAND IT. Sometimes people think they can require others to accept who they are, and they feel justified in resenting others for not doing so. Never forget that acceptance is entirely a gift from God and others. We cannot demand it because we do not deserve it. What we do deserve is terrifying: "The soul who sins is the one who will die" (Ezek. 18:4). This is a hard truth. Never ask for what you deserve—you really don't want that. Instead, model yourself after Gary in the story at the beginning of the chapter: Humbly ask God and safe people for acceptance, so that you can accept yourself, confess, and grow.

DON'T CONFUSE ACCEPTANCE WITH AGREEMENT. When someone in the growth process opens up and becomes vulnerable, and another person gives her honest feedback, she commonly feels persecuted and wrongfully judged. She thinks, "That criticism proves he does not truly accept me." Many people will even leave relationships because they feel unaccepted. They will say, "That church/group/counselor is so unaccepting of people. I need to find a place where there is grace." What they are asking for, in reality, is license, which God forbids (Rom. 6:15; Gal. 5:13).

While some criticism can be judgmental, direct loving criticism is a necessary part of spiritual growth. In fact, where there is no confrontation, growth is seriously hampered (Eph. 4:15). Agreement and acceptance are not equal. You can and should be in an environment in which both total acceptance and clear honesty are operating. Use Jesus' stance toward the churches in Revelation 3 as a good model for confrontation in the context of support. Further, the Bible teaches that any relationship that avoids necessary truth telling must take on some responsibility for the results (Ezek. 3:18–21). Don't be afraid of truth; it hurts but heals.

CREATING A CONTEXT FOR ACCEPTANCE: FOR THE HELPER

IF YOU ARE A facilitator of growth, such as a pastor, leader, counselor, or teacher, you are probably aware of how difficult it is to create an accepting environment in which people open up, give up the law, and confess. Here are some ways to foster acceptance in your growth setting.

LET PEOPLE KNOW THAT ACCEPTANCE IS THE NORM. Talk to your members about the importance of acceptance. Many of them are expecting you to hold them to perfectionist standards, so they aren't about to open up. Instead, let them know that acceptance is the way God treats us, and therefore it is the way we are to treat others. Let them know that condemnation and judgment will not be acceptable.

I recently accepted an invitation to speak at a church where I had never been before. I asked the people who were sponsoring my talk about the spiritual culture of the church. One person said, "You're going to have a challenge. The people here are taught that they have no problems, so nobody talks about them." Fortunately, those who held that view were open to biblical teaching on acceptance, and we had some fruitful dialogue. Therefore require acceptance, and then within that safe environment encourage confession.

TIPS FOR GROWERS:

- Work on understanding the biblical meaning of acceptance. Be aware of any tendencies to see acceptance either as negating our true badness or as being based on our goodness, neither of which is real acceptance.
- Take an inventory of how acceptance or its lack has affected your life. For example, how has being with unaccepting people kept you from opening up to grace? How has resisting the acceptance of God and others kept you disconnected from growth? How has entering into relationship with acceptance helped you grow?
- Investigate what specific parts of your soul exist outside of acceptance, and find out why they do and how you can bring them to acceptance.

TIPS FOR FACILITATORS:

- Help your growers to see that receiving God's acceptance is a necessary first step to personal growth. Be aware that some will not yet know the depth of their need for acceptance, and some will be afraid of that aspect of themselves. Make it safe for that reality to emerge.
- Work with them on understanding the difference between acceptance and approval, so that they can safely own sins, badness, and immaturity without losing acceptance.
- Confront tendencies to avoid the need for acceptance or to hide from the necessary confession that coexists with acceptance.
- Deal with tendencies for people to have a condemning, nonaccepting stance with others who need acceptance, and help point them to their own need.

BE VULNERABLE. If your role permits, be open about your own failings and how acceptance has been important in your life. People identify with strugglers, not supermen or superwomen. You need to judge on a case-by-case basis, however, as some roles, such as that of a clinical counselor, are not well suited to being vulnerable.

DEAL WITH ACCEPTANCE PROBLEMS AS INTERNAL ISSUES. If you find someone has a hard time accepting weaknesses in others and constantly criticizes or judges, this person may have a judged aspect of his own soul that he can't tolerate. Therefore he externalizes it onto someone else. As Jesus said, he looks at the speck in his brother's eye and not the plank in his own (Matt. 7:1–5). For example, someone who gets upset by another person's neediness may actually be quite critical of his own dependency, perceiving it as being irresponsible or lazy. His inability to accept his own dependency makes him resentful of others who don't hide that trait. When you see this, address it and help the judging person investigate what he might be reacting to inside.

DISTINGUISH BETWEEN THE SIN AND THE SINNER. Although you want to foster an environment of acceptance, you also need to help people confront wrong attitudes, behaviors, and values. As the old saying goes, "Love the sinner and hate the sin." There is a basic order to this also. The sinner will probably not admit and be open about struggles until he knows his soul is accepted. Grace should precede truth. But don't make the mistake of either extreme: avoiding confrontation in an attempt to avoid judgmentalism, or injuring someone's soul by not accepting who he is.

MAINTAIN A HUMBLE STANCE TOWARD GROWTH. Nothing is worse than the person who is "growing spiritually" who then feels she can't relate to others in her life because they are now in two different worlds. It is a condemning attitude. Help her to see that all growth is a gift from God and that as we are accepted at deeper and deeper levels, we are driven to accept others in our lives even more fully. Truly accepted people become truly accepting people. Use this as a yardstick for your growers: Are they becoming more or less accepting of all those unfinished people in their lives? Confront spiritual nonacceptance directly and quickly, before it has a chance to flower.

KEEP A PROCESS ORIENTATION TO ACCEPTANCE. Bear in mind that acceptance and being accepted don't come easily to anybody. They are processes that take time to develop and mature. Be patient with your people as they struggle to accept others and be accepted by God and others. Help them tolerate what they can bear right here and now, then nudge them toward further acceptance.

In the group I was in with Gary, I saw the process deepen over time. At first, everybody was nervous about what was and wasn't safe to talk about. After a time of working on it, however, we were not only admitting real struggles, but even joking about those that could be appropriately joked about. I had never dreamed you could say, as a woman did, for example, "I really want to kill my husband today. So let's talk about it so I won't." I am glad to say she talked, and he is still alive!

The safety of acceptance promotes spiritual growth. In the next chapter we deal with an obstacle to acceptance: condemnation.

9

GETTING TO
THE WARMTH
OF FORGIVENESS

*A "guilty Christian" is an oxymoron. But Stephen still
feels guilty. What's his problem?*

No matter how many times I read that I'm forgiven, I just don't
feel like it," Stephen said. "I know the Bible tells me God accepts
me. I know it in my head, but I can't feel it in my heart."

"What have you tried to do to change that?" I (Henry) asked.

"Well, I've tried memorizing verses and focusing on how God loves
me and accepts me. I just have to believe it more, I guess."

"So you think you can't feel it because you don't believe it?"

"Well, I guess so. That's what my friends tell me. They say if I don't
feel God's forgiveness, I'm not taking him at his word. It comes down
to a lack of faith, I guess. I need to believe him more."

"Do you *disbelieve* him?"

"What do you mean?"

"Well, do you have any reason to doubt God forgives you? Do you
not believe it?"

"No, I believe it. He says so. I just can't feel it."

"Well, then, why do you say you need to believe it more? Why do you think it's a 'believing' problem if you already believe it?"

"Because my friends tell me the Bible says the truth will set you free, and if I don't feel free from guilt, then I don't know the truth. That's why I think I need to believe the truth better."

"Well, you're partly right," I said. "The Bible does say that the truth will set you free, but it doesn't say that knowing the truth comes from believing it better. Jesus says it comes if we 'keep obeying my teachings' [John 8:31–32 NLT]. In other words, if you live out all he said, you will 'know' the truth. That's a lot different from just getting information into your head."

"How do I do that? How do I live in a way that will fix this?"

"Well, that's what we are going to have to find out and do."

Stephen had been acting out sexually. Every now and then he would have a "slip" (as he called it) and go to the Internet and view pornographic web sites. At other times he would have one-night stands and feel horribly guilty later. Even after he had confessed and asked God to forgive him, the guilt would remain for days, and he would be unable to shake it. What he *knew in his head* about forgiveness was different from what he *felt in his soul*.

He is not alone. We have talked to many people who ask God for his forgiveness, receive it, and then find they cannot feel it. They try to feel forgiven, but instead find that, even though the Bible says they are forgiven, guilt plagues them for a long time. Sadly, they do not know what to do other than what they have tried, and that is to ask God again and to read what he has said. So they pray and read over and over again 1 John 1:9, which says, "If we confess our sins, he is faithful and just and will forgive us our sins and purify us from all unrighteousness." This helps for a moment, but when the guilt remains, they often do not know what to do.

Stephen would get caught in a cycle. When he could not get rid of his guilt, he would act out sexually again to find relief. But instead of relief, it would bring more guilt, and the cycle would begin all over again. We see this same cycle in other behaviors, such as overeating. People will overeat and feel guilty, and then to feel better they will overeat again. Then the guilt comes back, because they are traveling in an endless circle.

So how are we to help Stephen? And what do we do when we *are* Stephen, for many of us can identify with not feeling as forgiven as we are? What are the steps he asked about, and how do we take them? That is the subject of this chapter. We will look at the causes of guilt and how the spiritual growth process can resolve them. We will look at where guilt comes from, some misconceptions about dealing with it, and what works.

THE SOURCE AND RESOLUTION OF GUILT

TO FULLY UNDERSTAND HOW our guilt is resolved, let's take a short look at theology. Remember our discussion of the Fall in chapter 2. When we fell, we went into a state of death, or separation, which the Bible refers to as sin. In the beginning God created us to be in relationship with him, and in that state we felt not a hint of guilt. We were not even aware of good and evil. We were connected to God and we were ourselves, totally vulnerable. The question of whether or not we were good or bad never entered our minds. Instead of judgment, we had love and connectedness with God.

But then we turned against him, and as a result we became separated from him. The relationship was broken, and we lost his love. For the first time, we knew guilt and shame.* As Genesis says, Adam and Eve hid because they were afraid because they were naked. That was the beginning of guilt and shame (Gen. 3:10). They lost their connection with God. In other words, guilt and separation from him were one and the same.

Later in the Bible, Paul explains that this separation from God was a state called *death* (Rom. 5:12). It was not cessation of life, however, as we normally think of death. Instead it was separation from life. We

---

*Historically there has been great debate regarding the differences and nuances between guilt and shame. Often that discussion links shame with being and guilt with doing. While there is truth in that view, in an overall sense the distinctions are more complicated than that. Therefore it seems beyond the purpose of this book to address the differences and nuances from either a theological or psychologically technical viewpoint. Our purpose here is to address for people in the growth process, or those who help them, the general experience of "badness."

were living, but we were dead because we were separated from Life itself. As a result, we were under the wrath and condemnation of God and his law; we were found guilty in the cosmic court of God. And as the Bible puts it, that law brings about two things: guilt and wrath (Rom. 4:15). We feel guilty, and, in addition to being under the wrath of God, we have our own anger at our imperfection.

But God provided an answer to this problem. Since the wages of our sin against God is death (Rom. 6:23), someone had to pay the death penalty. This is what Jesus did. He paid the penalty for our sin against God, and as a result he solved the problem of our death, our separation. We were guilty and separated, and instead of our having to pay the ultimate price, Jesus paid it for us. We were made "right" with God; we were declared "not guilty." As Paul puts it, "This righteousness from God comes through faith in Jesus Christ to all who believe" (Rom. 3:22).

The resolution of our guilt did not come from our "being good." It came from Jesus dying and paying the death penalty. As a result, we are reconnected to God. We now have an unbroken and alive relationship with him. There is no longer any separation and death. As the apostle Paul says, nothing can come between God's love and us ever again:

> Who will bring any charge against those whom God has chosen? It is God who justifies. Who is he that condemns? Christ Jesus, who died—more than that, who was raised to life—is at the right hand of God and is also interceding for us. Who shall separate us from the love of Christ? Shall trouble or hardship or persecution or famine or nakedness or danger or sword? As it is written:
>
> > *"For your sake we face death all day long;*
> > *we are considered as sheep to be slaughtered."*
>
> No, in all these things we are more than conquerors through him who loved us. For I am convinced that neither death nor life, neither angels nor demons, neither the present nor the future, nor any powers, neither height nor depth, nor anything else in all creation, will be able to separate us from the love of God that is in Christ Jesus our Lord. (Rom. 8:33–39).

Notice the key points here. *No charges can be brought against those who are justified by believing in Jesus, and nothing can separate them from his love.* This is why Paul says in the beginning of that same chapter, and in the midst of a struggle that sounds a lot like Stephen's (Rom. 7), that "Therefore, there is now no condemnation for those who are in Christ Jesus" (v. 1).

No condemnation. The verdict is "not guilty." No separation. No anger or wrath. In other words, those who have a relationship with Jesus have no reason to fear condemnation or guilt. The New Testament makes this point over and over again (see John 3:18; Heb. 10:13–14, 17–23).

The point we are making here is that guilt came from being separated from God and guilt can be resolved by being reconnected to God through Jesus. The guilt was total and legal, and the resolution is the same. We go from guilty to not guilty by believing. Separation equals guilty, and reconciled equals not guilty. This is the theology of guilt in the Christian faith. A "guilty Christian" is an oxymoron.

But Stephen still *feels* guilty. What's his problem?

Two Sides, Two Experiences

THE BIBLE TALKS ABOUT our legal standing before God, about how God feels toward us. It does not talk much about how we feel within ourselves. How *we* feel in response to how God sees us is the other side of the equation. In this way our relationship to God is like any other relationship. A husband, for example, can love his wife deeply, but this does not ensure that his wife is going to *feel* loved. She may be deeply cared about and accepted and yet unable to experience the love her husband has for her.

Have you ever been in a relationship where someone needed constant reassurance of your love? Your loved one asked you over and over again if you cared, and no matter what you did to show your love, it did not get through. After a while you realized that your reassurances were not all that was needed to help the other person. She had a problem in her heart. She had a block to feeling love. To tell her a thousand more times would not solve her problem. If she were ever going to feel your love, she was going to have to find out what inside of her was keeping her from feeling it.

It is the same in our relationship with God. Our hearts can condemn us even when God does not (1 John 3:20; 4:18). So we have to ask, "What is wrong with our side of the equation? What are the conditions inside of us that prevent us from feeling forgiveness even when we are surely forgiven?" This was the question Stephen had to ask and find answers to, and it is the question we all have to ask if we struggle with guilt. Let's look at some of the answers.

Wrong Teaching

Wrong teaching can keep us from feeling forgiven. The first question we always ask someone who is struggling with guilt is, "What do you know about what the Bible teaches?" After working with many Christians over the years, I have been amazed at how many do not know what we have just written above. Many have been taught that we are forgiven until we sin again and then we have to be forgiven all over again. Then they struggle with whether or not their confession was good enough. The Bible does not say that we go into a state of legal guilt when we sin. In fact, it makes light of the old sacrificial system that could never relieve us of feeling guilty. "[The law] can never, by the same sacrifices repeated endlessly year after year, make perfect those who draw near to worship. If it could, would they not have stopped being offered? For the worshipers would have been cleansed once for all, and would no longer have felt guilty for their sins" (Heb. 10:1–2).

Some have never been taught how forgiven they are when they believe in Jesus. They truly have been forgiven "once for all," and there is truly "no condemnation." So the first thing we have to make sure of is whether people understand that if they are reconnected to God, they are not guilty. Their problem may not be that their emotions are not following their knowledge. They may just not know.

In cases like this, it is crucial that people learn what the Bible really says about forgiveness and God's grace. Meditating on and memorizing Scripture verses about forgiveness and grace should be a part of their regular diet until they understand what God says about "no condemnation." They need to be able to answer their internal accusations with God's truth.

But all of this assume that a person is confessing his sin to God and asking for forgiveness (1 John 1:9). In some circles, confession of sin is a lost art. We can only receive God's forgiveness to the degree we are confessing. So make sure confession is taking place. If it is, God will cleanse and purify us (1 John 1:9).

Disconnection from Grace

Jake struggled with overwhelming guilt because of his depression. He had been working on his depression for some time, but was not getting well as fast as he thought he should. In his mind, he should not still be struggling. I would talk to him about giving himself some time and some grace, but he would still feel guilty about not having it all together. He just could not "cut himself any slack."

After watching him struggle with this for a while, I knew his depression was not going to get better until he had the grace to allow himself to be depressed. One can't fix something under the attack of guilt. He needed grace before his depression could be resolved. So, since he was praying and getting all the grace he could directly from God, he must have been cut off from grace from other people. (As we saw in chapter 7 on the Body, God gives his grace directly, but also through his people. They are part of his grace-distribution system.) Peter says that people "administer God's grace" (see 1 Peter 4:10). I figured Jake needed more grace from God's people, so I put him in a group.

The difference was profound. He found that he was not the only one whose struggle with depression took some time to resolve. He found acceptance from the other people in the group. Their grace touched him. He internalized it as he experienced their love. The Body was doing its work in his soul. They had the acceptance for him that he did not have for himself, and it was "getting in." He found that as others gave him grace, he could give himself more space to be where he was.

God has mysteriously wired us so that what was once outside of us comes inside. Based on our past relationships, we learn how to accept or reject ourselves. Our relationships and their messages are internalized in our brains. If people reject themselves or some part of themselves, part of the answer is encouraging them to join a supportive, accepting community so they can internalize new ways of feeling toward themselves. This is what Jake found. As others accepted him, he exchanged his critical voices inside for accepting ones. As James says, "Therefore confess your sins to each other and pray for each other so that you may be healed" (James 5:16). As we do that, we internalize from each other the grace we need.

When people are in grace settings and truly confessing to each other, their bad parts get totally known, accepted, and integrated. When all of our badness is known—and loved by grace—it loses its power. The goal is for grace to know all of our bad parts, and confession to God and others achieves that. The result is that guilt is dissolved.

False Standards

In addition to receiving grace from others in the group, something else happened to Jake. He discovered that his standard of "I should be over this by now" was false. It was easy to criticize himself as long as he compared himself with an unreal standard inside his own head. But when he got into a group, he found that others struggled as well; he was not the only one. He was not defective.

People who grow up with unrealistic standards from their parents, the media, or the culture often have an "ideal" person in their head to which they compare themselves, and the result is relentless guilt or shame. Their perfectionist standard beats them up daily. The reality is that we struggle to the degree we should, given what has happened to us. As Jesus said, we are broken and sick and need a physician. However, people have difficulty accepting their brokenness. Yet this is the standard the Bible tells us to use. David says,

> As a father has compassion on his children,
>   so the LORD has compassion on those who fear him;
> for he knows how we are formed,
>   he remembers that we are dust (Ps. 103:13–14).

God remembers the standard he measures us by; he knows we are a bunch of broken strugglers. Often we forget that. Anytime I hear "I shouldn't feel depressed" or "I should be making more progress," I know these clients are listening to the accusing voice of a false standard. While they might not want to be where they are forever, this is truly how they feel at the moment. And there is a reason why they feel this way.

As Jake found, no matter how he thought he "should" feel, he did feel depressed for very good reasons. So, when he got more in touch with reality by being with others, his internal false standards changed, and the crippling guilt went away.

People who struggle with making a career or other life endeavor work often operate under false standards. They expect to be able to do things on the first try, when the reality is that gaining skills and success takes time and effort. When they hear stories from others about how hard it was to succeed and how many failures and false starts were endured, they can give themselves more grace. Testimonies and support groups are a great source of encouragement for people. They find that others did not just "arrive" at success but had to work very hard and fail many times to get there. In short, *community helps us see failure as normal.*

The Bible is filled with stories of people who were real "Bozos." The people listed in the hall of fame in Hebrews 11 were real people with real problems, yet God lists them as models for us to emulate. God has never looked for perfect people, just faithful ones. The biblical standard is not people who have never failed; it is people who, when they failed, got reconnected to God and went on in faith. All of us should be comparing ourselves with this standard, not the one of perfection. Resolving guilt and shame always involves getting people to see themselves as fellow strugglers instead of super humans. As Paul says, we experience nothing that is not in some way common to humankind (1 Cor. 10:13). The problem is that in our isolation, we rarely find out that what we experience is common.

When people confess to one another (James 5:16), they find that out. They find out they are not weird and different, but are just like everyone else: fellow sojourners, fellow strugglers. This cuts down tremendously on guilt. If you are divorcing, get together with other people who have gone or are going through a divorce. If you are an addict, get together with other addicts. Strugglers need to be with strugglers. And in reality, that's all of us.

Weak Conscience

A weak conscience can keep us from feeling forgiven. On face value, when we think of a "weak conscience" we probably think of one that does not work well. We assume it is one too weak to stand up to our impulses. But in the Bible's view, it is just the opposite. A "weak conscience" is one that is *too* strict and is confused on the issues of right and wrong. Sometimes a weak conscience can convict people of things that are not even real issues (1 Cor. 8:7–12).

Usually the weak conscience comes from too strict a background, wrong teaching, a fear of losing control, or not enough safety for someone to find out what is helpful and real. If people feel guilty for things that are not even issues, they need the safety and grace of an accepting environment—first, to find out what the Bible really teaches, and second, to face their own appetites and impulses. As they gain the strength that comes from maturity and community, they will not need rigid rules to hold them in check. Self-control takes the place of guilt as the gatekeeper of impulses.

Idealization of Conscience

An issue related to a weak conscience is the idealization of conscience. An idealization of conscience can also keep us from feeling forgiven. When people think that just feeling bad about something means they really are bad, they might be idealizing their conscience. They blindly accept what their conscience says. In other words, they think their conscience is ideal, or without flaw.

This happens especially in controlling or hurtful relationships. A controlling person can "make" people who idealize their conscience feel bad about saying no, setting a boundary, or exhibiting freedom, and they cave in to the guilt feelings. Their immediate reaction is "I'm bad for saying no" or "I was selfish." The truth is, the other person is being controlling and giving guilt messages that should be confronted and resisted.

People who idealize their conscience, however, never question what they feel or think. They just accept it as true. But the Bible does not affirm this. As the apostle Paul says, his conscience could very well be wrong, and it is God who judges us (1 Cor. 4:4).

Confusion of Conscience with the Holy Spirit

Another related issue occurs when someone feels guilty about something and says, "The Holy Spirit is convicting me." They equate their guilt feelings with the voice of the Holy Spirit. It may or may not be true that the Holy Spirit is convicting them, but their guilt is definitely *not* the conviction of the Holy Spirit. Their guilt is their own feeling, not his.

A conviction of the Holy Spirit is something he says and does. It is his imparting of truth to us. What he feels when he does that is his feeling, not ours. Sometimes he is grieved, sometimes concerned. But his convicting is his sending a message. What we feel about that message, however, is a different matter. We may feel guilt, or we may feel something else.

Some people feel nothing because they ignore the Holy Spirit. So he is convicting, but they are not listening. They don't feel guilty. Yet, just because they are not feeling anything does not mean he is not talking. They have closed their hearts to him. So it is easy to see that guilt feelings are not his voice.

Others feel extraordinarily guilty when the Holy Spirit points something out to them. Again, this guilt is not his doing. He is convicting. What they feel is their own response to his voice. If it is guilt, they have not yet realized they are not condemned for what he is pointing out.

Godly Sorrow Versus Worldly Sorrow

Worldly sorrow can keep us from feeling forgiven. Guilt is not the proper response to the conviction of the Holy Spirit. The proper response is godly sorrow because it is based in love. Paul distinguishes between two kinds of sorrow: "Godly sorrow brings repentance that leads to salvation and leaves no regret, but worldly sorrow brings death" (2 Cor. 7:10).

The angry, condemning conscience is worldly sorrow at work. It is not based in love and does not bring about lasting change and repentance. Worldly sorrow is the kind Judas expressed after he betrayed Jesus. He went out and killed himself. Worldly sorrow is not based in love, but on oneself and one's own badness. Godly sorrow is the kind

Peter expressed after he denied Jesus. Heartbroken for the hurt he caused someone he loved, he moved toward the relationship and reconciled. He made up.

Whenever we talk in our seminars and on the radio about guilt being hurtful, people become upset. They think you need guilt to keep people in check. "People should feel guilty when they do wrong. It is healthy guilt," they say. But the Bible does not say this. *The Bible says we should not feel guilty, but we should feel sorry. There is a big difference.*

On the one hand, guilt focuses on me. It focuses on how bad I am, not on what I have done to hurt you. If I am feeling guilty, I am concerned about feeling good again, not about the destructiveness of the problem or the way I may have hurt someone. Guilt is self-directed.

On the other hand, godly sorrow focuses on the offended party. Those who express godly sorrow empathize with how their behavior has affected someone else. This is why the Bible talks about the wrath of God for the nonbeliever who is still truly guilty, contrasted with his being "grieved" when believers sin. There is no mention or room for guilt, wrath, or condemnation for the believer. Instead of our feeling guilty, he wants us to be concerned with how we have hurt him with our sin. Godly sorrow is "other directed."

The difference is astounding. As Paul says, godly sorrow ends up in repentance. When we realize we are hurting someone we love, we change. Love and empathy change us. We treat others as we would want to be treated. Love constrains us. But guilt actually causes sin to increase. It does not keep anyone in check. It only makes people rebel more. As Paul says, the law causes sin to increase (Rom. 5:20; 7:5).

This happened to Stephen. The guiltier he felt and the further he put himself under the law, the more his sin would increase. Guilt failed to keep him in check. If he could have gotten in touch with how he hurt the women he was acting out with, this could have changed him. His care for breaking their hearts, splitting their souls, and keeping them from God could have turned him around. Instead, he was too concerned with how "bad" he was.

The bottom line is that guilt is about the law and godly sorrow is about love. And the conviction of the Holy Spirit and our response differ in this way as well. The Holy Spirit is always about love—how God loves us and how he wants us to love others. When he convicts us, he is not trying to make us feel "bad and condemned" or, in short, "guilty." He is trying to get us to see how we are hurting God, others, or ourselves by our behaviors or attitudes. And if we can see that, love will "cause repentance."

Let's look at an example of someone who finally got in touch with this truth and how it changed his behavior.

Tom lied to his wife about their finances. He would not pay the bills, and he would lie about where they stood financially. Then a late notice would come in the mail or the electricity would be turned off, and she would explode emotionally, having felt horribly let down and betrayed by him. And then he would feel horribly guilty, talking about how bad a husband he was and how he would never do it again. He would promise over and over again. But it would happen again.

Finally, when they went for marriage counseling, the counselor had the good sense to focus on what was important. She got Tom to see not how "bad" he was, but how much he was hurting his wife. She got him to empathize with his wife and to understand what it must be like to live as she had to live, never knowing where things stood because of his lying. She got him in touch with his wife's heart and fear. When he got in touch with that, he could not lie again. He could not hurt her like that. He had never seen that before, because all he had thought about was how bad he was.

God is not interested in our seeing how bad we are (he has already done that), but instead in our seeing how we have betrayed and hurt him. As Paul says, "Do not grieve the Holy Spirit of God" (Eph. 4:30). If you have ever been in a relationship with someone who fails you and is overly concerned with how bad she feels as opposed to how she is affecting you, you understand how God feels. Get off the guilt and onto how your behavior affects other people. This is love.

THE NATURE OF CORRECTION

OUR CONSCIENCE MAKES US aware of right and wrong, and when we violate a standard, it corrects us. Conscience, however, can be flawed in many ways. Sometimes it can misjudge what is right or wrong, as we saw above. At other times conscience, which has an emotional tone, can be wrong in its corrective tone.

A proper tone is as loving and kind as it is firm. It is clear about what is right or wrong and does not let a person slide, but it is also kind. We call this a "New Testament tone," because in the words of the New Testament, it corrects with "grace and truth." It is not only honest but also kind and accepting.

If someone is getting beaten up from the inside by a harsh conscience, the growth facilitator has to help this person change the tone of his conscience by gaining insight into the nature of the tone as well as internalizing new, loving voices from new relationships.

Take the example of Summer, a woman in a group I used to lead. One night she came to the group and confessed a failure in her growth path. She had gone back to a destructive boyfriend for a night and had slept with him.

"I'm so stupid!" she said, angrily and harshly. "I'm so *stupid*!" She said it over and over and was very angry at herself for being duped by him. She also called herself derogatory names for sleeping with him.

The group immediately helped her with her issue of being drawn back to this relationship. They asked her how it had happened, what had tempted her, what she had been feeling, why she had allowed him to seduce her, and why she had not remembered what he was really like.

"You know, I bet she knows all of that," I said. "I bet you anything she knows all of that. We have talked about it a lot. But I bet you something else. She can't use it."

The group stopped and looked at me as if I were crazy. They were not expecting me to devalue all of their wisdom.

"I don't think she can use it because of what we just heard. The voices in her head that correct her and warn her are meaner than her boyfriend's. No wonder his seductive voice is more appealing to her than that harsh screamer."

"What?" they collectively asked.

"Summer's conscience is so mean that she runs away from it just like she ran away from her screaming parents. We are seeing her teenage years repeat themselves. I think what the group should help her with is learning how to tone down the way the voices in her head talk to her, or she will never listen."

This was not a new concept to them, as I had talked about the problem of critical voices before. What was new for them was to see how it works. They realized that having harsh voices inside did not keep someone in line.

What the group did for her then was to correct her lovingly and talk through the issues in a way that communicated that they did not want her to get hurt again. They were good, kind, protective voices. They also helped her evaluate the critical issues and see where they came from.

A few months later something happened. Summer could hardly contain her excitement as she told the group.

She had been doing well, and then the old boyfriend reappeared. He made his play for her, and she was very tempted to go with him. Then something happened. "I was getting into him, and I felt that familiar pull. Then—and I know it sounds strange—I could hear your voices talking to me in my head. I heard you say, 'Summer, we are just saying this because we are your friends: Don't do it! He will hurt you. Don't give yourself to someone who will not commit to you. We will be here for you.' It was as real as if I were sitting here. So I told him no, went home, and watched a movie. And I tell you, the next morning I felt a lot better than if I had woken up in his bed."

The tone of their correction had been different. It had not called her stupid and had not been angry with her. Instead, the tone was "for" her. This is what grace is, and we can respond to it better than an adversarial, critical, mean tone. The group had done its work. They had transformed her conscience from an enemy into a friend.

True Guilt and False Guilt

As Christian counseling grew popular during the seventies, people became increasingly aware of the problem of guilt. They noticed that sometimes people felt guilty for no good reason. In an attempt to help them, they coined the term "false guilt." For things that were not really "bad," people should see their guilt as inappropriate, label it "false guilt," and give it up. Great advice: No one should feel bad about things that are not bad.

But the problem was on the other side of the equation. These people also taught that people *should* feel guilty for the bad things they did. They called this "true guilt."

There are behaviors, attitudes, and choices that are wrong. There is no question about that. When we commit an offense, *we are guilty of committing this offense.* But this does not mean that our proper response is to feel guilty and condemned. Instead, we should feel "godly sorrow," which, as we have seen, focuses on the other person.

The problem with "true guilt" emotional response is that it is still self-focused. When we are wrong, we should feel distressed, but we should not feel bad and condemned. We should feel sorrowful remorse and concern for the party we offended. This true godly sorrow is not angry and condemning of the self, but instead empathic with and concerned for "the other." And it leads to change.

In addition, the guilty party should be concerned with the problem itself.

I recently talked to Trevor, another young man who was feeling guilty about sleeping around. He had had a few breakups with girl-friends, and he had retreated to sex instead of relationship. What was concerning him most was his guilt over his sexual behavior.

I did not condemn Trevor; I felt sorry for him. As I saw what he was doing, however, I looked into the future. I saw he would never have a satisfying relationship in life unless he changed his relational patterns with women. He would get close to a woman and then withdraw, or he would feel overpowered, become passive, and then move away from her. As a result, he kept picking the wrong kind of woman and then leaving her. As long as he avoided these issues, he would always be lonely and feel powerless with women. His sexual exploits, which gave him a feeling of power and intimacy for the moment, would never cure his soul or fetch him what he truly wanted and needed.

When Trevor talked to me, the problem he was most concerned about was his guilt. From the Bible's perspective, however, *this is not even a problem. Jesus died to end that problem, once and for all, so that we could deal with the* real *problems in our lives and souls.* His real problem was his inability to relate deeply and the way in which his sexual acting out split his soul in half. His power and assertiveness were part of his sexual exploits only and not part of his love relationships. He needed to bring his sense of interpersonal power into real relationship, put it together with love, and express it to someone he felt close to and needed. But that was too risky. So, instead, he expressed those assertive parts of himself in non-love relationships, thereby sealing his fate and reinforcing his split. This is how the sex outside of a loving marital relationship was hurting him, and it is one of the reasons God is against loveless sex. (For more information on this, see *Boundaries in Dating*.)

This was the problem I wished he would get distressed about instead of his guilt. "There is therefore now no condemnation," but there is a lot of dysfunction. And that is what the New Testament says in so many ways. Forget the guilt and solve the problems, because if you don't, you are going to reap death.

The verse about "no condemnation" comes at the beginning of Romans 8. It annihilates our guilt all together, but the chapter does not go on from there to say we have nothing to worry about. In fact, quite the opposite. It says we have to worry a great deal about how we are living and what we are doing, for we are either producing life or death by how we are living our lives. It has nothing to do with guilt, but with what sin does to us:

> Therefore, brothers, we have an obligation—but it is not to the sinful nature, to live according to it. For if you live according to the sinful nature, you will die; but if by the Spirit you put to death the misdeeds of the body, you will live, because those who are led by the Spirit of God are sons of God. For you did not receive a spirit that makes you a slave again to fear, but you received the Spirit of sonship. And by him we cry, *"Abba,* Father" (Rom. 8:12–15).

So the Bible tries to talk us out of being afraid of God and out of feeling guilty, and into living the life of spiritual health and growth. Guilt pushers do not like to get rid of guilt, for they fear that if people do not have guilt to stop them, they will do whatever they want.

But the Bible is clear. Condemnation has no place, but serious worry about sin does. When Paul preached total acceptance, he ran into the same problem we do, for it is a radical concept: "What then? Shall we sin because we are not under law but under grace? By no means!" (Rom. 6:15). He then talks about the seriousness of sin, and that is the whole point. Guilt does nothing to help. But getting a picture of what sin is doing to one's life does. And that is one of the big reasons why we have to help people like Trevor see that guilt is not the issue; sin is.

Guilt as an Old Voice

"I just feel mean telling her that," Joyce said.

She was referring to a conversation she had had with a friend about that friend's marriage. Her friend was not confronting her husband on how he was treating their teenage son. He was going back and forth from ignoring their son's behavior to confronting him angrily, and the problem was getting worse. Joyce was concerned, and rightly so, that her friend was sitting back, passively letting her husband hurt their son. So Joyce had told her friend she was being too passive and her son was going to get worse if she did not do something.

"Why do you feel mean?" one of the group members said. "That was a very loving thing to do, and you did it in a nice way. I wish I had a friend like you who would tell me when I'm not doing what I should be doing with my son. He can be a nightmare, and I could use the help. You were being such a good friend."

"But I felt horrible after I left her. I felt like I had hurt her feelings."

"Did she act like it?" another member of the group asked. "Did she get mad?"

"No, she acted fine. In fact, she said I was right, and she asked me to help her figure out what to say. But I just feel so bad, so mean." Joyce seemed to become more depressed as she talked.

"Well, someone's accusing you," another member said, "but it's not her, and it's not us. And it's surely not God. He tells us to do what you did. That was an act of love."

"What do you mean 'someone'?" she asked.

Good question. As Joyce talked, she began to see a pattern. Every time she would be lovingly honest with someone (Eph. 4:25), she would feel bad. And she was even doing what the Bible told her to do—a good deed. But her honesty had not been seen as good in past relationships. Her mother could not handle confrontation, and if Joyce ever said anything negative to her, she would punish Joyce by withdrawing emotionally. Her siblings acted similarly. Her father having died when she was ten, Joyce really needed her mom, and she would fold under her guilt messages.

What we said earlier holds true here: What was once outside is now inside. In other words, external relationships are internalized as part of our conscience (the "voices in our heads") that can accuse and condemn. Joyce had to see the reality of those past relationships and work through them. She had to gain insight into them, work through some feelings about them, blame them appropriately for their sin, forgive them, grieve them, and let them go. Then she had to internalize the new "voices" of her support group and others who loved and valued her for telling the truth. When she had done this work, she no longer experienced guilt when she confronted those she loved.

This is one of the most important dynamics about guilt. Internal ties and old relationships are replayed inside the soul, and people feel the same feelings they felt with those people until they work through those feelings. And usually the guilt has to do with the expression of some aspect of one's personhood, as Joyce experienced. She felt guilt about her truth-telling parts.

Here are some examples of aspects of personhood around which people have internalized guilt messages:

- Needs
- Weaknesses
- Failures
- Anger
- Sadness
- Sexuality
- Talents
- Strength
- Honesty
- Success

- Separateness
- Autonomy
- Independence
- Pain

Any aspect of ourselves that is disapproved of or attacked in a significant relationship can come under "judgment," and then guilt attacks that part of the soul from the inside. If a parent, for example, belittles a child's need for affection, a punitive voice against that part of the child gets internalized in the child. This is partly how our conscience is formed. Then, until the conscience gets modified, this person will feel guilt whenever he expresses that aspect of himself, even if it is a good part. So, many times people have to express themselves in new, safe relational settings to get the healing and encouragement God provides to restore the soul. A new conscience has to be internalized and developed in new relationships. Again the Body of Christ does its work.

Anger

We saw above how aspects of the self can be paired with guilt messages, and certainly anger is one of those. Some people feel guilty whenever they feel themselves getting angry. But there is another problem with anger.

Anger is a state of protest and fight. God wired this emotion into us to be "against" something. We use anger to fight injustice, unrighteousness, evil, and other bad things. As the Bible says, love what is good and hate what is evil. It is a good thing to hate bad things (Rom. 12:9). Anger is a problem-solving emotion designed to protect what is good and what is valuable.

But sometimes people have not expressed anger toward bad things that have happened to them because they have happened in a context in which expressing anger would have been dangerous. So these people deny their anger.

The problem is that anger is directional. It has to be aimed at something. It is supposed to be aimed at injustice or the person who is being unfair. But if this is not possible—for example, in cases of child abuse—people will aim the anger at themselves instead. Abused children feel, "I am bad if this is happening to me." They turn the anger that should be aimed at the abuser toward themselves. Other instances of oppressive relationships, like hurtful parenting, cause the same dynamic. As Paul says to parents, "do not provoke your children to anger" (Eph. 6:4).

So sometimes the cure for guilt has nothing to do with helping people feel "forgiven." It has to do with helping them resolve their anger, to feel it toward whomever or whatever deserves it. When they do that, the guilt is resolved because the guilt was only anger turned toward themselves, making them seem "bad" when they are not.

The big point to notice here is the misdiagnosis. Many people suffer for a long time at the hands of others trying to get them to "believe" they are forgiven when what they should be working on is the resolution of their anger. (This shows again how inappropriate guilt is for a Christian. Anger and guilt are basically the same force, coming from different directions. Since God is not angry with Christians anymore, guilt does not apply. He took the anger out in propitiation with Jesus, and it is gone. So there is no guilt.)

THE CHILD POSITION

SOMETIMES GUILT IS NOT a problem to be solved; instead, it is a symptom of the position one lives in. If adults have not emotionally grown up to be equals—siblings—with other adults, as the Bible teaches (see Matt. 23:8–9), they will experience peers as parental figures. They will feel "one-down" to others and therefore subject to people's approval or judgment. It is a perpetual "guilty" state, as they are always under the judge. (For more on this read the Adulthood section in my book *Changes That Heal.*)

People stuck in this position must see guilt as a sign that they have given other people the position of God-the-parent in their lives. They must move out of the position of being a child under parental approval and be adopted by God and answerable to him (Gal. 4:1–5). In this way they get free from the disapproval of others and its resulting guilt.

The spiritual growth community can be the bridge to adulthood for people who are stuck here. Normally, when someone goes through adolescence, they have a peer group that encourages independence from the parents and helps them make the bridge to adulthood. For people with this sort of guilt, the transition was interrupted in some way, usually by an overly controlling parent. So these people are essentially "pre-adult" in development. The spiritual community is a good safe place to ease into adulthood and take the risks necessary to grow up.

Skills like being assertive, being honest, embracing sexuality, taking risks with talents, thinking for oneself, separating from one's parents are all essential to coming out from under the child position. The spiritual community and the growth steps the Bible advocates (such as the ones above) are the formula for resolving this kind of guilt. (Unfortunately, many times spiritual communities have functioned like another controlling parent instead of a launching pad to maturity. The community should be helping people to grow up and think for themselves.)

Again, the issue here is that the problem is not always the problem. Guilt was never the issue. Guilt was just a symptom of a person who had never grown up, and the task is to grow up. The responsibility of the community is to help that happen, not to focus on guilt.

ISOLATION

ONE OF THE MOST misunderstood aspects of guilt is the theological one mentioned above—that guilt is basically about separation from love. As John says, "There is no fear in love. But perfect love drives out fear, because fear has to do with punishment. The one who fears is not made perfect in love" (1 John 4:18).

Guilt and the resulting fear are not about feeling "bad about oneself." They are basically about being separated from love. If people know they are loved, they are not afraid of their "badness." They feel accepted and safe, and they do not have to feel "good" about themselves to be safe. Love does that. Love is everything. *In the Bible, the opposite of "bad" is not "good." It is love.*

So if people are feeling bad about themselves, the answer is never to get them to feel better about themselves. The "self-esteem" trip is a dead end. The answer is to have them feel connected to love. If they feel connected and accepted, they do not have to feel good about themselves.

TIPS FOR GROWERS:

- Review your view of guilt and see if it squares with what the Bible teaches. Is there a disconnect in what your head believes and what your heart experiences? Determine why.
- See the source of guilt's power as separation from God, love, and other people. See where that has happened to you and what is keeping it going.
- Examine faulty teaching you have received.
- See where you are disconnected from grace, either from being cut off from others or from being unavailable to the grace offered.
- Examine where these causes of pathological guilt are operating in your life: false standards, weak conscience, strict background, idealization of conscience, worldly sorrow versus godly sorrow, the tone of your correction, true guilt versus false guilt issues and not seeing the real issues that are the problem, old voices, resolving anger, the child position, isolation.
- Determine what contexts and activities with God and others you will undertake to reverse the separation from love you are experiencing and to experience the sources of healing needed.

TIPS FOR FACILITATORS:

- Examine prayerfully your theology of guilt. See whether you have a view of "no condemnation" or are subtly still teaching and communicating law to the people to whom you minister.
- Make spaces and opportunities for people to overcome the separation from God, love, and other people that ultimately fuels guilt. Provide an atmosphere in which people can confess and can feel safe, and design activities to promote confession and safety.
- Teach the theology of "no condemnation" aggressively, as the Bible does. Do away with guilt as "a good thing," and teach the value of godly sorrow and its orientation toward love.
- Confront people's hiding from grace and emotional unavailability. Encourage openness.
- Provide contexts and activities that help people learn about, talk about, and face the causes of guilt: false standards that you might be under, weak conscience, strict background, idealization of conscience, worldly sorrow versus godly sorrow, the tone of your correction, true guilt versus false guilt issues and not seeing the real issues that are the problem, old voices, resolving anger, the child position, isolation.

- Remember that the more openness and confession you can encourage with your people, the more guilt will be overcome.
- Confront any cancers of judgment in your group that prevent grace from touching people's hearts.

In fact, they stop being so concerned about themselves altogether and get into love instead. Adam and Eve were not concerned about their badness until they lost love. Feelings of badness are not something to be overcome. They are another symptom of the basic problem of our disconnection from love. Don't fall into the trap of trying to make a person with "bad" feelings develop "positive" feelings. That is not the answer. Getting loved is.

One of the most destructive causes of "guilt" is emotional and spiritual isolation. The maxim to remember is this: An alone self is a bad self. If someone feels alone, he or she is going to feel "bad." The answer is not "goodness," or more self-esteem. The answer is love.

That is the reason we have a gospel of reconciliation of relationship with God and others instead of a gospel of being "better" people. If we get reconciled, we will be better, but we won't be obsessed with it. The "knowledge of good and evil" will not be the big issue; love will be.

In helping people grow in the area of resolving guilt, make sure that you are on a mission to end internal isolation. If you find people who feel "bad" about themselves, find the isolated part of their heart and give them grace, love, and connection. If you do that, you will cure a lot of the guilt.

This is one reason why abuse victims feel so bad about themselves. The abuse has made getting close to others and trusting very difficult, and isolation takes over their soul. As a result, they feel like a "bad" person, even when that is the furthest thing from the truth. Love will do away with that state, whereas positive affirmations, although important, will fall short. Reconciliation to love is the answer for guilt of any kind.

THE GOOD NEWS

JESUS SAID THAT HE did not come into the world to judge or condemn it (John 12:47). If this is true, how on earth did the institution he

began turn into one of the guiltiest places on earth? This is a big problem. The One who came to end guilt has it dished out in his name over
and over. As we have seen in this chapter, the Bible teaches there should
be no guilt for the Christian. Instead, there should be the freedom of
"no condemnation" along with a deep concern for real problems and
issues.

So as you work on your guilt or the guilt of others, remember that
it is not a problem, but a symptom. It is a symptom of being separated
from Love. And the solution to this problem is always reconciliation to
Love. It is simple, yet sometimes very difficult—but as the apostle Paul
tells us, it "never fails" (1 Cor. 13:8).

PART IV

THE PATH OF
GROWTH

THE GARDENER'S HANDBOOK: THE BIBLE

The Word of God is alive and life-giving.

Years ago, when I was a seminary student, I walked into the restaurant where I was employed as a waiter. The hostess, a young woman named Cindy, greeted me. She and I were friends, even though we didn't know each other very well. She was always kind and cheerful, and she made my job easier.

After we said our hellos, Cindy said, "You're a God person, aren't you?"

"Yes," I replied. I wasn't sure how she knew I was into God, but I figured someone had mentioned that I was studying at the seminary.

"Can I ask you a God question?"

Now, if you want to make a Bible student's year, ask that question. I thought I was in heaven. My entire existence was making sense! All that studying, and now someone had a question about the information in my brain!

I quickly answered, "Sure," wondering if she would ask about something I had been working on recently, like the nature of the Trinity or how Christ could be both human and divine. I had reams of biblical truth, on all sorts of subjects, ready to bestow upon Cindy.

Then she said, "When my boyfriend does a lot of cocaine, he beats me up. What am I supposed to do?"

I was stunned. I didn't know what to say. In my heart, I felt a deep compassion for the hurt and confusion Cindy must have felt. But in my head, I was racing through every Bible verse and principle I knew, hoping to land on something that would help her.

In the end, all I could muster was a paraphrase of Romans 8:28, that all things work together for good for those who trust God. Cindy politely thanked me, and we both went to work. But I knew, and I think she did too, that I hadn't really helped her.

I remember driving home that night thinking, *I was in a divine moment, and something went wrong.* I thought about how God must have brought Cindy and me to work in the same place. How God must have planted seeds in her to wonder if he could provide help for her horrible situation. How he must have prepared me to help her seek him and his kingdom. Yet nothing truly godly had happened that evening.

The problem certainly wasn't that Romans 8:28 is not true. It is true, but it was not the particular truth that I now think would have helped Cindy.

And the problem was not that the seminary taught me the wrong things. I learned to study and understand the Bible for myself, and I am still very grateful for the training I received and the relationships I formed there. The benefits I experienced in those years are foundational to my life and work today.

The problem was *me*, or more accurately, *how I viewed the Bible's work in the lives of people.* I believed that the Word of God is living and active (Heb. 4:12) and that it does not return to God empty (Isa. 55:11). I had no doubt of the power of God through the Scriptures. And I believed and practiced the biblical disciplines of study, reading, memorization, prayer, commitment, and surrender.

However, I had an incomplete idea of how the Bible addresses the spiritual growth process. Similar to Henry's experience, I thought that understanding theology, our position in Christ, and how much God loves and values us were the key to solving problems and becoming a victorious, thriving Christian.

Yet Cindy had not walked away with hope after our conversation, and as I reflected on that, I realized I faced the same dilemma. Although God's Word had given me much hope, security, and faith, I still had personal struggles and failures that were not being transformed deeply and completely. I found myself fighting the same battles, trying to manage things through recommitment, coping, and trying harder.

At this point I went to God and asked him for help. I said something like, "God, I really do believe you have healing in your Word, but I am not finding it for myself or others. Please open my eyes." With that, I embarked on a long-term study of the Bible, this time with no assumptions about what growth is or is not. I just wanted to examine the Scriptures with an open mind (Acts 17:11).

What I found as I studied, and as Henry and I thought out loud together, forms much of this book. I found that the Bible is complete. It contains all the principles we need to understand for both growing spiritually and resolving personal struggles. And it asserts the same theology I had learned in school. However, I saw this theology in a new light, the light of God's process of growing his people.

This chapter talks about the specific and unique part the Bible plays in the growth process.

THE POWER OF THE WORD

THE BIBLE STANDS ALONE as God's only perfect guide to life and growth. Through the miracle of forty or so authors over the course of fifteen hundred years producing a magnificently consistent set of ideas and stories, God laid out all the elements for us to understand how people grow. Since the Bible has been written down, it can be scrutinized and checked objectively. It is a trustworthy and dependable book of life for us (Ps. 119:138).

The Bible has authority. Many, many scholars over the centuries have concluded that the Scriptures are the Word of God. (The book you are reading now is not the place to go over the research behind these conclusions. A good Christian bookstore or church library can point you to these sorts of resources.) However, if the Bible were not what it claims to be, its teaching would not have the power that people throughout the centuries have attributed to it. Life and light are within the Bible.

So when people expose themselves to the pages of the Bible, something profound happens. They come into contact with the God of the universe and with the way he sees the world and us. Reading the Bible is one of the main ways God speaks to our lives and hearts. Although learning principles and truths is very important, coming close to God personally through the Bible is a higher value (Ps. 119:27).

A friend of mine recently went through a very painful divorce that she did not desire. I asked her how she was doing.

"It's not easy, but it's okay," she said.

"What do you mean?"

"Well, I get a lot of support from my friends. They have really been there for me. And, while I don't want to sound hyperspiritual, the Bible has been so important to me. I would be at some crisis point in the divorce, and I would sit down and read the Bible, and God would speak to what was going on. I might receive comfort and love from him, or correction or wisdom in some decision. I have felt so close to God at such a distressing time."

My friend is psychologically sophisticated and mature. And she faithfully clings onto the words of God like a little child.

The Bible Points to God as the Source of All Growth

Most importantly, the Bible anchors God as the source of all growth. All the way through the Bible we read that everything we need in life comes from him, not from ourselves (Acts 17:28; 1 Cor. 4:7). This essential and defining reality helps to humble us and make us dependent on God. For example, read Psalm 119 in one sitting. It will give you a picture of our dependency on the Word and, ultimately, on God: "Save me, for I am yours; I have sought out your precepts" (v. 94).

When we see that the Bible points to God for all growth, we understand that *all growth is spiritual growth.* From groups that study the

Bible to those dealing with relationships to those helping people with depressions or addictions, everything that fosters growth is ultimately from God.

Growth can even occur when the Bible is not given credit, though the process tends to be more successful when it is. For example, people may be involved in a support group not intentionally based on biblical principles, but inadvertently practicing some of them. As members trust each other, they share vulnerabilities and weaknesses. As they do, they find that they feel safer and that their internal worlds are less empty and isolated. The group may not know it, but they have been applying the biblical practice of confession (James 5:16), which opens the soul up to being loved by others. This is how wonderful, powerful, and spiritual the Bible's growth principles are. At the same time, how much better for groups to understand that what they are doing is from the Bible! They are then better able to surrender to the designs of the One who designed the growth process.

In contrast, some Christian schools of thought teach that if you know the Bible well enough, you will automatically grow spiritually. These groups often frown on counseling as heretical, and they tell strugglers to "get into the Word" instead. The strange thing about many of these groups is that they don't practice what they preach. Instead of turning struggling people away with exhortations to study more, they provide relational support for their hurts, such as listening, comforting, and empathizing. They spend patient time with them, taking hours out of their week to meet with them, give them structures to guide their lives such as principles of right and wrong and organized ways to make decisions, help them in the forgiveness process, and pray with them. These very things, the Bible says, help grow people up, and yet from the pulpit you often hear, "All you need is the Bible." It's an interesting paradox: They don't preach what they practice.

The Bible Prescribes the Path of Growth

The Bible clearly presents a process for pursuing spiritual maturity. It refers to the process in different ways, such as sanctification (being progressively set apart for God's use, Rom. 6:19), transformation (being changed from the inside out, Rom. 12:2), and growth (maturing spiritually, 1 Peter 2:2). At heart, the idea is that we are designed to become increasingly more of who we were created to be (2 Cor. 3:18).

THE ELEMENTS. As we discussed in depth in chapter 2, the Scriptures teach that relationship—both with God and with others (Eccl. 4:9–12) —truth (Eph. 4:15), and time (Mark 4:26–29) must be present for someone to grow. Anytime you see someone growing spiritually or personally, these elements are operating.

THE TASKS. In addition, the Bible identifies the tasks required for growth. As anyone who has been applying biblical principles for a time can tell you, spiritual growth is anything but "let go and let God." It is hard and sometimes painful work; yet it is always worth it, for "it produces a harvest of righteousness and peace for those who have been trained by it" (Heb. 12:11).

Here are some of the grower's tasks:

- Submission and obedience to God (Rom. 12:1). This means we are to present our lives to him and his ways rather than our own ideas of how life should be.
- Need and dependency (Prov. 3:5–6). We are to go to him continually as the source for all that we need for light and growth.
- Responsibility and ownership (Luke 9:23). We are to take on the tasks and burdens of what he calls us to do in life.
- Forgiveness (Matt. 6:12–15). This involves both asking forgiveness from God and others and also canceling the debts others have with us.

These tasks are in addition to the traditional disciplines of Bible study and prayer.

THE RESOURCES. Finally, Scripture also points us to the resources available for the growth process. God, as we mentioned above, is the ultimate source of all we need; however, we also find his ingredients for growth in other places. The Creation itself is a resource of good things. For example, we have food to sustain us (Gen. 1:29), work to fulfill us (Gen. 1:28), and nature to cause us to marvel at the wonder of the Lord

(Ps. 33:6). Many people who are growing spend time in nature regularly to help them feel close to God.

People are another major resource of growth. The Bible teaches that the Christian who is not deeply connected to others as well as God is not a complete Christian (as we saw in chapter 7). We are all called to faithfully administer God's grace to each other (1 Peter 4:10). In other words, people are also a source of the grace of God so necessary to growth.

The Bible Helps People Grow

The Bible, in and of itself, is one of the resources for the growth process. The Bible does not stop with teaching *about* growth. It is actively involved *in* growth. Let us take a look at how the Scriptures directly assist maturing.

A central passage in which the Bible talks about itself is 2 Timothy 3:16–17: "All Scripture is God-breathed and is useful for teaching, rebuking, correcting and training in righteousness, so that the man of God may be thoroughly equipped for every good work." This passage gives four uses of the Bible that have different emphases.

1. TEACHING. The Bible's teaching helps us understand the ways of God and his relationship with us. People need a structure to know God and how he wants us to love him and conduct our lives. God instructs us on the doctrines and principles about himself and us, such as the Holy Spirit, the nature of humankind, and sin and salvation. He also teaches many realities concerning relationships, values, and the growth process in general. These provide an overview of the essence of spiritual life. They orient us toward living in God's ways. A regular and systematic study of the Bible helps us understand these truths.

For example, a leader who is facilitating a spiritual growth group may want to study the book of Ephesians systematically because it teaches much about relationships. Or if people struggle with feeling that God is distant, they might find it valuable to study Christ's nature in Colossians, especially his incarnation as a person, so that they might identify with him.

2. REBUKING. We need more than teaching to grow, however. We stray, rebel, are self-centered, and are in denial. No amount of teaching

is enough to cure these tendencies. So we need rebuking, or reproof, to confront us with our transgressions. Just as it is necessary for a parent to confront a child clearly and directly with a wrongdoing, we must be rebuked for our wrongdoings.

The Bible has many passages that perform this task. They are more direct and exhortative than informational or comforting in nature. They get our attention and direct it to a problem area. For example, the Bible rebukes our tendency to withhold love and affection from others (2 Cor. 6:11–13). Jesus rebukes the sins of self-righteousness and pride (Luke 18:10–14).

In fact, God can use any part of Scripture to rebuke us when we need it, even those that were not written with reproof in mind. This is due to the illuminating work of the Holy Spirit (John 16:12–15; see chapter 6 in this book). Using a certain passage, the Spirit may open our eyes about a particular area of our life that is cause for concern, and may help us repent and change direction. Many people have had an experience in which a certain familiar verse simply "jumped out" at them and reproved them concerning some issue they were dealing with.

During one period in my life I was engaged in a million religious activities, but I was doing it all on my own, without checking in with God, without consciously relying on God's help and strength. I was in a self-sufficient mode. One day I read John 5:19: "Jesus gave them this answer: 'I tell you the truth, the Son can do nothing by himself; he can do only what he sees his Father doing, because whatever the Father does the Son also does.'" I had read that passage before, but this time it struck me how dependent Jesus was and how much of a Lone Ranger I was. This verse rebuked me for my distance from God and helped me change my ways.

Be careful, however, how you use the Bible to rebuke. Some people have been seriously wounded by "Bible bashers" who use the requirements of God to put people further under the law. As a seminary professor of mine once said, "It takes little work to preach the law, and a lot of work to preach grace." Use the Word gently, prayerfully, and at the right times and in the right amounts. At the same time, rebuke is sometimes necessary. I have seen many growth processes go awry because someone was afraid to rebuke another due to his or her own anxieties. Be a graceful *and* truthful person.

3. CORRECTING. The Greek word for *correcting* means "straightening up." The meaning here is to straighten out someone's error, not necessarily an error due to sin or rebellion, but the mistake someone makes out of ignorance or lack of awareness.

As in the case of rebuking, the Bible can correct our ways both through correcting passages or simply through the Spirit's work. A good example of a correcting passage is 1 Corinthians 5:12–13. Here Paul corrects the idea that believers are to judge nonbelievers, and he says we are to be stricter with our own kind in the church.

The Bible can also open our eyes and correct us with other passages. I was in a group with a man who desperately wanted to live the life of God and was very committed to him. Yet certain habits hindered his walk with the Lord, one of them being pornography. This man tried many things to deal with his addiction, including surrender, prayer, accountability, and Bible studies on lust. These all helped, but the sin kept returning and, at best, would subside for only a short time. He was discouraged.

One evening, as we were discussing his addiction, into my head popped 1 Corinthians 13:11, which says, among other things, "When I became a man, I put childish ways behind me." I mentioned the verse to my friend and explained how I thought it applied to him.

"I think you have the cart before the horse," I said. "You expect to put this addiction behind you, yet you are broken in your ability to take in love and support. This brokenness keeps you from fully becoming the man God wants you to be. It is an immature, wounded part of you. I believe you go to pornography to take in the love you can't safely receive from people. I would like to see you continue all the disciplines you are doing, but I want you also to work on how you keep yourself emotionally distant from receiving the grace God and people have for you, and let's see what happens."

My friend understood the point immediately. He worked on becoming an open, vulnerable person. For example, when he was lonely or had a stress at work, he called friends for love and support instead of acting out sexually. In time, his craving was completely gone. He still points to this Scripture passage as a key turning point for him, in which God corrected his mistake of trying to stop sinning without growing.

4. TRAINING IN RIGHTEOUSNESS. *Righteousness* literally means "upright." When used in growth contexts, it refers to our becoming godly, mature, and upright people. The Bible trains us in this process. We are to learn to turn from evil and do good (Ps. 34:14). It produces the fruit of wise and sound judgment (Prov. 2:2). It involves deepening and maturing (Heb. 6:1–2).

As I wrote this chapter, I asked my sons Ricky, age eleven, and Benny, age nine, what we would miss if there had never been a Bible. They said, "We wouldn't know what was right and what was wrong." This is a pretty good summary of the goal of training in righteousness!

The Bible has these other uses besides the four already mentioned:

COMFORT AND STRENGTH. As we grow spiritually, we need encouragement and support. We need to be able to receive love and comfort from the outside to bear what we must bear. Our burden may be learning to speak up and tell the truth when we are afraid. Or it might be a heartbreak or loss in life that deeply hurts us. Whatever the cause, we cannot tolerate pain and struggle for very long without comfort.

Through the centuries, when people have come to the end of themselves, they have found much in the Scriptures to keep them going. "I have remembered Your ordinances from of old, O LORD, and comfort myself" (Ps. 119:52 NASB). In the same way that we receive strength from God in prayer and from friends who listen and love us, we can be refreshed through the Scriptures.

IDENTIFICATION WITH FELLOW GROWERS. One of the unique contributions of the Bible to spiritual growth is its many narratives of the faith lives of people in the past. The stories about Abraham, Sarah, Moses, Ruth, David, Mary, Peter, and Paul, to name a few, help us identify our struggles, sins, and victories with others. One of the most growth-producing realities in my life was when I read through the life of David and saw all the horrible messes he got himself into. Yet he was described in the Bible as a man after God's own heart (1 Sam. 13:14).

Be sure not to skip over the character flaws of the heroes of the Bible and make the mistake of idealizing them. You will miss one of the great reasons for their being there: to see that God doesn't grow perfect people, but rather people who are unfinished. This provides hope for us who read about them: "For everything that was written in the past was written to teach us, so that through endurance and the encouragement of the Scriptures we might have hope" (Rom. 15:4).

SPIRITUAL WARFARE. The Bible is an important tool to help us in this area.

Jesus focused on the Scriptures when he was tempted by the Devil (Matt. 4:1–11). Also, the Word is the only offensive weapon in the listing of the armor of God, "so that you can take your stand against the devil's schemes" (Eph. 6:11–17). Satan has more power when there is a lack of truth and light. The Bible sheds truth and light in our lives and hearts so that he has less purchase on us. I have experienced situations in which I could tell that there were dark forces at work; when I quoted Scriptures, the effect was a lessening or ending of the attack.

THE BIBLE AND THE GOD OF THE BIBLE

SOME PEOPLE MAKE THE mistake of missing the One to whom the Bible is directing them. They become enamored of learning the depths and complexities of the Bible, and they forget that it points us toward God. This problem is technically called "bibliolatry," which means making an idol out of the Bible. This occurs in some circles that emphasize doctrine or Bible study to the point of neglecting a personal relationship with Jesus, who said that the Scriptures actually bear witness to him (John 5:39).

A preacher once said this is like the man who goes into a restaurant and reads the menu. Then, exclaiming how great the menu is, he puts salt and pepper on it and proceeds to eat it. Bibliolatry also points up certain character issues in people, such as valuing intellectual pursuits over relationship, or needing closure and black-and-white answers to theological puzzles rather than relating to the God of mystery. The point here is that while we need to diligently study the Bible, it was not written to satisfy our intellectual curiosity. It was written to give us the path to God, life, and growth. Keep that as your goal, and ask God daily to bring life to you through its pages.

THE BIBLE AND PSYCHOLOGY

A GREAT DEAL OF discourse in Christian academic, discipleship, and counseling circles concerns the relationship of the Bible to psychology. People ask whether the two deal with different areas of life (spiritual versus emotional), whether the two are parallel disciplines, and whether one or the other is unnecessary for helping people grow so that we can make do with only one of them.

Many books, articles, and sermons have been dedicated to these questions. This book doesn't have enough room for a complete treatment of the issues, yet in a way, this book is our answer to these questions. We would take the following position: *The Bible teaches everything that people need to grow.* All the principles and truths necessary for spiritual growth and for relating to God and others, maturing, and working out personal issues and problems have been provided. God did not begin maturing people only in the twentieth century. He has been leading, healing, and growing his flock ever since he created us. This is why we view all personal growth as spiritual growth, whether it be religious, emotional, relational, or behavioral. We do not see psychology and the Bible as two equal disciplines that should be blended together. Psychology always bends the knee to the Scriptures.

At the same time, although all the processes of growth are in the Bible and it is a complete guide to spiritual growth, psychology can and does assist. Sound research and theory can serve to illustrate and support the realities of Scripture. People in the behavioral sciences observe people and come to conclusions about what motivates them, how problems develop, and how to solve them. These conclusions are not based on the Bible, but they are based on observations about the way people operate as dictated by rules taught in the Bible.

For example, the Bible teaches that we need each other, that life is not at its best when we are isolated: "The LORD God said, 'It is not good for the man to be alone. I will make a helper suitable for him'" (Gen. 2:18). Psychologists have reached the same conclusions, that people who do not have healthy, deep relationships are at increased risk for emotional and medical problems.

Psychology's sound research and theories have been very helpful in dealing with people's problems, but they actually only serve to illuminate and support the principles of growth and healing that have always been in the Bible. This reality is what started our own study, and it is the basis for our own biblical counseling, writing, and teaching.

BIBLICAL ILLITERACY

ONE CONCERN TROUBLES US, however. Many Christians who have found help in growing spiritually and emotionally are not well grounded in the Bible. Even though they believe the Bible is true and powerful, they don't really know the doctrines, key passages, book themes, or ways to navigate through it. This biblical illiteracy is a problem because the Bible is so central to God's process of growth.

This is a problem for a couple of reasons. First, some people from conservative backgrounds were taught a lot of Bible content, but not in helpful ways. They might have experienced legalism, judgmentalism, or profound guilt in their study of the Bible. Thus, they were wounded by errant teachings on the Book that is meant to heal them. Often, later in life, these people receive help from nonbiblically based growth or counseling circles, and they experience healing. Now they are in a double-bind: Either they stick with the Bible and don't get well, or they leave the Bible and grow. As a result, some of them negate their scriptural backgrounds and are not able to connect with God or grow through the Word. This sad dilemma we address in our book *12 "Christian" Beliefs That Drive People Crazy.*

Second, some people don't have a lot of Bible in their background, and when they get into growth and support contexts, they simply don't get exposure to how biblical teachings relate to real life. They may attend a church in which the Bible is preached from the pulpit, but there is very little biblical content in the support groups and pastoral counseling situations. These people learn the basics of the Bible from the Sunday service, but it is not carried over into their spiritual growth process. They aren't wounded, as in the case of the first group. Rather, they are uninitiated.

Either way, we encourage every person interested in personal growth, or in helping others grow, to invest deeply in the Bible and its doctrines. So many people who have taken the time to study the Scriptures have found that this simple endeavor can help them make authentic and heart-based changes within their lives forever. They are permanently and "thoroughly equipped for every good work" (2 Tim. 3:17).

PRACTICALITIES

YOU CAN EXPOSE YOURSELF to the Bible in several ways. Each of the specific means listed below has its own unique benefit. These suggestions only touch the high points, and we recommend that you explore some resources to dig deeper.

- **Listening.** Listen to Bible messages at church and on tape or on the Internet, or listen to the Bible in some media form. Do some research to make sure that the speaker is theologically sound and reputable. Ask balanced individuals to recommend speakers whom they read and trust.
- **Reading.** Reading is the most direct and simple approach to getting exposed to the Bible. Make a plan to read the Bible every day for the rest of your life. Find a "one-year Bible" (designed with a program for reading it through in twelve months) with a translation that people you trust recommend. I have a friend, a businessman, who last year read the Bible through for the first time; it transformed his life. For example, he began seeing his marriage as a spiritual reality. He began opening up his heart more to his wife's heart, as he came to understand that this was a way of growing closer not only to her, but also to God.
- **Quiet time.** Also called devotional time, this is a time of the day that you set apart daily when you can regularly get away from things. Read the Bible and think about what it might mean for your life. Pray about what you are reading, and pray also for your growth and that of your loved ones. People often find help in journaling their quiet times. They write

their observations, reactions, emotions, experiences, problems, and questions. Many well-done devotional programs are available at Christian bookstores.

- **Study.** Bible study, in which certain subjects are broken down and discussed, moves you more deeply into the Bible. Two basic kinds are book study and topical study. The first involves understanding the themes of a particular book of the Bible, its context, the needs it addresses, and its applications to life. The second covers the various passages that relate to a subject, such as relationships, holiness, parenting, the person of Christ, or future events. Some studies are already organized and come with prepared lessons. Some people like to study without helps. Also, some people like to study alone, and some like being in a group. We suggest that whichever way you choose, make sure you are regularly connecting with people and the Bible on a deeply personal level.

- **Meditation.** In this spiritual discipline you intimately personalize a small portion of Scripture, from a verse to a paragraph or so. Read the passage several times, perhaps in different translations. Pray over it, break it down into all the things it might teach, and ask God to show you himself through the words.

- **Memorization.** Memorizing passages in the Bible has great benefits in that you store up Scriptures in your head so that God can bring the relevant ones to your mind at the right time of need: "I have hidden your word in my heart that I might not sin against you" (Ps. 119:11). To defeat the Devil, Jesus quoted passages he had memorized (Matt. 4:1–11).

- **Formal study.** Many seminaries, Bible schools, and churches offer courses in scriptural studies for academic credit. You can find these on campus or online.

Experiment with different methods and preferences. See what suits your style and reaps the most benefits. And take note of whether you find that your heart, life, and relationships are being connected to God and his love for you.

TIPS FOR GROWERS:

- Explore how you have related to the Bible in your life: Have you seen it as being about religion and not the rest of life? Or have you experienced it as a book of prohibitions to deprive you? Begin to look at the Bible as bringing life and light to your soul.
- Make a study of the scope and nature of the Bible—its uniqueness and power in people's lives over the course of several millennia—in order to understand how it is a resource to your everyday life.
- Ask God to show himself—not just information—through the Scriptures. Ask him to show you his ways that will help your growth and path.
- Understand that the teaching "All you need is the Bible" is itself an unbiblical concept. Learn that the Bible teaches that, more than just reading it, we need to get out and live it out in our lives and relationships.

TIPS FOR FACILITATORS:

- Help your people to see that their everyday lives and struggles are not only reflected in the Bible, but also addressed by it. Show them that good theology and doctrine are very relevant to struggles and growth issues.
- Find contexts for them to make the Bible a part of their lives and to enter the discipline of learning the Scriptures, on the basis of grace rather than performance.
- Help them understand that the Bible contains the growth principles we need for spiritual and personal maturity and that psychology serves only to illuminate what is taught in the Scriptures.
- Help those who have been hurt by distorted teachings about the Bible to see that life is in its pages and they need not be afraid of it. Help those who have little experience with the Bible to see how a systematic understanding of the great truths offers major healing for them.

RESTAURANT REVISITED

REMEMBER CINDY, MY RESTAURANT friend? Let's revisit that conversation, and let me show you what I would have said to her today, knowing what I know now about what the Bible teaches about life.

"You're a God person, aren't you?"

"Yes."

"Can I ask you a God question?"

"Sure!"

"When my boyfriend does a lot of cocaine, he beats me up. What am I supposed to do?"

"Cindy, I am sorry your relationship with your boyfriend is so difficult and painful. God does care about your situation, and he has solutions for it. First, you need to reach out both to him and to caring people, because you need spiritual and emotional support. Notice what it says in 2 Corinthians 1:3–4: 'Praise be to the God and Father of our Lord Jesus Christ, the Father of compassion and the God of all comfort, who comforts us in all our troubles, so that we can comfort those in any trouble with the comfort we ourselves have received from God.'

"Second, you need to gain the strength to set limits with your boyfriend, because what he is doing is not okay, and he probably won't change until you can be strong enough to be firm. Proverbs 19:19 says, 'A hot-tempered man must pay the penalty; if you rescue him, you will have to do it again.'"

And at that point, I would have invited her to spend time with spiritual and supportive friends who could flesh out what I had just told her.

CONCLUSION

THE BIBLE POINTS US to the life of God in so many ways. Delve deeply into its life-giving truths and stories. And find in the chapters that follow many essential elements of growth about which the Bible teaches us.

II

NO PAIN, NO GAIN: THE ROLE OF SUFFERING AND GRIEF

"Suffering produces perseverance; perseverance, character; and character, hope."

Grief is the one pain that heals all others. It is the most important pain there is.

Ihate exercise, but I do it. I hate lifting weights and riding my exercise bike, but I do it. I do it because, if I do, I will be healthier, will live longer, and will feel better. Plus I (Henry) have an eleven-month-old daughter who would like to have a father who lives long enough to know her children. My love for her makes me exercise to stay healthy.

Why bring up exercise in a chapter on suffering and grief? Well, first of all, it shows you that I am naturally lazy. But seriously, I bring it up because physical exercise and suffering is analogous to personal growth and suffering. *Pain can bring health*. As we go through the pain of exercising our bodies, we gain strength and good things happen. But there is something else at work.

Physiologists tell us there is a reason I am sore after I lift weights; in fact, as I write this, I am really sore, as I just resumed weight lifting after several months off. I am sore because I have worked my muscles past their ability; I have stretched their capacity. After my workout they re-create and rejuvenate and grow back to a higher level of development than before. I tear down to rebuild. And through the process of pain, growth happens. I hate it, but it is good.

The same God who designed and created our muscles designed and created our souls. He also created the process of growing them and rebuilding them from their fallen, crippled state. Just as we stretch our muscles to make them stronger, God stretches our souls to grow them into something stronger and better. Sometimes he literally "wounds" and "heals" (Isa. 30:26). And it is true that "blows and wounds cleanse away evil, and beatings purge the inmost being" (Prov. 20:30). Certain suffer-ing tears down aspects of our character that need to be torn down and builds up new aspects that we need in order to live as we were designed to live. So suffering can be good. It can take us to places where one more season of "comfort" cannot.

But suffering can also be terrible. Some suffering is not a "wound . . . to heal." Such suffering inflicts evil on a person's heart and soul and is totally outside God's desire. Although God can bring good out of the experience, the experience itself is no good at all.

I sometimes use this analogy when I speak: "If one of you walked out of this meeting and a guy with a mask walked up to you in the dark parking lot, took out a knife, stabbed you in the stomach, took all your money, and left you in an unconscious state, you would call him a mugger. Someone would call the police, and they would try to find the perpetrator.

"But if you left this meeting, drove down the street to the local hos-pital, and a guy with a mask came to you in a brightly lit room, took out a knife, cut your stomach open, took all your money, and left you in an unconscious state, you would call him a doctor and thank him for helping you. One is a mugging, and the other is surgery."

Suffering is a lot like that. There is therapeutic suffering, and there is destructive suffering at the hands of evil people. The key is to be able to tell the difference between the two and to apply the right kind of experience to each. Too often in the church those who have been "mugged" have been told that God is trying to teach them a lesson or that what they are going through is a result of their own sin or that it is part of the growth process.

This is what happened to Job. His suffering was not the result of some sin he had done; in fact, he suffered because he was doing such a good job in life. God pointed Job out as an example of righteousness (Job 1:8), and then God allowed him to suffer for his purposes (see also John 9:2–3).

But his friends did not know that. In fact, what they told him regarding his suffering reminds us of some things we hear in churches today. He was told that he did not have enough faith, did not trust God enough, had sin in his life, did not know God's Word well enough, and so on. All the reasons for his suffering were based on something being "wrong" with his spiritual state. And God was angry about the advice Job's friends gave to him, declaring that they were not right (Job 42:7).

So the first thing we want to do is to distinguish between the muggings and the "growth sufferings." When life mugs someone, we need to give him or her healing, support, love, and comfort. We need to give strength and life support to those who are weak from things that have happened to them (1 Thess. 5:14). We are to "bear one another's burdens" (Gal. 6:2 NASB) and help each other through tough times. (Chapter 14 goes into this in more detail.) We hurt, and we need help.

When dealing with your own suffering or that of others, therefore, first ferret out hurt and suffering that needs healing and support. Get that for yourself, or give it to those you are helping. Make sure you are not getting the wrong advice—advice that does not in anyway fit the pain. This is "worthless" medicine, and it would be better if your friends would just be quiet (Job 13:4–5). Also check yourself before giving advice to others who are suffering. Make sure you are not ascribing fault where there is none. God does not like that, and neither will the recipient. In fact, it may even drive him or her away from God. As Job said, "For the despairing man there should be kindness from his friend; so that he does not forsake the fear of the Almighty" (Job 6:14 NASB).

GOOD PAIN

AS WE JUST SAID, some pain is "good for nothing" and should not be treated as if it has purposeful value. Our character does not grow in the same way, although we may develop the fruit of faith, perseverance, and a deep capacity of empathy for others.

But other suffering does have value and produce growth. I call this "good pain." Dan is an illustration of how good pain can lead to growth.

Dan was a success in life. He had built a big business, made many "friends," and had a beautiful family. He was respected in his community and was a leader in his church. To many, Dan had it made.

Then two unexpected things wounded Dan deeply. First, he experienced business problems. He had highly leveraged himself for some growth opportunities right before a major downturn in the market. Without warning, he found himself on the brink of insolvency. His behavior became erratic. He lost his temper with the people he worked with. Concerned about his leadership—as well as for him as a friend and a person—his colleagues went to his board of directors to let them know that all was not well. At first the board was divided on what to do. A few men on the board were "yes man" types for Dan, and they were very reluctant to intervene and tell him that he was wrong.

But then something else happened. Dan's wife, Abi, left him. During the crisis at work, Dan's erratic behavior had spilled over into his home. He frequently lost his temper and then withdrew from his wife more and more. For a long time Abi had been dissatisfied with the marriage. Dan had always worked too much, and he had always been perfectionistic and difficult to get close to, but she had felt these things were not important enough to leave her for.

Yet now the situation had gotten much worse. The more stress Dan felt at work, the more he exploded at home with her and the children. More than his usual distance, a real wall had been erected between the two of them. She felt she could no longer make the marriage work. So one day she decided to leave. She packed up, took the kids, and flew to her parents' home five hundred miles away. She left a note that said, "I'm safe, but I just can't take it anymore. I'll call you. Don't call me."

These developments at home put Dan over the edge at the office, so finally the board stepped in. They told him they were relieving him of his duties immediately, both because of the company's performance as well as the staff's complaints. Dan hit the roof. He screamed betrayal. He fought and lobbied the board members to allow him to keep his responsibilities. They held the line. They told him they were open to his coming back, but only after he got his temper under control.

Dan's anger turned to despair. He did not know what to do with a situation he could not control or perform himself out of. His charm and salesmanship were not working, on either his board or his wife. He pleaded and begged. But nobody was listening. He became more and more depressed and finally stopped going out of the house.

At this point one of Dan's advisers suggested he call me. When he did, I recognized his name. I had heard about his life and career, and he was an impressive figure. During the initial phone call I did not ask him what was happening, but just agreed to see him and his wife as he requested.

When I met with them, I could tell this meeting had not been his wife's idea. His adviser had talked Abi into coming in with him, but she had very little hope for the relationship. She said she had tried for years to reach him, to no avail. "Why would it be any different now?" she asked. As she told her side of the story, she surprised herself at how disgusted, hurt, and hopeless she felt. Having always tried to be the "good Christian wife," she had never let herself realize how bad things really were.

When Dan told his side of the story, he was full of promises to Abi of being different and wanting her back. This is standard behavior for a previously oblivious husband shocked into reality by a potential divorce.

What I saw was the depths of dysfunction into which this "pillar" of leadership had sunk in a few short months. Not long before, people had sought his friendship, advice, and company. Now he was a wreck. He hid from everyone who cared about him.

As I asked him about his background, I began to understand the "whys." His father had died when he was very young, and his mother was an angry and difficult woman. Early on, he had learned to nurture himself and use his talents, brains, and charm to make it through life. His being a star athlete in high school and college had led to good connections later, and hard work had parlayed those into business success. And having been in a religious culture that valued status more than true spiritual maturity, he had risen in the ranks of leadership in his church as well.

What I saw was an entire life, identity, and security base built on sand—the sands of performance, admiration, and status. (The Bible refers to these things as wood, hay, and stubble.) When the difficulties came, this foundation could not withstand the winds and the rains of tribulation. And the house crumbled (see Matt. 7:24–27). This is what had happened to Dan.

So, in spite of his difficult nature, worthless panic-driven bargaining, and defensiveness, I empathized with him. I knew he had become who he was by trying to hold things together the best he knew how. But I knew something else that was very good news indeed.

As I reflected on Abi's rhetorical question of "Why would it be any different now?" I had an answer for her. While Abi and Dan had had difficult times in the past—what I would call "bad pain," that is, pain that produces no change—this time would be different. For what they were both going through now was something I would call "good pain." This time Dan had been reduced to a place where his old coping methods no longer worked. They were all gone.

Dan used to make up for the emptiness inside by performing, winning, and charming others into admiring him. One victory after another kept him afloat emotionally, but he always needed another fix. This time another fix was not coming, and he was trapped; the pain and lack of an internal life had caught up with him. All of the struts that had propped him up for years had been taken away. And Abi, who had always been there to make him comfortable and secure without his relating or getting close, was no longer playing the placating role. So Dan was left with his pain.

Abi did not have to worry about his old coping methods coming back to haunt her. The old Dan was dying. God himself was putting him to death. But whenever God crucifies one of his children, he resurrects them to glory. This is what I thought was happening to Dan, to her, and to their relationship if they could stay the course and let suffering do its work.

At first, Dan wanted me to make it all go away. I had to "convert" him to the idea that the only way "out" was "through." He was going to have to face some painful realities, and if he did that, he would never have to do it again. In the end, he would not be standing on sand, but on solid ground.

So we went to work. Dan had to face the pain of his isolation. He had to face the anxiety of giving up all his controlling behaviors. He had to face the pain of the losses and hurts he had been hiding for all those years. He had to deal with strong underlying feelings of inferiority for which he was always trying to compensate with his performance.

It took a while, but in the end, Dan got to a much more "complete" state than if he had never crashed. He and Abi learned to connect at much deeper levels. For the first time he found more satisfaction in going on a walk with her than in making that next business deal. He also learned how to work in a saner fashion and to treat people better at work. The ways that he dealt with stress changed completely. As a result, he was able to go back to work and do it all very differently this time. He retained his talents, but he lost his former driven style.

I was reminded of the words of James: "Consider it pure joy, my brothers, whenever you face trials of many kinds, because you know that the testing of your faith develops perseverance. Perseverance must finish its work so that you may be mature and complete, not lacking anything" (James 1:2–5).

Dan did not "consider it pure joy" when it all first hit him and his life became a world of trials. He thought he was going to die. And he was right, just not in the literal sense. What would die were his old character patterns. It was God's design for those to die. As a result, Dan was resurrected into a new life, one that truly was "the life of God" (Eph. 4:18). In many ways, because of the death he died, he was alive for the first time.

As James puts it, when Dan persevered through the trial of the breakdown of his old ways of coping, he worked through the issues and was made "complete." He got to a place where he was not "lacking anything." He now had love within his soul and the ability to connect with others, to be real, and to find healing. The fiery trial had done its work. Although his own patterns caused his downfall, God organized the circumstances that would force him to face them.

This suffering is like that caused by the surgeon, not the mugger. Dan was not a healthy man, stabbed and left for dead and in need of a Good Samaritan. Dan was a sick, incomplete man in need of major surgery. And that is what God did in his life. The circumstances were the "wounding" from the surgeon's knife; the deep work in the soul was the constructive surgery itself. In the end, Dan was put back together much better than before.

STRETCHING THE SOUL AND PUSHING THROUGH

WE ALL HAVE COPING mechanisms that cover up pain, help us deal with fear, enable us to cope with relational inabilities, and help us hold it all together. Trials and suffering push those mechanisms past the breaking point so we find out where we need to grow. Then true spiritual growth begins at deeper levels, and we are healed. Righteousness and character take the place of coping.

This kind of suffering is good. It breaks down and stretches the "weak muscle" of the soul and replaces it with stronger muscle. As Paul tells us, "We also rejoice in our sufferings, because we know that suffering produces perseverance; perseverance, character; and character, hope" (Rom. 5:3–5). In this suffering, the prize we win is character—a very valuable prize indeed.

When we exercise, we have to push through. The runner feels as if she cannot take another step, but she keeps going to reach a higher level. The weight lifter does not think he can take another repetition, but he keeps pressing to get to a new level.

The same thing is true in character growth: We stretch to grow. We push through the fear, the vulnerability, and the pain. We embrace suffering to reach a higher level. We have to ask others and ourselves to push through some very painful and scary things:

- Reaching out from a vulnerable heart
- Making a vulnerable heart available to be known
- Confessing sin and failure to oneself and others
- Facing hurt and pain and allowing others to see it and be there in it
- Taking risks in new areas of performance
- Taking risks to be more honest
- Taking risks in relational confrontation
- Dealing with trauma and pain from the past
- Becoming assertive

- Becoming active in life to get one's needs met
- Taking responsibility for our weaknesses and growing beyond them
- Learning to grieve
- Learning to forgive
- Learning to ask for forgiveness and to make amends
- Learning to reconcile difficult relationships

The list goes on and on—to just about as many areas as there are verses in the New Testament! God requires a lot from us. In fact, he requires it all. Maturity and completion are our goals. He does say that we will not get there completely, but at the same time he tells us to press on toward those goals at all times (Phil. 3:12; Eph. 5:13–16). This is good pain—pain that leads somewhere. As we have pointed out elsewhere, discipline does not seem joyful for the moment; it seems painful. But in the end it yields the peaceful fruit of righteousness (Heb. 12:11). What was true for Jesus is true for us:

> During the days of Jesus' life on earth, he offered up prayers and petitions with loud cries and tears to the one who could save him from death, and he was heard because of his reverent submission. Although he was a son, he learned obedience from what he suffered and, once made perfect, he became the source of eternal salvation for all who obey him (Heb. 5:7–9).

Suffering is the path Jesus modeled for us, and he modeled how to do it right. He went through it all without sin and with obedience. This is the difference between those who suffer to a good end and those who suffer to no good end at all.

Every day a million Dans go through the kind of suffering he did, with no good end at all. They do not do it according to the will of God. They do not do it as Jesus did, being obedient all the way to death.

In our lives, as Dan found, the death of certain aspects of character has to happen to get to the healing we need. Jesus modeled going the distance, even to death. He modeled facing suffering with an eye toward his father, knowing that he could deliver him if he desired, but that God had a greater purpose in having him go through the process instead. This is what our attitude toward suffering has to be as well.

So, as you are working through things in your own life or are helping others, make sure that you teach and value this kind of suffering. Have people look at their trials with the question, "What can I learn through this?" As James 1:5 says, have them look to God for wisdom to find out what steps of maturity and growth have to happen in their lives. If those steps are taken and completed, they will not have to take the same course again.

BAD PAIN

BAD PAIN COMES FROM repeating old patterns and avoiding the suffering it would take to change them, because many times people suffer because of their own character faults. Then other people come alongside them and give them comfort or a spiritual pep talk about how God is with them in this testing. They usually frame the experience as the testing of an innocent person. "Keep the faith," these people say, "and God will reward you for persevering."

The problem is that these people don't tell the sufferers that the suffering is the fruit of their own character and is of no value unless they see it as a wake-up call. This is false martyrdom. It happens when the divorce recovery group comes to the aid of the "victim" of that "bad ex" instead of making the person see the patterns he or she needs to face to keep from repeating them in a new marriage.

It happens with the false support that people get when they lose a job because of performance issues and their friends and family see them as a "victim" of a bad boss or company. The friends would do well to say instead, "Have you thought about what is true about what they said? Have you thought about the pattern in your life of work and jobs that is not going well? Have you thought about the fact that you are the common denominator with all of those 'bad' bosses?"

Bad pain is basically *wasted* pain. It is the pain we go through to avoid the good pain of growth that comes from pushing through. It is the wasted pain we encounter as we try to avoid grief and true hurt that needs to be worked through. It is the wasted pain of trying to get a person to love us or approve of us instead of facing the loss of this love and moving on.

But in too many support circles, people are supported in ways that do not make them face the growth steps they need to take to keep from repeating their mistakes. They are seen as victims and are then set up for failure all over again. Here are some examples of "bad pain":

- Pain that comes from avoiding pain, such as psychological depression that comes from avoiding grief, and anxiety that comes from not facing troublesome things inside one's soul.
- Pain that comes from not facing a character pattern that needs to be changed. Codependent people, for example, who lack boundaries and allow themselves to be used, suffer wasted and needless pain.
- Pain that comes from picking the wrong kinds of people to be close to, in friendship or romance. This pain usually comes from not facing patterns of denial in one's own life and then having relationship blindness when looking at others.
- Pain that comes from repeating failing patterns in work and performance. This comes from not facing weaknesses, irresponsibility, or undeveloped skills or talents.
- Pain that comes from addictions and other clinical syndromes.
- Pain that comes from avoiding growth in general. Life makes demands, and if we stay immature, we can't make life work.
- Pain that comes from not separating from destructive family of origin patterns, the "sins of the fathers." Thus, patterns are repeated for another generation.
- Pain that comes from lack of forgiveness and not letting go of bad relationships and injuries.
- Pain that comes from desiring things from the past that will never come true.
- Pain that comes from isolation and not learning how to become interdependent.

The list goes on. But the point here is that a lot of pain comes from not facing our own issues that repetitively cause pain. As the Bible says, "As a dog returns to its vomit, so a fool repeats his folly" (Prov. 26:11). Or as Jesus said, "When an evil spirit comes out of a man, it goes through arid places seeking rest and does not find it. Then it says, 'I will return to the house I left.' When it arrives, it finds the house swept clean and put in order. Then it goes and takes seven other spirits more wicked than itself, and they go in and live there. And the final condition of that man is worse than the first" (Luke 11:24–26).

As Jesus implies, something needs to happen inside this man's house. He needs to fill his house with spiritual growth, and then there will be no room for darkness to come back in. Not facing the growth that we have to face always leads to further suffering—and the further suffering is usually progressively worse. If a person is not facing things, the dynamics and symptoms and relationships get worse as time goes on.

HOW TO AVOID BAD PAIN AND EMBRACE GOOD PAIN

FOR THOSE GROWING AND for those who minister to them, the call is threefold. First, *do not refer to pain and suffering caused by character patterns as "growth pain."* Unless you can use this pain as a wake-up call, it is worthless. If you see it as valid suffering God is putting someone through, or as God's testing someone's faith, or as someone being the "victim" of someone else's mistakes, the pain will be wasted, and it will continue or return. It is not legitimate suffering. It is the fruit of a lack of growth.

Not long ago I ran into a friend of mine, who caught me up on someone I hadn't seen for ten years. His was a sad story. He basically was stuck in the career misfires he was in the last time I had seen him. What stood out for me was a particular character pattern. Literally every conversation I had ever had with him was dominated by his talking about how someone else was to blame for whatever was going on in his life. It was his last boss or his graduate school professor or his church or certain friends or people in the community who had done him wrong. It was *never* him. Never. I never once heard him say that any of his problems had anything to do with his performance, his procrastination, his lack of initiative, or his lack of action. It saddened me that he had not learned his lesson, and it did not surprise me that he was still stuck ten years later.

None of the pain and loss he had experienced for the last ten years was redemptive. None of it had taught him anything. But it could have, just like Dan's, if he could have seen the lessons his troubles could teach him. Part of the blame probably belonged to the people around him, including his wife, who were not pointing out those lessons to him. The Bible tells us that if we do not confront people to take ownership of their problems, we share in the guilt of those problems (Ezek. 3:18–21; Lev. 19:17).

The second call is, *help people own worthless pain so that it can be redeemed and turned into "good pain."* If people can see the character patterns causing their pain, they can redeem and change them. If a pattern can be owned, a pattern can be changed. But as long as we mistakenly see it as "legitimate suffering by a victim," nothing good can happen.

This kind of redemption happens frequently in codependency movements. When codependents recognize that they are suffering from lack of boundaries and poor choices, they often join a group where group members can help them confront their codependent patterns and own them. Then they go into the legitimate suffering of making difficult changes in themselves and their relationships. When they do that, they can transform their worthless suffering into the suffering of growth, and good things happen.

This brings us to the third call: *Help convert worthless suffering into redemptive suffering.* In other words, help them resolve the issues. Help others see that they are not just victims like the man in the story of the Good Samaritan. Help them to see instead that their suffering is coming from trying to avoid the legitimate suffering of growth, and help them with *these issues.* It is a very human trait to try to avoid the suffering of discipline and growth. We all do it. But the wiser we become, the more we value the pain of growth and despise the avoidance patterns in our lives. Help them face what must be faced and deal with it.

PETER: THE RELUCTANT SUFFERER

I WAS TALKING TO a group of about a hundred experienced pastors and church growth leaders in a training seminar. The topic for the day was how to help people grow spiritually in ways that affect real life. I began by giving them a hypothetical problem to solve.

"If you had to arm your parishioners with protection from sin, how would you do it? What do you think is the best armor they could wear? What do you think would best equip them to not act out sinful patterns in their lives?"

Hands went up. I called on them one by one.

"I would teach them to pray."

"That's good," I said. "Prayer is good."

"I would teach them to stay in the Word."

"That's good, too," I said. "Being strong in God's Word is a big part of the picture. Any others?"

"Fellowship."

"Not placing themselves in temptation."

"Getting lots of support."

"Those are all good," I said. "Those are very important aspects of spiritual growth and becoming strong. But there is one aspect of spiritual growth that is particularly stated to be 'armor' against sin. Anyone know what that is?"

No one raised a hand.

"That's okay!" I said. "I did not notice it for a long time either. But let me read it to you. It is from 1 Peter 4:1–2: 'Therefore, since Christ suffered in his body, arm yourselves also with the same attitude, because he who has suffered in his body is done with sin. As a result, he does not live the rest of his earthly life for evil human desires, but rather for the will of God.' What the Bible says is that having an attitude of embracing suffering will protect against sin. Let me tell you how that works."

What I told them was the story of Peter, the reluctant sufferer.

The apostle Peter changed from a man who avoided suffering to one who valued it. In the beginning he was not into the idea of suffering at all. When Jesus said that he was going to suffer and die, it was Peter who told him there was no need for that (Matt. 16:21–22). Jesus promptly told him, "Get behind me, Satan! You are a stumbling block to me; you do not have in mind the things of God, but the things of men."

Jesus did not stop there. He taught a profound lesson on the value of suffering: "If anyone would come after me, he must deny himself and take up his cross and follow me. For whoever wants to save his life will lose it, but whoever loses his life for me will find it" (vv. 24–25).

Right in the midst of Peter's attempt to get Jesus to avoid the suffering he came to do—the suffering he came to model for us as the path to resurrection—Jesus calls us not to avoid suffering, but to embrace it. He says that we must forsake the pattern of trying to save ourselves and instead pick up our cross and die. Think of what this means in terms of growth.

Dan had tried for years to "save himself." He thought he could perform his way around the growth needed in his soul. He thought he could avoid the pain of facing his hurts, losses, and character patterns. Depending on his wit and abilities, he thought, would get him through and offer healing and salvation for life. Instead, Jesus' words proved true. Dan's attempts to save himself were the very ones that ended up costing him everything. His attempts to avoid his pain and save himself by performing promoted the growth of the cancers eating away at his soul, his career, and his marriage. And he was close to losing it all.

When Dan decided to pick up his cross and follow Jesus, he "learned obedience from what he suffered" (Heb. 5:8). As he faced his cross and went through the death experience of things he had lost and the character patterns that needed to die, he found life as he had never known it before. By suffering, by picking up his cross and being obedient to the suffering of growth and character change, he experienced salvation from his sin.

This is exactly what Peter found out. The same Peter who, like Dan, thought suffering and death should not be included in the plan later said, "Therefore, since Christ suffered in his body, *arm yourselves also with the same attitude, because he who has suffered in his body is done with sin.* As a result, he does not live the rest of his earthly life for evil human desires, but rather for the will of God" (1 Peter 4:1–2).

Peter came to see suffering as *armor!* He came to see suffering as *protection* against sin. He came to see that if we go through the suffering we need to go through, then we are "done with sin" (or at least the sin that had to do with that particular growth step). As for Dan, he had no armor against the pressures of marriage and stress. Because he had never done the necessary suffering of growth, he was vulnerable to the failures of the cracks in his soul and character. But when he learned to embrace the suffering, he was done with the patterns that were wrecking his life. This is the lesson that I had hoped the friend I had not seen for ten years would have learned.

THE REAL SUFFERING OF CHRIST

"ARM YOURSELVES ALSO WITH the same attitude, because he who has suffered in his body is done with sin." Most likely we will not face a brutal execution as Jesus did. So how are we to identify with the sufferings of Christ? How can we arm ourselves with his attitude and purpose? How can we help others to do so? There are many ways, but a few are intimately connected to the growth process.

The Kenosis, or Emptying Experience of Godhood

The first way to arm ourselves with the attitude of Christ is to "empty" ourselves. Jesus emptied himself by giving up "equality with God." Paul describes this emptying (*kenosis* in Greek) this way:

Your attitude should be the same as that of Christ Jesus:

Who, being in very nature God,
did not consider equality with God something to be
grasped,
but made himself nothing,
taking the very nature of a servant,
being made in human likeness.
And being found in appearance as a man,
he humbled himself
and became obedient to death—even death on a cross!
(Phil. 2:5–8)

It is a humbling, suffering, lifelong experience to empty ourselves of the wish to be godlike. We saw in chapter 2 what happens when we try to play God. We cannot "grasp" being the source of life to ourselves, or being in control of everything, or being the boss, or being the judge, or writing the rules, or any of the other aspects of Godhood. It is impossible for us to play God, yet we try. *To humble ourselves constantly and to take the role of God's bondservant is the path of all growth.* When we become a servant and take the obedient position, we grow by getting smaller. We ascend by descending. This begins it all. Assuming the humble position of bowing to God instead of trying to be him starts the process. We first obey the Spirit of Grace by accepting his love and forgiveness. We then continue by humbling ourselves to obey the rest of his desires and will for us.

It was a suffering, humbling experience for Rich and Stephanie (whom we met in chapter 3) to give up their "godlikeness" to grow. But it saved their marriage because *God designed marriage—and the rest of human life—for humans, not for himself.* Life only works when we are being human. It does not work when we are playing God.

"Not My Will, But Yours Be Done"

The second way to arm ourselves with the attitude of Christ is to submit to God's will. We can identify with Jesus' suffering by identifying with what Jesus experienced in the garden of Gethsemane. When Jesus realized that the time of his crucifixion was drawing near, he sweat "like drops of blood" and in deep anguish asked God for his suffering to end. He did not want to go through what he had to go through. Yet he submitted to the path God had placed before him and went through it. This submission to suffering was the key. He prayed to God to be relieved, yet he said, "Not my will, but yours be done" (Luke 22:42).

In all growth we have to bend the knee to God's path for us rather than going our own way. Just as Jesus could have bailed out on going through what he had to do, so can we. And we often do. But if we don't—if instead we submit to God's will—then we grow.

The most basic means of choosing our own way and not God's is to decide not to suffer. Instead, we choose our own way by taking Satan's solution and giving in to the temptation to medicate the pain instead of dealing with it. Sex, substances (the lust of the flesh), performance (the pride of life), and materialism (the lust of the eyes) help us avoid suffering. But none of these serves as the armor we need. They lead to suffering that is not redemptive, and eventually they cannot carry the weight of the problems they try to mask. To choose God's will, not our own, is to turn from those options directly to the problems themselves.

A more subtle way we choose our own way and not God's is to rely on our old defensive maneuvers. Adam and Eve used a fig leaf to hide from what was inside (as well as outside), and we continue to do that. To choose God's will and not our own is to face our defense mechanisms and give them up. When we do so, we find that we have to deal with our problems. Then some of the deepest character growth happens.

Tony found this to be true. He came to counseling to find out why he had never been able to sustain a romantic relationship all the way to marriage. He had had some wonderful girlfriends, but for some reason, with each one he would always lose interest and move away from the relationship.

The more we looked at Tony's patterns of relating, the more we saw something. Whenever a woman Tony was dating would confront him, he would argue with her and become defensive. To ward off the criticism, he would label her "controlling" or "demanding" or "critical." I watched him go through a few relationships, and the pattern was clear. He was seeing as "controlling" and "demanding" women who were not even close to this description.

As this pattern emerged, I asked him to take a close look at it. At first he fought me. He said that I just did not see what his girlfriends were really like, because if I did, I would agree with him. I could not get Tony to see that he was distorting his relationships with women. So instead of that route, I took another one.

"Tony, let's say that you're right," I said. "So what? So she is being critical. How does that justify your getting argumentative and withdrawing from the relationship? Every woman is going to do something you don't like."

"Yeah, but this is really bad," he retorted, trying to justify his pattern.

"This still doesn't change the fact that you are acting like a baby," I said. "What is your problem that you cannot stand there when you are being criticized and deal with it? Why do you have to run? Who is the man in the relationship? I thought you were supposed to be the strong one."

He at first tried to justify his defensive behavior, but finally I got him to see something important: *Just because someone else does something wrong does not mean that I have to.* Jesus taught us this lesson in his handling of relationships. He did not return "evil for evil." Instead, no matter how he was being treated, he responded in grace and truth.

So I got Tony to see that even if his girlfriends were being critical and controlling, this did not give him the excuse to be that way. If he were going to get well, he was going to have to get "righteous"!

But Tony did not want to get healthy in this relationship, he told me. He thought that I was asking him to put up with a critical woman. I reassured him that I was not asking him to marry anyone. I was just asking him to be who he was supposed to be and see what he learned. It did not matter if he married her or not, I explained. He still was under the command to learn how to relate as God wanted him to.

Tony worked on his defensiveness. He had to suffer to say, "Not my will, but yours." He had to confess that his pattern of defensiveness was not what God wanted of him, no matter how the other person was acting.

So he suffered—through many interactions. He had to confess his patterns of detaching when things got heated and of withdrawing when things got uncomfortable. And when he did, he found out some things. Underneath all of those defensive character patterns were fear and hurt. He had been hurt and controlled a lot when he was young, and three things had happened. First, he had never faced the wounding and fear inside of him. Second, he had learned some maladaptive ways of handling relationships to keep women away from him and feel a false sense of power. Third, he had never learned the right way to feel powerful in a relationship, which is to stand there and be honest.

When he decided to suffer and say no to his defensive character patterns, doing God's will and not his own, Tony found his soul. But he was not happy at first. He found a soul that had to face its hurt, weakness, and fear. It also had to face its inability to relate directly with conflict and had to develop some new skills. In the process, some other things changed as well.

As he became stronger and less wounded, Tony saw women differently. They were not so threatening. He was able to take criticism and stay in a conflict. He stopped withdrawing defensively and learned to be direct and honest. He even learned to own it when his woman friend was right and apologize instead of just seeing the criticism as part of a "controlling woman's" problems.

It was not long before Tony fell in love, this time for good. He met a wonderful woman and got married.

What is really interesting to me is that the woman he married was much stronger than many of the others he had dated. This time, when she would get upset or assert herself, he would see it as cute, or he would empathize with how she must be feeling and try to do something to help. But he never saw her as controlling or demanding. He just loved her and contained all of her strong reactions. Not only did he not run in a defensive way, but he now was strong enough to do what Jesus did in tough situations: "the will of God."

Not Returning Evil For Evil

The third way to arm ourselves with the attitude of Christ is to not retaliate. We saw the way Tony discovered the dynamic of not "returning evil for evil." The breakthrough for him did not come by my helping him to see that the women he dated were good and not bad. Although this was an important insight, it was not the most important one. For even if he could have seen that, which he could not (see Matt. 7:5), it would not have helped in the long run. What would have happened if that "good" woman had ever done anything not so good? Then he would have thought he was justified in his own dysfunctional, defensive, and even sinful responses. It would have just set him up for more broken relationships in the future, because he would have needed "goodness" from the other to be good himself.

What he had to see was this: *His level of health and maturity could not be dependent on someone else's. If it were, he would be a slave to someone else's immaturity.*

I had to show Tony that regardless of how he was treated, he had to give back better than he received. He had to overcome evil with good, and in that lay his "salvation" from other people's problems. It did not matter how "controlling" someone else was or wasn't. As Paul said, "Do not be overcome by evil, but overcome evil with good" (Rom. 12:21).

The only question Tony had to be concerned with at that time was his ability to deal with conflict and relationship. My challenge to him was this: "If every time a woman is upset with you, you get defensive and run away, you don't have a chance of ever getting married. You are a dependent child, and children should never get married."

Ultimately, we are only as healthy as our ability to relate as God relates. He is honest, loving, and forgiving, communicates well, is able to be vulnerable, and so on. This is health. This is righteousness. Good relating equals good health. So if I can be drawn into sick patterns or sick relatedness by someone else's sick patterns, then I am not healthy at all. I am dependent and at the mercy of whatever treatment I am receiving at the moment.

This is one of the main problems with people leaving marriages without working on the issues from their own side of the equation. Many marriages break up because one spouse determines that the "other" is making her miserable, or is too difficult, and leaves. As a result, two things happen. First, the person never grows past her need to have another person be healthy for her to be okay and to relate well. Second, the marriage does not have a chance to work because she did not work on her patterns that could have changed the entire relationship and brought the other person around.

We have received testimonies and talked to thousands of people who have read our book *Boundaries* and who have learned to relate as God would have them relate and, as a result, have turned a hopeless marriage around and saved a family by changing themselves.

Jesus suffered through the dysfunction of others and did not allow it to turn him into one of them. The Bible is clear about our need to do the same as we follow his example of suffering:

> For it is commendable if a man bears up under the pain of unjust suffering because he is conscious of God. But how is it to your credit if you receive a beating for doing wrong and endure it? But if you suffer for doing good and you endure it, this is commendable before God. To this you were called, because Christ suffered for you, leaving you an example that you should follow in his steps.

> *"He committed no sin,*
> *and no deceit was found in his mouth."*

When they hurled their insults at him, he did not retaliate; when he suffered, he made no threats. Instead, he entrusted himself to him who judges justly (1 Peter 2:19–23).

Jesus was concerned with doing the right thing, no matter what was done to him. If we would identify with that suffering, we would get well and grow much faster than not. We would transcend the immaturity around us and grow in spite of what is thrown at us. And we would save some others in the process.

Picking Up the Cross

As we saw above, when Peter tried to get Jesus to forgo suffering, Jesus told us two things. One is that each person will have to pick up his cross; the other is that if a person tries to save himself, he will lose, but if he loses himself for Jesus' sake, he will gain his life. This is the essence of the suffering of Christ as we have looked at it here. We have to identify with that cross. We have to be obedient to the suffering that will bring about holiness. We have to give up our own defensive and offensive attempts to save ourselves.

Identifying with Jesus' suffering has meant many things to believers over the years. For some it has meant giving it all and dying for their faith. For others it has meant leaving the comforts of this world and going to faraway and difficult places on mission fields. For still others it has meant persecution in various ways for taking a stand.

But for all, no matter what the "outside life" brings in suffering, the internal suffering of character growth is a constant for everyone who does it his way. It means that we humble ourselves and give up playing God. It means we are able to say "not my will, but yours." And it means we will not return evil for evil, but overcome evil with good (Rom. 12:21). All of these responses are a very real part of how people grow.

GRIEF: GOD'S CURE FOR WHAT ISN'T RIGHT

GRIEF IS THE TOUGHEST pain we have to deal with. It is not the worst human experience, because it leads to resolution, but it is the most difficult for us to enter into voluntarily, which is the only way to get into it. The rest of our human experience just happens "to us." Hurt, injury, anxiety, alienation, and failure all break through, and we suffer. Grief does not "break through." It is something we enter into.

But its voluntary nature is not the only thing that sets grief apart from other kinds of suffering. The other difference is that *grief is the one that heals all the others. It is the most important pain there is.* This is why God calls us to enter into it voluntarily. It heals. It restores. It changes things that have gone bad. Moreover, *it is the only place where we get comforted when things have gone wrong.* So, God tells us and our counselors tell us, "Go there." Listen to Solomon: "Sorrow is better than laughter, because a sad face is good for the heart. The heart of the wise is in the house of mourning, but the heart of fools is in the house of pleasure" (Eccl. 7:3–4).

Why is that? What is so special about grief? Why is it the "pain that heals"? Because grief is God's way of our getting finished with the bad stuff of life. It is the process by which we "get over it," by which we "let it go." And because of that, because it is the process by which things can be "over with," it becomes the process by which we can be available for new, good things. The soul is freed from painful experience and released for new, good experience.

The soul is designed to finish things. It is designed to grieve. Just as a computer is programmed to run a particular path, so our soul is designed to go down the path of grief. Therefore, since it is the way we are made, Solomon tells us, basically, to "get on with the program." Be sad, and your heart can be made happy. Cry it out, and it will get out. It will be over.

So what is this process that we are wired to do and that can save our hearts from misery? What does it look like? Let's take a look:

The Loss Itself—Reality

For grief to occur, something bad has to happen. Everyone is wired for grief and is a candidate for healing, because bad things happen in life. As Jesus said, "In this world you will have tribulation" (John 16:33). It is a reality in everyone's life. Here are some examples:

- Death of a loved one
- Death of a dream
- Death of a season of life (caring actively for children, employment, and so on)
- Death of a relationship
- Death of a plan
- Failure
- Not attaining the love or approval of a significant person
- Not being the person one wishes he or she were (loss of the ideal self)
- Not getting what we want
- Loss of health due to illness
- Financial reversals
- Death of anything we need, want, or desire, good or bad

Protest—I Don't Want This to Be True

The second thing that happens is that we protest the reality. One way we protest is by becoming numb or denying what is happening. Often when people lose a loved one, they initially feel "unreal." They feel that "this isn't really happening." Their emotions have not caught up with the reality. These feelings are a form of protest. We naturally do not want what has happened to be true.

Another way we protest is by screaming, "No! This cannot be happening!" We have all seen traumatized people who lose someone and their first response is to scream, "No! No!" It is the natural protest against that which is bad. It is the "anger phase" of the grief process.

Then we usually try to change reality. We try to make it not so. The protest turns into bargaining. We try to bargain our way out of the reality. We do everything we can to make it all not be true. Many people have seen a loved one being led out by a doctor who is saying, "It's over. There is nothing more we can do. He's gone." And the family member naturally protests the reality. "Keep trying. Keep shocking him." It can't be true.

We all recognize this normal, common protest. Less recognizable is the protest and bargaining of less tangible losses. For example, if someone does not feel loved by a parent early in life, he or she might live many years "bargaining" to make that reality not be true. "If I were to perform more, the love will be there. If I were prettier or thinner or smarter, the love would be there." Then he or she finds other people with whom to live out that bargain, hoping to ward off the reality of what was lost a long time ago.

Despair or Depression — The Giving In

When our protests and bargaining do not work, we realize that what has happened is really true. It is hopeless. It is not going to change. This is the beginning of grief proper; it is an embracing of the loss.

Despair in this sense does not mean a total loss of hope—a state of hopelessness—but rather a loss of hope that this is really not happening. We become aware that this reality is not going to change, no matter how much we bargain, wish, or try to make it so. It is reality. When we realize that, we hit bottom.

We have the wish and the reality at the same time. We wanted it, and it is gone. This is a death experience, a real loss. It is giving up the hope that this is not going to be true. And this is the experience no one wants. It is the truth. It is the sadness of the reality itself kicking in.

So we ward this one off, either by reverting to more bargaining or protest, or by acting out in some way. We try drugs, a new relationship, a return to an old one, more trying to perform, or whatever other mechanism is available to us to get away from that truth. The wish raises its head for one more round when it should bow its head to the reality instead. When we bow to this reality, all the air goes out of the balloon.

Sadness, Loss, and Grief Proper—Letting Go and Saying Good-bye

When we hit bottom, when we realize that this really is true, we "lose it." We break. And we cry. This sadness is the letting go of the reality. It is saying good-bye to what can never be.

But it is the beginning of true healing as well. It is the aspect that Solomon was talking about when he said, "A sad face is good for the heart." The emotional investment in whatever was lost is being given up. The wish and desire are being "counted as loss," as Paul said. We are letting go of what cannot be. Reality and our heart, mind, and soul have all come together, and we cry. Tears are shed, and after many, many tears, we let go. "I will never have it, so I will let go of the wish." And like a leaf falling into a stream, free of the tree that lost it, it goes away.

Resolution and Resurrection — Understanding and Becoming Available

The sadness does go away. And, as Solomon said, then the heart is happy. It is happy because it is now available for new things: new desires, new attachments, new hope, new energy, and everything that springtime brings. Winter has past, and it is the time for sowing new seeds of life.

We also bring to the new year the learning and understanding and experience that we learned in the old. Whether good or bad, what was lost was an experience, and from it we take understanding and wisdom for the rest of life. The process is complete, the person has grown, and the past is now the past and is not affecting the present, except in greater wisdom or the pleasant memories of a loved one who has passed on. The death experience has given way to the resurrection of a new life.

If Grief Is So Good for Us, Why Don't We Grieve?

If grief is the answer to so many of life's problems, why don't we just do it? If a sad face can make a heart happy, why don't we have "sadness parties"? Well, we do. They are called funerals. They are gatherings where we can be sad and begin to process our grief. Funerals were a regular part of God's family practices with the children of Israel, and we have continued that practice, although we have limited funerals severely. In Israel there was a prescribed period of mourning and people were assigned to carry out the task. "The Israelites grieved for Moses in the plains of Moab thirty days, until the time of weeping and mourning was over" (Deut. 34:8). The phrase "time of mourning" is one that appears several times. The Israelites saw it as the right thing to do. And Solomon says, there is a time "to weep and a time to laugh; a time to mourn and a time to dance" (Eccl. 3:4).

We usually hold funerals only when someone dies, but we also need to grieve other things. The problem is that we don't often see those experiences as losses. So we stay in denial or protest for a long time. Tony, for example, was still protesting that he did not have the "all

TIPS FOR GROWERS:

- Examine your view of suffering to see if you have "muggings" and the suffering of growth figured out. Determine whether you have been blamed for the muggings of life or have not seen the value of growth sufferings. Examine the counsel you have received.
- Make sure you have space for "good pain" in your view of life so that you can embrace it.
- See if there are specific changes you need to make in the list we mention on pages 213–14. Which ones do you relate to?
- Determine if there is bad or worthless pain in your life that you need to face and see differently. Convert it to helpful suffering. Take a look at what issues you should embrace.
- Make sure that you are not seeking consolation for things you need to change.
- Look for repetitive patterns in your life that you should own up to.
- Convert to Peter's attitude toward suffering—that it is armor.
- See whether the roles of the suffering of Christ are present in your life: kenosis, not my will, facing pain and stopping medicating or using defenses, not returning evil for evil.
- Take an inventory of the grief you need to face. Get the support you need and go through it.

TIPS FOR FACILITATORS:

- Examine your view of suffering to see if it is balanced. See whether your view has room for suffering that is totally innocent as well as for suffering that is needed. Examine the experiences people have had in which they might have been blamed for the muggings of life.
- Teach the value of good pain, and develop a culture that is open to entering into it. Provide contexts and activities that promote it.
- Provide teaching and contexts for facing the issues in the list we provide on page 207–8.
- Confront bad pain squarely. Provide contexts and activities in which bad pain can be confronted and converted into good suffering.
- Confront repetitive patterns. See them as destructive, and communicate that. Call people to repentance.

- Teach what Christ taught Peter and what Peter teaches us—that suffering is armor against sin. Offer that protection.
- Provide experiences and contexts for the sufferings of Christ: *kenosis*, not my will, facing pain and stopping medicating or using defenses, not returning evil for evil.
- Teach the value of the grief process and make contexts available for people to go through it. Make grief normal and teach it as a powerful tool to resurrection. Build the support systems that can make this happen.

loving mother" in each and every girlfriend he encountered. He continued to stay in the protest and bargaining phase, and therefore he never could get to a new life.

Another important reason people cannot grieve the way they need to is that they lack resources. In short, grief is a letting-down and a letting-go. And we cannot let down and let go if we are not being held up. If there is not enough love to sustain us, both inside and out, then we cannot let go of anything, even something bad.

This is the answer to the age-old question that people ask every day, "Why doesn't she just let it go?" Or, "Why doesn't he just get over it?" The reality is that often they can't because they don't have the resources, either internal or external, to do it. A good analogy is the trapeze: You can only let go of one trapeze if there is another to grab on to. Or surgery: You can only go under the knife if there is life support keeping you alive while the surgeon does her work.

We basically need two things for grieving. First, we need love, support, and comfort. As Paul says, "Mourn with those who mourn" (Rom. 12:15). The Bible recognizes that grief is only done in community. Otherwise we stay stuck in the despair or the wishing because we do not have the love to hold us up in order for us to let go of what we have lost. You don't throw even rotten food away in a famine. But if a new truck of food shows up, you can let go of the stuff that has died.

Second, we need structure. We need time and space for grieving. We need structured activities. This is why good support groups that meet at a regular time and do regular tasks are effective in getting people through grief. There is a time, a place, a space, and some tasks to do that structure the experience.

This is why I tell people that God put our tear ducts in our eyes. Grief is a relational experience, and our pain has to be seen eye to eye with another person. Someone should be looking at us when we are crying, and we should be looking at him or her. Then we know that we are not alone and our tears are seen and heard. Then, as Jesus tells us, "Blessed are those who mourn, for they will be comforted" (Matt. 5:4). Being heard, empathized with, understood, and supported gives the life support needed to go through the surgery of grief.

I wish that I had understood this process when I was younger. When I lost my dream of playing golf, I did not enter into grief soon enough. If I had, I would have saved myself a lot of pain. Instead, I tried to protest by finding a new life without grieving for the old. I tried to find a new dream. I tried to find new meaning. But until I found the God who designed grief and got me into the support and structure I needed to face my losses, I did not have losses—I *was* lost. Then, when I found the process of grief, with the support and structure that God and his Body gave me, I could finally have losses. I could process them, and then I was found.

So in your own life and the lives of the people you help, grief may be the answer to your rut. You may be denying a reality lost long ago. You may be protesting something that will never come true. Maybe it is time to give it up. Maybe it is time for you to mourn so that your heart can be made happy again.

To do that, however, you are going to need to get out of the vacuum. You have to have support and structure to get to a new life. If you do, the dead truly are raised. The mourners truly are comforted. The Psalmist was right when he said, "Weeping may remain for a night, but rejoicing comes in the morning" (Ps. 30:5). The Bible affirms it and commands it, and science proves it to be true. There really is such a thing as "good grief."

12

GROWING TASTY FRUIT: BECOMING A RIGHTEOUS PERSON

We need to seek God's kingdom and righteousness, not to be good, but to stay alive.

When I (Henry) hit bottom, Matthew 6:33 turned my life around: "Seek first his kingdom and his righteousness, and all these things will be given to you as well." This verse invited me to believe that God could help me put my life together. The way I heard this verse at that time was that I should seek God because he is the answer to all I ask. I had been looking to make life work on my own, and I thought that if I sought God, he would help me make it work. It sounded like a deal!

Somehow I skipped over the "his righteousness" part of the verse in putting together my theology of life change. I can't remember what I thought about the "his kingdom" part, but I do know that I did not think much about righteousness that day. I was just thinking about finding God and having him do something for me.

I soon found out that seeking God's righteousness meant I would find a legal righteousness—forgiveness before God—through *faith,* not through *works.* I would be made "right" with God, not by working hard, but by faith. This was clear. God accepted me on the basis of what Jesus did, and I was declared "righteous" by him (Rom. 10:4).

What I did not immediately discover, though, was that for me to have all of the things I needed "given to me," I would also have to seek righteousness in another way. I was going to have to become a person who not only was righteous in the sight of God, but also was living out that righteousness in my soul and in my life. This was not part of my plan.

When most people turn to God to improve life, they look at what he is going to do for them. If they struggle at work, they ask God for a new job or career or account. If they struggle in relationships, they look to God to bring them a relationship or change the person they are with. If they are depressed or addicted, they look to God for healing and deliverance. We all look to the sky and want him to make our lives better. And he will. But the tough reality is that while he does give us jobs, relationships, and blessings, he also wants to make *us* better as well.

The implications of this are twofold. First, some of the things we want from God are fruits of our becoming more mature and righteous as we work with him. If we don't possess these things, the reason may be that we are not changing and growing in the needed ways. For example, I may want a job, but if I am not becoming responsible, I won't get one. Second, God often only gives us things we are mature enough to use. So until we grow, we will not have them.

One thing I was seeking from God was relief from significant depression. I did not know at the time that I was depressed; I just knew that every morning when I woke up, I felt a heaviness that would not go away. By the time I found myself in that chapel at SMU, I hoped that God could do something about that heavy feeling.

While I hoped that he might just "heal" me, this is not what happened. What happened is that God put me through a process of growth whereby he showed me many things about myself. Two things in particular stand out about my depression. First, as I related in chapter 7, I carried around some unresolved pain, but as God led me through resolving it, I felt better. Second, while I was a very relational and social person, I really did not let people get close to me. My heart was cut off from others even though I had what I considered "close" friends.

I did not know what God was doing at the time. Now, as a psychologist, I know that two of the biggest causes of depression are unresolved grief and emotional detachment. God healed both of these, not through some lightning bolt from heaven, but through my changing into a more mature person. As I grew in seeking his kingdom and righteousness, guess what? Emotional wellness was "given" to me, just as the verse promised.

I found the ways of his kingdom, such as deep, abiding relationship with others, but I had to make changes in my own personality and character to be more like him, more "righteous." As I did these things, I found emotional healing from my depression. In saying I became "more righteous," I do not mean that I became a perfectly holy person or better than anyone else. Far from it. But I changed many dynamics and patterns in my life that were contributing to my problems. And things got better.

One particular evening, the group I was in turned their attention toward me. Someone had asked me something about my life, and I told the story about my illness as a child, when I had been in a wheelchair and leg braces and unable to walk for a few years.

I must have made a joke about being the "crippled kid" and then just continued on with my story. But the group would have none of that. They confronted me as being "cut off" from my feelings. I guess they sensed I could talk about really painful things without showing any emotion. So they went after me. They questioned me as to what being in a wheelchair and leg braces was like, and they would not settle for the "uninvolved" response on my part. They made me face how I felt.

This was really painful to do, but what happened as a result of that incident and others in which I had to be more real with what I felt, is that I got my heart back. I could feel again and begin to trust people. So, over time I became more open with people and allowed them to get closer to my heart. I was learning the part of righteousness that Paul refers to in Ephesians 4:25, where he tells us to put off falsehood and be more honest with each other.

Changing meant turning from doing things my way to doing things God's way. I had to learn to be honest about myself and my feelings. I had to stop hiding my hurt. I had to become more responsible. I had to learn how to confront some people and to stop controlling others. I had to learn to delay gratification. (The list could go on and on, as I was not then nor am I now short on dysfunction.) But the point here is that having the life and the growth we're looking for involves our changing into people who do things God's way.

The following three Scripture passages about righteousness illustrate the characteristics of our goal of becoming that kind of person:

> 1. "You were taught, with regard to your former way of life, to put off your old self, which is being corrupted by its deceitful desires; to be made new in the attitude of your minds; and to put on the new self, created to be like God *in true righteousness* and holiness" (Eph. 4:22–24).

> 2. "This is my prayer: that your love may abound more and more in knowledge and depth of insight, so that you may be able to discern what is best and may be pure and blameless until the day of Christ, filled with the *fruit of righteousness* that comes through Jesus Christ—to the glory and praise of God" (Phil. 1:9–10).

> 3. "No discipline seems pleasant at the time, but painful. Later on, however, it produces a *harvest of righteousness* and peace for those who have been trained by it" (Heb. 12:11).

In other words, these are the three characteristics of people who do things God's way:

1. They put off the old ways of doing things and turn to the ways that God does things (repentance).
2. They seek more and more to understand and gain insight into what is best (understanding and insight).
3. They commit to the pain of discipline in order to grow (discipline).

Let's take a look at each of these three—repentance, understanding and insight, and discipline—in greater detail.

TURNING FROM WORLDLY WAYS TO KINGDOM WAYS

THE FIRST CHARACTERISTIC OF a person who does things God's way is *repentance*. We talked earlier in greater detail about how repentance works. What is relevant here, however, is that when people look for the life they want, they must understand that this life is found in doing things God's way. But how do we communicate to people the importance of seeking the ways of God, and how do we motivate them to do it?

Two basic ways to motivate people to change are the "religious" way and the "reality" way. In the religious way we tell people they should do the right thing because it is the right thing and it is wrong not to do the right thing. But being "right" has never been a very strong motivator for people to change. They have always been more interested in doing things "their" way than the "right" way. The other problem with the "religious" way is the human response to "should." When we tell people they "should do this and that" because it is right, they naturally rebel. Remember how the apostle Paul puts it: "Once I was alive apart from law; but when the commandment came, sin sprang to life and I died. I found that the very commandment that was intended to bring life actually brought death. For sin, seizing the opportunity afforded by the commandment, deceived me, and through the commandment put me to death" (Rom. 7:9–11). Something about being under the commandments—the "shoulds"—inspires the sinful nature to rebel. When someone says, "You should be good," we will find a way to be bad.

Paul tells us to give up this approach, and he reaffirms the "reality" way. He does not tell people to do the right thing just to be good or because it is right. He tells them to do it so that they will live. As he says a little later, "For if you live according to the sinful nature, you will die; but if by the Spirit you put to death the misdeeds of the body, you will live" (Rom. 8:13). To live—to have the life we desire—we have to live according to God's ways. It's reality. It's effective!

It is truly amazing to see what happens in people's lives when they shift from seeing the right way as something they "should" do to seeing it as the only way they will have life.

- They see honesty not just as a virtue, but as the only way they will ever have intimacy.
- They see facing pain and suffering not as something that their counselor wants them to endure, but as the only way out of a depression or an addiction.

- They see confession and ownership of their faults not as something humiliating and guilt inducing, but as the way to grow and reach their goals.
- They see listening to feedback and correction, not as someone telling them they are bad, but as receiving a gift that is going to bring them life.
- They see living a life of sexual purity not something they should do to avoid God's being mad at them, but as the only way to find satisfying love.
- They see forgiveness of others not as a law, but as a path to freedom and reconciliation.

In other words, these people see the right way not as some religious rule God is handing down, but as the way to life.

It is always interesting to see nonbelievers change their ways because of the consequences of that behavior and not because God is telling them to. For example, many couples now practice sexual abstinence and avoid living together before marriage. This is not for religious reasons; rather, they see the staggering divorce rate of people who do live together before marriage. People do not turn from drugs, alcohol abuse, and smoking because these acts are "sinful," but because of the death and destruction those behaviors bring. People take a harder look at divorce because of the research concerning the long-term effects of divorce on children and because of the high divorce rate of second and third marriages.

For any of us to be motivated to grow, we must see doing things the "right" way as the only way life is going to work. Otherwise, doing things the right way is just too much work and, in the short term, not as gratifying—like the guy who knows for years that he "should get healthy," but never does until he has a heart attack and almost dies. After that, he sees health not as a "should," but as the way to stay alive.

Therefore the lesson for ourselves and for the ones we help is to make the message of "seeking his kingdom and his righteousness" not one of having to "be a good Christian," but one of finding the true path to life.

As Jesus said, "I came that they might have abundant life" (see John 10:10 NASB). And as the Israelites were told,

> In the future, when your son asks you, "What is the meaning of the stipulations, decrees and laws the LORD our God has commanded you?" tell him: . . . The LORD commanded us to obey all these decrees and to fear the LORD our God, so that we might always prosper and be kept alive, as is the case today. And if we are careful to obey all this law before the LORD our God, as he has commanded us, that will be our righteousness" (Deut. 6:20–25).

God gave the Israelites all of these "religious laws" so that their lives would work well and they would prosper. He does the same for us. This is one of the toughest things to understand. In our own lives we need to seek God's kingdom and righteousness, not to be good, but to stay alive.

For people to grow and find life worth living, they must do the two things to which kingdom and righteousness refer. They must seek the ways of God (how his kingdom operates), and they must live and internalize those ways for themselves. To *find* his ways is to find the kingdom; to *live* his ways is to find righteousness.

In the Sermon on the Mount Jesus describes this path:

> "Blessed are the poor in spirit, for theirs is the kingdom of heaven.
> Blessed are those who mourn, for they will be comforted.
> Blessed are the meek, for they will inherit the earth.
> Blessed are those who hunger and thirst for righteousness, for they will be filled.
> Blessed are the merciful, for they will be shown mercy.
> Blessed are the pure in heart, for they will see God.
> Blessed are the peacemakers, for they will be called sons of God.
> Blessed are those who are persecuted because of righteousness, for theirs is the kingdom of heaven.
> Blessed are you when people insult you, persecute you and falsely say all kinds of evil against you because of me" (Matt. 5:3–11).

People who want to experience the true growth revealed in the Bible will shift 180 degrees from the ways of the world to the ways of the kingdom, because only the ways of the kingdom work.

The kingdom of God, which seeks weakness, brokenness, righteousness, and purity of heart, is altogether different from the kingdom of this world, which seeks power and victory. From a growth perspective, the only path to make it all work is the path of the kingdom, not the path of the world.

If we could see things the way the Bible presents them, we would not be so opposed to "holy living." In fact, just a cursory glance at what Jesus teaches about kingdom ways after the Beatitudes is a good blueprint for the good life. Look at this list of teachings in the Sermon on the Mount:

- Live a life of good deeds in the community, where they have an effect, and show what God is really like.
- Keep God's ways and show others how to do the same.
- Be better than the hypocrites.
- Don't just avoid killing people; avoid also the internal attitudes that kill, such as anger, hatred, and name calling.
- Make amends with those you have hurt and work out your conflicts with others.
- Don't just not cheat on your spouse, but stop cheating inside your heart with lust and pornography. Love your spouse purely.
- Run from the things that will destroy your life.
- Keep your marriage commitment, and work it out. Don't just ditch a spouse for no good reason.
- Be a person of your word, and people will trust you.
- Don't return evil for evil. If someone is bad to you, don't hurt them back. Try to give something good.
- Don't just do good to those who do good to you. Be a good person. Do good to everyone.
- Don't do good things just to get attention, but to help other people.
- Don't be religious for show. Be spiritual in the privacy of your own heart.
- Pray to God with real words in a real way. Revere him, ask for what you need, ask him to bring good to the world and to protect you from evil. Confess what you have done wrong, and ask for forgiveness. Then give that same forgiveness to others who have wronged you. This is only fair.

- Don't be materialistic. Invest time and money into things that will last forever, like God's ways and people.
- Get your spiritual sight examined so you see life correctly.
- Don't worry about life. Seek God, and become the best person you can be. The life that happens when you do that is the one you would want anyway.
- Stop judging other people. Worry about your own behavior first.
- Guard the good things of your life and heart from those who would want to hurt you.
- Seek life and what you desire and need. Go to God, and ask him to lead you. Then you will find it. Trust his care for you.
- Treat other people in the exact way you would want to be treated. If you do that, you won't need a lot of other rules in life.
- Remember that the path to real life is not easy and not a lot of people find it.
- Beware of false spiritual teachers. You can tell the real ones from how they live and what happens to the people who follow them.
- Be real and true about your spiritual life with God. Those are the only people he will acknowledge.
- Build a life on what Jesus taught and you will have a solid life on which to stand. No matter what happens, you will make it through it.

This is not about "religion," but about a healthy life: reality. If everyone who is trying to make life work would just do these things (not to mention the rest of the New Testament), it is hard to imagine how healthy people would be. This is one of the messages of this book: *Getting righteous and aligned with the ways of the kingdom and getting healthy are one and the same thing.*

Understand and Gain Insight

THE SECOND CHARACTERISTIC OF people who do things God's way is that they seek understanding and insight. We must find out what is best and gain insight into our lives to apply it. Let's listen to Paul again:

"And this is my prayer: that your love may abound more and more in knowledge and depth of insight, so that you may be able to discern what is best and may be pure and blameless until the day of Christ, filled with the *fruit of righteousness* that comes through Jesus Christ—to the glory and praise of God" (Phil. 1:9–10).

The phrase "knowledge and depth of insight" means at least two things. One is that people should always be learning the ways of the kingdom and all the things God tells us to do. People need to be taught the principles of relationships, healing, and life. This is why teaching, Bible studies, growth groups, books and tapes, and seminars are important in the process of growth. We need to know what God wants us to do.

But knowledge is not enough. Therefore, the second thing is that we need to know how to apply that knowledge to our own lives in an in-depth way so that we can develop the purity that will lead to the fruit of righteousness. Gaining insight includes work, feedback, correction, digging inside our hearts and souls, and prayer, specifically about our own character dynamics and patterns.

We have discussed all of these things earlier in the book. The point for now is that in order for people to become righteous, they need to be gaining deeper insight into what is best for them. Whatever system of growth you are applying to your life or the lives of others, it must include ways for the participants to gain insight into the destructive dynamics of their lives so that they can be exposed and can learn and apply new dynamics.

As David said, "Who can discern his errors? Forgive my hidden faults. Keep your servant also from willful sins; may they not rule over me. Then will I be blameless, innocent of great transgression" (Ps. 19:12–13). We are not able to see and understand ourselves by ourselves. Insight comes from God and others. David asked God to show him the hurtful ways in himself and lead him into good patterns (Ps. 139:23–24). In other places the Bible tells us that we need to gain insight about ourselves from other people. "The purposes of a man's heart are deep waters, but a man of understanding draws them out" (Prov. 20:5).

Patrick was an elder of a large church, and he had actually begun many of the different ministries of the church. Most of them were heavily steeped in the Bible. He had a really strong commitment to the

Scriptures, and it was important to him that everything that was done was "true to the Word."

During the recovery movement, his church started a few recovery groups for people who wanted to go deeper and look into their "issues." People spoke of learning things about themselves and God in a new way and of "growing personally" through the ministry. As an elder, Patrick was really happy about these reports and happy that people were touched by what was going on, but he was not into these groups himself. They seemed to have more of a "counseling" emphasis than he wanted. He would leave those types of groups for "people with problems." He was content to stay "strong in the Word" and continue to go to his small group Bible study that studied the doctrines he considered meaty and for the really mature.

But over time, even with all of his Bible knowledge, parts of Patrick's soul were not growing. In his relational life, specifically with his wife, he was stagnant. He had been gaining a lot of head knowledge about the Bible and the major doctrines, but he was not changing in his ability to meet his wife's emotional needs. Finally his marriage was in trouble and his wife was demanding that he go with her to counseling. They came to see me.

I enjoyed my work with them as a couple, and they did very well. But the marriage counseling was secondary in helpfulness, in my opinion, to a group Patrick joined with some other men. Several men in that group had for years been committed to giving each other difficult but honest feedback about what they saw in each other. In that group Patrick was forced to see patterns in his relational style that were less than honoring to the Scriptures he had been so committed to teaching. He found that he was not always honest about how he was doing, hiding struggles from others with an attempt to perform and act as if all were okay. He learned he could be harsh and critical. When he confronted and dealt with that problem, he had to admit that he felt self-critical and fell way short of realizing the grace of God he had taught others about for years.

Patrick also began to get real about some ways in which he was argumentative and defensive whenever he felt threatened or people challenged him. This particular dynamic was affecting his marriage, as he would often become defensive when his wife would talk to him about problems in their relationship. His group strongly confronted him on his defensiveness, his emotional immaturity, and his arrogance hiding behind his "leader façade."

What was most surprising to Patrick, as well as to me, is that these things were really true. He was so successful as a church leader and such a "good guy" that the only ones who would ever have been able to make him aware of those "unrighteous parts" of him would have to get close and below the surface. His wife had been in this position, but he had not been able to hear her. The group was able to get through.

A key for Patrick was finding out that the righteousness the Bible talks about is not just to be learned and preached, but to be realized at personal

---

TIPS FOR GROWERS:

- Take a look at your own attitudes about righteousness. See if you resist the concept in your heart. Be converted to the idea that "right truly is good for you." It is the way you are going to get the life that you desire and is much more than just "being good." It is the way to the "good life."
- Take an inventory of the specific areas of your life that are not "righteous." See them as at best keeping you from what you desire and at worst destroying you. Repent of the lack of righteousness in these areas.
- Get rid of the "shoulds" thinking and get to the "I need to" thinking about righteousness. You need to get "right" with God, not because it is the thing you "should do," but because it is the thing you truly "need to do."
- Develop a context in which you can get deeper insight and understanding about yourself and what you lack in terms of righteous living. The process is much deeper than just knowing the concepts. The concepts must interfere with where you are and call you to change.

TIPS FOR FACILITATORS

- Communicate "righteousness" as essential to the way life works as opposed to "law." Breed an atmosphere of righteous living and successful life and relationships as being one and the same.
- Give ways and contexts to seeing what "right" is in the areas of their lives that need to be changed. Provide for people experiences and settings to take a deeper look at themselves and discover where change is needed.

levels as well. He had never been in a context, or had a need, to find that out. He became a spokesperson to others about getting their internal lives to line up with the righteousness of God.

People are never going to grow by listening to a sermon once a week and then just go about their business. They must gain deeper knowledge about God's ways (his kingdom) and also find out how those ways apply to their own issues in life (his righteousness). They need to discover what is true about them, and they need feedback about how their patterns work and what to do differently. Then they can grow. This is why we are such big supporters of structured groups that take people through biblical teaching on specific issues like relationships. These small-group participants receive both knowledge and feedback from others who observe them. They gain insight, and they find out how best to proceed. This is what the Bible says to do, and research shows that it works.

DISCIPLINE

IN CHAPTER 19 WE talk about discipline as a process that takes time on the path of growth. But it is also important to talk about this disciplinary "process and time" with regard to seeking righteousness.

We look for the "quick fix." We want what we want right now. We may want our pain to end, our career to take off, or a relationship to get better. But the clear teaching of the Bible, life, and all the research is that growth takes time. Listen again to the verse quoted above: "No discipline seems pleasant at the time, but painful. Later on, however, it produces a harvest of righteousness and peace for those who have been trained by it" (Heb. 12:11).

We all want the "harvest of righteousness." We want to be well, and we want the fruit it brings to "give us" the good things of life, as Matthew 6:33 says. But we must realize that to receive the fruit we want, we must commit to discipline. We must go to a group for many seasons. We must see a counselor for a while. We must enroll in classes to learn about our profession and to grow our business. We must call on clients to build sales. We must invest in our marriage to build intimacy. We must dig around in our souls week after week to change the dynamics that are ruining our lives. All this takes time, and often it is not fun. It doesn't seem "pleasant." But what true growers learn, as we talk about in chapters 11 (suffering) and 13 (discipline), is that the pain is temporary and the fruit is long-lasting.

Therefore, in your own work as well as your work with others, be an evangelist for the process. Be an evangelist for the fact that it all takes time. Be an evangelist for pain and suffering. Pain is the path to greatness. Someone once said that pain is dysfunction leaving the body. It is like that for whatever weakness or sickness we possess. It hurts to grow past it or out of it or to have it removed. But this kind of pain is good, and it will not return again. And the lessons we learn will last forever.

PUTTING IT ALL TOGETHER

A RELATIONSHIP WITH GOD is the answer to all we seek. That's what I began to discover the day I ended up in that little chapel. As Jesus said, and as we have seen in this book, if we seek first his kingdom and his righteousness, all the things we are looking for will be provided. But as we have also seen, this is not a one-step dance.

Seeking God first means that we know him as the God of grace who is for us. He is the one who will provide what we need, and we must give up our own self-help programs. But we can't just have him and have it all done. We also have to be changed into people who can produce the fruit of the life we desire, and we do that by finding his ways and learning to live them.

God is not only a God of grace. He is also a God of truth. And getting well means that we have to discover a lot of truth and follow it. Seeking righteousness truly does bring it full circle. And that is not some sort of religious mumbo jumbo any more than to tell an airplane designer that he must seek the laws of physics. If he does not know them and apply them to his work, the plane is going to crash.

Life and righteousness are exactly like that. Life is designed with laws that govern relationships and success. Laws govern healing and growth. For those "planes" to fly, we have to learn the laws that govern them. Seeking righteousness is not at all a religious trip. It is about learning and becoming life itself, and in the end the "right" way is the only way.

13

THE VALUE
OF PRUNING:
DISCIPLINE

Discipline provides the structure for love to grow us up.

Ayoung woman named Kara came to my office to talk about her home life. "Here is my problem," she said. "I tend to be a flake. I have a hard time getting organized, I'm terrible with money, and I'm late for everything. It never bothered me until I got married and had small kids. Now it's really bothering me."

"Any ideas on how things got this way for you?" I (John) asked.

"Well, my parents loved me as a child, but they did everything for me. I never learned how to handle schedules and money, or even how to keep my room clean. Now I'm married to this loving, supportive guy, and I really like my marriage and my life, but try as I might, I can't keep it together. I have a to-do list for parenting, cleaning, and errands, and so much of it just doesn't get done. The house is always a total mess, and the errands don't get done. And it's not like my kids are that demanding or the tasks are that unrealistic. I have friends in my situation who pull it off. It's me. I will get bored or get on the phone with a friend, and nothing gets done."

"So a flake is a person who has trouble being organized, disciplined, and focused?"

"Yes. And I really hate the disappointment I see on my husband's face when he gets home after work. He's not a controlling person or a perfectionist or anything. He helps out a lot. All he wants is a little order in our life. But I can hardly get any of my list done. I feel like I'm not ready for the grownup world."

"What have you done to try to deal with this?"

"Well, I was tested for ADD [Attention Deficit Disorder], and the results were negative. I pray a lot, and make resolutions and commitments to God. They help for a while, but not for long."

"If you told your toddler to try really hard to make dinner, what would happen?"

Kara looked confused, then said, "He would fail."

"Right. Why?"

"Because he doesn't have the ability."

"So how does he get the ability?"

"I suppose he has to work on it over a long period of time." She paused. "Are you saying that's what I have to do?"

"In a way. I'm saying you don't have the ability to be self-disciplined. It's not inside you. So when *self-discipline* is found wanting, we need *other-discipline* from outside of us so that we can take it in and develop it."

"So what do I do?"

"Well, at this point it doesn't seem to me as if you have some unknown resistance to being organized, or are sabotaging yourself, so I would suggest you ask some friends, including your husband, to check in with you at certain times during the day to encourage you and to see how your to-do list is going. This will break the day up into manageable pieces and will also keep you aware that you'll be answering to someone soon, not in a parental way, but in a friendly way. Try that for a while.

"If, however, you are still not able to pull off the tasks," I continued, "I would move to an arrangement in which you have to lose something if you don't get the tasks done. Maybe you have to shine your friends' shoes or drive to their house with an ice cream."

"That sounds like how I'm raising my kids."

"It is, because you are somewhat like your kids inside. The only difference is, you are initiating this approach rather than someone doing it to you."

Kara went to work. One of the things I loved about her was that she had no problem submitting to her friends and being honest about her "flakiness." She cared more about growing up than looking good or self-righteous. And God always honors that attitude, as in the story of the tax collector and the Pharisee (Luke 18:9–14). So I wasn't surprised when she called me a while later and said things were much better. She had to do more shoe shining than she had expected, but she was seeing more of an ability to stay on task in her life.

WHY THE PAIN?

NOT ALL PEOPLE IN the spiritual growth process have Kara's problem. However, the Bible teaches that everyone needs discipline and correction to grow: "My son, do not despise the LORD's discipline and do not resent his rebuke" (Prov. 3:11). Along with all the other elements of growth we deal with in this book, discipline is a necessary—in fact, a principal—one.

Let's understand what we are talking about. The Bible has many meanings for the word *discipline*, such as chastening, correcting, instructing, reproving, and warning. The word *disciple* refers to one who is in the learning process. The idea for our discussion is that discipline in its broadest sense is *training for a person to learn self-control in some area of life.*

Actually, the word *discipline* describes both the process and the result. God disciplines us so that we will be disciplined people—that is, we go through external correction and consequences so that we will make discipline a part of our internal life and experience. *We become disciplined by being disciplined by God and others.* Why do we need to be disciplined to learn self-control? Because we are not in control of ourselves. Like children, we go astray, make mistakes, and need parameters. One of the fruits of the Spirit is self-control (Gal. 5:23), and it comes from God over time so that we can run our lives under his rule. And like children, we know when it has borne fruit inside us, *when we are not as dependent on the outside structure to stay in control.*

So discipline is one of the necessary ingredients of spiritual growth. Our need for discipline applies to much more than problems in organization and structure, as in Kara's case. It applies to every area of life in which we are not operating as we should, from attitudes to relationship conflicts to faith struggles. For example, a very highly organized and focused person might have a problem being emotionally available. When he is upset or stressed, he might have a pattern of withdrawing love from those who need him. Loving correction and reminders from others when he is doing this can make him more aware of it so that he can take responsibility for the issue.

Self-control provides a structure for love. People who have internal discipline have learned to run their lives in such a manner that God's love flows through them in very fruitful, fulfilling ways. They display qualities such as honesty, responsibility, faithfulness, and dependability. They are not slaves to their impulses. *If love is the heart of the person, discipline is the skeleton, giving a person form and protection.*

Yet discipline is painful. Many people enter a growth group, for example, with the idea they will be loved, supported, and understood. And any good growth context provides these things. But if this is all a group provides, members can become well-loved infants, unable to solve the life problems with which they struggle. Often it is because they lack the necessary elements of discipline and correction.

Some people fear that discipline means punishment, condemnation, judgment, or even abuse because others may have hurt them in the guise of discipline. Thus they avoid discipline. But God's view of discipline differs greatly from that. One of the Greek words used in the Bible for *discipline* has a meaning that includes "nurture." That is to say, discipline assists in loving and growing us up. It is driven not by anger or punitiveness, but by caring, "because the Lord disciplines those he loves, and he punishes everyone he accepts as a son" (Heb. 12:6).

For example, I never enjoyed my parents' "making" me do dishes and clean up after myself. I thought they were being mean and unloving.

However, today those tasks are automatic, and I do them without needing to be reminded (except sometimes by my wife). And I am truly grateful for the time my parents took to be an external support for discipline until it became a part of me.

Discipline is related to suffering, though it is not the same as suffering (see chapter 11). Suffering involves any discomfort we go through, be it as serious as the loss of a loved one or as trivial as getting a traffic ticket. However, while suffering speaks more to the *experience* of discomfort, pain, or loss, discipline is more concerned with the *goal* of growth and self-control. For example, you suffer through a diet and exercise regimen, experiencing hunger, temptation, deprivation, and fatigue. While suffering through that, you learn the discipline of being the master of your body. It becomes a fruit, or result, of submitting to that regimen.

Submitting to discipline is difficult because we must allow something to be done to us. We are *being disciplined.* Like Kara, we can't provide discipline for ourselves; it is just not inside us. We have to let it occur to us, and then we grow from it. This might mean giving someone permission to confront us when we are unloving, or agreeing to be in a group that will tell us the truth about ourselves. A certain loss of control and self-protection is necessary when we want to learn discipline. God never makes growth a process we can fully control. It takes faith (Heb. 11).

Although discipline is a process we receive, it does not mean we are passive in it. We also need to take initiative and be active. Paul says it this way: "No, I beat my body and make it my slave so that after I have preached to others, I myself will not be disqualified for the prize" (1 Cor. 9:27). *We are an active part in the discipline we allow to happen to us.* For example, two women mutually agree to give each other feedback. One tells the other that she seems to be indirect and not forthcoming at times. That feedback is received. The next act is to begin taking steps toward being more emotionally honest with her friend. That is the active part.

THE INGREDIENTS OF DISCIPLINE

SEVERAL ASPECTS TO DISCIPLINE operate in our hearts and aid our spiritual growth. Some are qualities of the person being trained, and some are qualities of the process. When the discipline works as it should, these all add up to much growth in the person.

What the Grower Must Provide

RECEPTIVENESS. We need to be receptive to discipline's training. The more we embrace the necessary pains of growth, the more discipline bears fruit (Heb. 12:11). Receptiveness is highly important. I have seen people receive the lessons of discipline and grow from them to the point that they made major strides in their sanctification. I have also seen people refuse discipline, and their lives have suffered as a result. King David humbly received God's correction when he went off the path, and his kingdom was established forever. In contrast, the Pharaoh of Egypt, a man with a high position, hardened his heart against the discipline of God, and he came to a tragic end.

If you are a growth facilitator, normalize this receptivity in your growth context. Make sure that truth and loving confrontation are integral parts of the process, not exceptions. Help your people see that part of love is to be honest and direct. Receptive people will take initiative and ask for feedback on how they affect others. Less receptive ones might need to be encouraged to look at their resistances to discipline.

CONFESSION. To "confess" is to agree with the truth. When God or others are disciplining us, we need to agree on the issue or problem. When we confess, we are aligning ourselves with the process of growth and repair (James 5:16). When we do not confess, we can negate discipline's good effects.

I knew a man in a growth group who desired to be more intimate with God. The group tried to encourage him, but soon found he wouldn't let them in emotionally. When heart issues arose, he would talk about his thoughts and opinions instead of his feelings, or change the subject. For a while he disagreed, saying that his problem was totally "vertical" and that the "horizontal" had no bearing. And he experienced little progress in his quest for God.

Then one night he confessed how lonely he was, but at the same time how afraid he was of having others know him inside. The group grew closer to him, as they could feel his heart, and they had great empathy for him. A marvelous thing happened. He began to sense the presence of both God and others within. He was no longer blocking people out. His confession began the process of repair.

REPENTANCE. When we encounter God's discipline, we need to be willing not only to agree with the truth, but to live out the truth—that is, to turn around, or repent. Repentance means that we truly will change what needs to be changed. It is important to note here that this doesn't always mean fixing the problem itself immediately. If that were true, there would be no need for growth. Repentance would simply mean doing only the right things and avoiding all the wrong things—which can't be done, given our immature and sinful condition (Rom. 7).

It is better to see repentance as an attitude of turning both from what is not the best and toward the good. This may involve changing how we deal with life. For example, a person who is a spendthrift and wants to change will probably not have the internal structure to become frugal immediately. But repentance for him may mean that when he feels unloved or bad, he calls a supportive friend instead of spending money to feel better. This repentance helps us move from death to life.

What the Process Must Provide

A SOURCE. As we mentioned, discipline must come from the outside until we develop self-control and maturity. God provides more than one source of discipline.

First, he chastens and corrects us directly. It all started when he had to put his first kids in a permanent timeout from the Garden of Eden (Gen. 3:23–24)! This was a painful experience for Adam and Eve, yet one meant ultimately for their good. I remember a friend of mine losing a high-paying job during an industry slowdown. This loss was not because of any performance issue on his part. However, it happened during a time when he had been paying more attention to his work than his family and his inner life. He told me later that he believes his job crisis was a signal from God to get his spiritual house in order, which he did.

Second, people are a source of discipline. It is hard to overstate the importance of the Body here. We need caring, honest, perceptive people who will love us enough to correct us when we stray. David had Nathan (2 Sam. 12:1–14); Peter had Paul (Gal. 2:11).

Third, reality is also a source of discipline. God has constructed the universe to operate with certain laws. When we disobey those laws, we feel the pain of the consequences (see the Law of Sowing and Reaping in chapter 5 of *Boundaries*). For example, when we don't listen to the feelings of others, they will disconnect from us. This discomfort alerts us to the task of reaching out to others' hearts.

EMPATHY FROM OTHERS. Discipline must also be administered with gentleness and care. Knowing the one doing it cares for us lessens the discomfort of receiving correction. We can bear consequences when we know that God and others are doing it to correct us, not to punish us. Stay away from having parental or controlling attitudes toward those who are enduring discipline. Make sure they are treated as adults, with respect and freedom. Remember what it feels like when you are admonished.

PAIN. Discipline generally requires pain to be effective. Pain signals a problem to which we should pay attention. God, people, and reality administer that pain in the right dosages for us to see what is going on, and then we correct ourselves.

The kinds and dosages of pain differ according to our need. A person with a receptive heart needs less pain to get the message. Someone who is egocentric or naturally strong-willed may need more. For example, one husband might hear his wife tell him that he hurts her feelings when he does not attune to her emotional state, and that will be all he needs. He empathetically feels the wound he causes her, and he doesn't want to hurt someone he loves. Her gentle words administer all the pain he needs to receive, and he submits himself to staying connected with her. In contrast, another husband may ignore his wife's words to the point that he almost has to lose the entire relationship to wake up to the reality that he needs to change. So our attitude toward growth and accepting discipline is a key character quality that dramatically affects the amount of pain we must endure.

If you are a growth facilitator, make sure the pain you are administering is given appropriately and carefully. Here are a few tips:

- Give grace (love and care) first.
- Be sure you are working on yourself to earn the right to say anything to others.
- Use gentle reminders.
- Speak before you give consequences.
- Give the person specifics so he or she can identify the problem.
- Stay away from judging or condemning terms.
- Be direct and clear.
- Distinguish between events and patterns. Events do not generally require much discipline; patterns do.
- Be sensitive to the emotional state of a person; we can bear only so much truth.
- Let the person know how his or her behavior affects others.
- If words don't work, administer consequences with care (see *Boundaries*).

Remember also that there are other kinds of pain in the world besides the pain of discipline. Losing a loved one, for example, may not be a wakeup call, but merely the sad reality of living in a broken world. People can hurt each other needlessly by always attributing pain to the need for discipline, such as "Maybe you lost your husband because you weren't listening to God."

TIME. Sometimes discipline performs its work very quickly, and sometimes not so quickly, depending on the following factors:

- The attitude of the grower
- The severity of the issue being dealt with
- How early in life the problem began
- The spiritual and emotional resources available to help

For example, on the one hand, a person who has recently developed a slight problem with disorganization, yet has a good attitude and a close group of supportive care, might take very little time to increase his focus and structure. On the other hand, a person who has always had severe problems in structure, blames others for it, and does not avail himself of help will take much more time to make progress.

INTERNALIZATION. Internalization is the process of emotional learning that means a person has made the experience a part of herself. She no longer needs the external structure and pain, because she has taken in the lesson and grown from it. It is more than simply memorizing a list; it requires both mind and heart.

For example, a woman in a group I led didn't realize that she dominated the conversation and always led the subject back to herself. The group members lovingly let her know how it distanced her from them and how much they wanted to get past it to be close to her. It hurt her to hear it, but she submitted to the process and asked them to remind her when it happened again. They did that faithfully. In time, she would catch herself controlling things verbally before anyone said anything. Then later, as she continued growing, she became much more connected with the group, with no hint of the controlling tendencies she once had. She had internalized many experiences of loving discipline from her group.

WHAT NEEDS DISCIPLINING?

HOW DO WE KNOW what to correct and what to let go? This is an important question, since many extremes exist on both sides. Some people function as moral police officers and constantly rebuke others to the point of hurting them. Others ignore the value of discipline and refrain from confronting people. Here are some guidelines for how to think about disciplining.

PROBLEMS ARISING FROM IGNORANCE. Some people struggle in life or relationships because they are ignorant of the issues. It's not that they resist or deny their issues. Rather, they are more innocent; they don't know they are a problem. For example, I have a friend who has a loud voice. She wasn't aware of it, but I noticed it in public places. When I mention it to her, she talks more softly, though it seems too soft to her. But she has become less ignorant of this (admittedly small) issue. She encounters discipline in my reminders to her, but she does not have a bad attitude. She is humble about accepting feedback.

PROBLEMS IN LACK OF STRUCTURE. The matter of lack of structure comes up often in spiritual growth circles. Like Kara, many people find they do not have enough internal structure to confront problems with others, stay focused on goals, make good choices, and think long-term. The discipline process can be extremely helpful to a person with these struggles, because the structure of the discipline creates what the person lacks.

Think of a child who can't attend to homework for more than a few seconds without darting off to play. You can nag the child all day, and she won't be able to stay on task. But when you design a disciplining structure that provides love, parameters, and appropriate consequences (for example, specific amounts of time required studying, with a consequence of loss of playtime if she doesn't stay on task), the child over time is more likely to develop the ability to work steadily. The same is true with all those who identify with Kara's problems.

CHARACTER PATTERNS. We need to be aware of, and discipline, disruptive character patterns. Some ways we interact with God, others, and the world do not work well. These patterns are often the cause of more external problems, such as depression, anxiety, marital and dating struggles, financial struggles, or substance abuse. Here is a partial list:

- Emotional detachment
- Passivity
- Devaluing love
- Controlling others
- Irresponsibility
- Self-centeredness
- Perfectionism

At their core, these are generally long-standing immaturities within us. But when we accept discipline for them, we observe them more, and we obtain wisdom on dealing with them and support for resolving them. Ultimately, they mature and are no longer issues.

Here is an example. Dave had a problem in devaluing the care of others. That is, when he was under stress or had failures at work or home, he would think, "People won't be there for me. They will think I'm being whiny and selfish." It would be obvious to his Bible study group members that he was having difficulty some evenings. They could see his sad countenance or would notice that he was withdrawn. Yet he would not respond to invitations to talk about his struggles. As the group became aware of this, they began to confront his pattern when it emerged. One night a group member said, "Dave, when you cut us off like you do, it's hard for us, because we don't feel like we can help you." Dave was struck by the fact that he mattered so much to this member and that he was so destructive to the relationship. As he became more aware of this tendency, he began taking more risks and allowing the group inside his heart.

ERRING TOWARD COMFORT. Be aware, however, that some spiritual growth concerns may need more love than correction. For example, people who are brokenhearted and needy may benefit from reminders of the issues, but what they need more are safety, comfort, and love. If you are a growth leader, pay attention to this so that you don't risk wounding someone with discipline who might simply need care.

A case in point is a man I knew who struggled with anger. His growth group corrected and corrected him. He tried to respond well, but felt more helpless and guilty each time they corrected him. Finally, his counselor diagnosed an underlying depression that was driving his anger. His depression had to do with deeply sad feelings of loss. When he was comforted in his grief, the depression and anger resolved.

DISCIPLINE BUSTERS

SADLY, WE ALL TEND to sabotage the growth process. Especially if you are a facilitator, be able to recognize the many ways we turn from God's growth paths, because more than anything, they can render spiritual growth null and void until they are resolved. Here are four.

DENIAL. Denial is not admitting the truth about a problem. There are two types of denial: One is when we keep something hurtful away from our awareness, such as trauma; the other is when we don't want to admit we have responsibility for something, such as how selfish we can be. The second is much more serious than the first. An example of this might be someone who has a habit of being critical of others, but when people say something about it, responds with "No, I don't do that."

TIPS FOR GROWERS:

- Take an inventory on how not having self-control has affected your life in some area—such as spiritually or relationally or financially or sexually or in parenting or career or home maintenance or food.
- Investigate why you have lacked discipline in those areas, whether from a lack of accountability with others or from over-harsh discipline or from a resistance to submitting to the process. Make a plan to enter discipline from a balanced, loving context of growth.
- Understand that discipline can't come from willpower and commitment, as those are on the inside. When we lack self-control, we must find discipline from other-control—that is, external structures that help us internalize discipline.
- See God as caring and loving, not punitive, when he disciplines you.
- Above all, look at any tendencies to deny, rationalize, minimize or blame your self-control struggles. Own the problems, and find good discipline sources.

TIPS FOR FACILITATORS:

- Be sure to present discipline as being a form of love and growth from God, not meaningless pain or punishment.
- Help people look at how their lack of being correctly disciplined, their resistance to accepting discipline out of pride or fear, and their not having self-control has affected their lives.
- Help them do an inventory of what areas of their lives need discipline and correction.
- Give them safe experiences with accepting discipline, from confrontation to consequences, to help them understand how this builds a sense of self-control.
- Clarify with them the tendencies to equate discipline with being abused or controlled, and help them learn to require discipline in their safe relationships.

RATIONALIZATION. When we rationalize, we make excuses for our problem to avoid being blamed. We may admit the problem exists, but it's not our responsibility. Using the above example, a person might say, "I do criticize you, but it's constructive."

MINIMIZATION. To minimize is to lessen the perception of the problem, or dilute it. For example, the person might say, "I really don't criticize you like you think I do. You're being oversensitive."

BLAME. Blame takes the responsibility squarely off the shoulders of one and lays it on another. It points the finger anywhere but toward us. For example, "I criticize because you provoke me to do it; you continue to show up late all the time."

At the heart of all of these "discipline busters" is our attempt to remove a bad aspect of ourselves from us. This is called "projection," and it is what Jesus referred to when he warned us to remove the plank from our eye before concentrating on the speck in our brother's eye (Matt. 7:1–5). People project so that they will not have to experience the discomfort of their own weaknesses and sins. Often this projection causes them to be afraid of those upon whom they lay their bad aspects. The other person is perceived as dangerous and, ultimately, as someone to control and keep at bay. This is why, when you become aware of denial, rationalization, minimization, or blame, you must lovingly but directly confront it. These projections divide people and disrupt the growth process.

CASE IN POINT

I AM A PERSONAL testimony to this chapter! While writing a section of this book, I encountered a time problem. Buried with other tasks and projects, I got behind in my writing schedule. Nothing I did helped me catch up. I put time aside, prayed, resolved to do better, and drank coffee late at night, all to no avail.

Finally, I called people in my growth group and asked them to do three things for me. First, I asked them to let me give them a copy of my writing deadlines so they would be aware of when I had to have what parts written. Second, I asked them to call me twice a day to see whether I was on schedule. Third, I asked them to decide what favorite charity they would like me to send money to, as long as it wasn't one of my favorites, so it would sting a little. And it worked. Knowing my friends were on my side and would be in touch with me helped me stay on task.

A friend who heard about this tactic said, "But why didn't you use rewards instead of discipline?"

I told her, "At this point, I couldn't take the chance."

The reward of relief came later when I made the deadline anyway.

CONCLUSION

GOD DISCIPLINES THOSE HE loves. A lack of being disciplined means a lack of being loved. However, if we stay in the correction process "correctly," we will grow in love, faith, and responsibility.

Discipline provides a structure for growth. However, there is another important element that helps make us open to growth and discipline: spiritual poverty. Find out about its benefits in the next chapter.

14

WATER FROM A DEEPER WELL: SPIRITUAL POVERTY

Spiritual poverty is experiencing the reality of our condition.

Henry and I were meeting with a large Christian organization, and the topic of small groups in the church came up. We strongly support and see much value in small groups. We were discussing the needs that groups meet, how they operate, and so on.

One of the executives of the organization, who is a friend of mine, asked, "What difference do you see between groups for people with problems and groups for normal people?"

Henry and I looked at each other and said, "There is just one kind of group."

This story illustrates a lingering problem in the church's view of spiritual growth. Just about everyone would agree that we all need to grow spiritually. We need to be close to God, love each other, read the Bible, and apply its truths. But many do not believe that a major reason to grow is that we are in a deep and severe state of neediness and incompleteness.

Yet the Bible teaches that all of us are in this state. The parable of the Pharisee and the tax collector (Luke 18:9–14) and Paul's personal anguish over his inability to do the right thing (Rom. 7:15–24) illustrate how much every person needs God's grace and mercy. By our very nature, we are a broken people, with no hope except for God.

Not everyone is aware of his or her neediness, just as the Pharisee in Jesus' parable did not recognize his. However, some are. Jesus described those who are aware of their neediness as *poor in spirit:* "Blessed are the poor in spirit, for theirs is the kingdom of heaven" (Matt. 5:3). The Greek for "poor in spirit" indicates a cringing beggar, absolutely dependent on others for survival. Not a flattering picture of us! You don't see people greeting each other in church with, "Wow, you're such a cringing beggar. I'd like you to mentor me." Yet the kingdom of heaven belongs to those who experience their dependency.

Spiritual poverty is about living in reality. A good way to understand this is to think of spiritual poverty as experiencing our state of incompleteness before God. This can be due to weaknesses, unfulfilled needs, emotional injuries and hurts at the hands of others, and our own immaturities and sins. It has to do with those parts of ourselves that are not what they should be and that we cannot repair in our own strength. When people experience at a deep level their neediness, incompleteness, and dependency—the way they actually are—they are often overwhelmed. Spiritual poverty is the cure for narcissism, self-righteousness, and a host of other problems. When our eyes are opened to our brokenness, we do not "feel better about ourselves"; rather, we feel that something is terribly wrong.

Yet Jesus calls this a "blessed" condition because it helps us get closer to God. Our state of incompleteness drives us outside of ourselves to God as the source of healing and hope. When we are comfortably independent, it is easy to avoid our need for God.

Brokenheartedness is related to spiritual poverty. Brokenheartedness is a state of being wounded or crushed by some loss, person, hurt, injustice, or circumstance. When a person is downcast because of an emotional, relational, or career injury, he is brokenhearted. God has special tenderness for this condition: "The LORD is close to the brokenhearted and saves those who are crushed in spirit" (Ps. 34:18; see also Ps. 147:3; Isa. 61:1). Brokenheartedness often brings about a sense of our spiritual poverty as it shows us our need.

When I tell strangers about the subject matter of this book, I glean information on their own stance toward spiritual poverty. I will meet someone on an airplane, for example, and we will talk about what we do. When I say that I write books, my seatmate may say, "So what do you write about?"

"I'm working on a book about spiritual, emotional, and personal growth," I'll reply, trying to cover all the bases.

Sometimes my seatmate's eyes will glaze over, and he'll say, "Sounds interesting," and we'll move on to sports or politics. But sometimes my companion will light up because the subject touched something important inside him. Then we will typically start talking about some struggle or issue he has had to face in life and how, through it, he experienced growth.

Now, I am not condemning the uninterested person. He may have been wounded in some growth group or process, or he may be one of those "together" people I have mentioned. The point I am trying to make is that all of us need to get to a needy place before growth can happen.

WHY SPIRITUAL POVERTY IS IMPORTANT IN HELPING PEOPLE GROW

MANY PEOPLE WHO HAVE a heart for God and growth have the same split idea of who goes in what group as that friend of mine had. They want to deepen their walk, become more Christlike, and know God more intimately. But they feel disconnected from those with life problems, such as depression, addictions, anxiety, a marriage/family/relationship problem, or a work obstacle. Those without these struggles may feel compassion and concern for those with them, but they can't relate to them. They will sometimes wonder why their friend can't just get it together, snap out of it, or trust God more, since these solutions work for them. And when they counsel others this way, they run the risk of disheartening their friend so much that she could despair of even her trust in God himself: "For the despairing man there should be kindness from his friend; So that he does not forsake the fear of the Almighty" (Job 6:14 NASB).

We are not saying that everyone with life problems is poor in spirit. Some are in denial. Others blame their problems on other people. Still others believe that, given enough time, they can solve their problems all by themselves. These people have not yet come to the end of themselves, to the humble acceptance of reality that causes them to grieve as a signal that they understand their position (James 4:9–10). We are saying, however, that those with life problems have more opportunities to recognize their need for God's healing, because the evidence is right there in front of them.

We are also not saying that those who don't experience problems are in denial. There are many believers who love God, have good marriages and relationships, and have reasonably good lives, without catastrophes. They aren't hiding anything. They aren't deceptive or mean people. But they may lack a sense of their own brokenheartedness, because they are not as aware of their neediness as the reality would indicate.

Recently I ran into an old friend who had been in the same Christian organization with me many years ago. As we were catching up with each other, he told me that he had had a radical spiritual change. Knowing that he had always had a very solid and committed faith, I was curious. "Tell me about it," I said.

"I went to a spiritual growth conference dealing with issues from the past. I didn't think it really would relate to me, but I wanted to be open.

"The speaker taught about how our family backgrounds can affect our spiritual lives. The short version is that I became aware of how my family background affected me. My parents were caring, responsible Christian people, but they were judgmental and distant emotionally. I grew up cut off from my feelings and tied to my work and ministry. And I tended to criticize others unfairly.

"I realized how this hurt my marriage, my kids, and my friends. All of a sudden, I became overwhelmed with sadness and grief over my own hurt and what I had unknowingly done to others. As time went on, I worked on getting emotionally connected, and giving up criticism and judgment of myself and others.

"By the way, I wanted to know if, back in the old days, I also hurt you with my distance or judgment."

Tears came to my eyes, not because he had hurt me, but because I could see how much he had carried inside for so long, trying as hard as he could to follow God, not knowing about all his issues. While I remembered my friend as very kind, I could feel that he was a different person from the man I had known. He was more approachable, more relational, and more open.

This is how spiritual poverty can help people grow. My friend became aware of his spiritual poverty, his particular hurt and emptiness, and his brokenness, and it changed his entire spiritual life, not to mention his relationships and ministry.

THE RICHNESS THAT SPIRITUAL POVERTY BRINGS

SPIRITUAL POVERTY HELPS US grow because it is literally *spiritual* poverty. The Greek term for "spirit" used in Matthew 5:3 ("Blessed are the poor in spirit") is the word indicating the spiritual dimension of life. In other words, the experience of poverty is both practical and spiritual. Being aware of our incompleteness orients us toward God and his ways, where he awaits us with all we need to grow and repair.

Spiritual poverty is a rich part of the spiritual growth process. Here is how.

SPIRITUAL POVERTY IS REQUIRED FOR A SAVING FAITH. No one can become a Christian who does not admit, at some level, her lostness and hopelessness in freeing herself from the prison and penalty of sin (Rom. 3:23). Otherwise, Jesus' death is meaningless and unnecessary. So to come to saving faith, we must be broken. What often happens, however, is that we accept Christ as Savior because of our brokenness and then we live our Christian lives as if we were whole. Although we have God dwelling inside us, we all still have unfinished parts that need to become mature and sanctified. This is why the Bible teaches us to continue in the faith walk as we began it: "So then, just as you received Christ Jesus as Lord, continue to live in him" (Col. 2:6).

SPIRITUAL POVERTY DEVELOPS A HUNGER FOR GOD. Spiritual poverty drives us to find solutions for our neediness and, ultimately, to find

God. Those who know they are truly needy are more motivated to look beyond themselves to the Lord. For example, those in need often become humble in spirit, due to the difficulty of their condition. From there, it is a short step to finding God in so many ways. There is a strong correlation between those who are humble and those who seek after him: "The humble have seen it and are glad; You who seek God, let your heart revive" (Ps. 69:32 NASB).

Many people who would not otherwise have invested much time in God's ways have sought spiritual solutions to their problems. Need and emptiness goad them toward him after they have exhausted their own resources. Reflect on the difficult times in your life, and see if those were also times when you sought out the Lord more.

This helps to explain why the Bible spends so much time blessing the spiritually needy and confronting the spiritually complacent. Without poverty, there is no motivating hunger. Lukewarmness is the hallmark of someone who has not yet become poor in spirit and therefore is not hungry. Jesus had harsh words for the lukewarm church of Laodicea: "You say, 'I am rich; I have acquired wealth and do not need a thing.' But you do not realize that you are wretched, pitiful, poor, blind and naked" (Rev. 3:17).

There is a paradox in spiritual growth: People who are more dysfunctional yet poorer in spirit tend to grow more than people who are less dysfunctional and less poor in spirit. One would think that people with more problems would struggle more with growing, and they certainly do struggle. However—and I have seen this more times than I can count in clinical and counseling settings—poverty drives hunger. You can't stop a needy person from grasping onto God, while many people in less severe circumstances easily fall away.

I once worked with a Christian couple who fit both these descriptions. The husband, on the one hand, had a drinking problem, a sexual addiction, and a raging temper. He was a mess, but he was hungry. When he understood the gravity of his problems and his spiritual condition, he went through a long, painful period of deep grieving over what he had done to himself, God, and his family. He made amends to all he could. He went to counseling and several support groups a week, and he voraciously read the Bible and all the books on growth he could get his hands on. He was as vulnerable, correctable, and humble as he could be in his growth relationships. His growth took a long time, but he is a new man. He is grateful for all the grace God gave him, and he now has a fruitful ministry to others.

His wife, on the other hand, was caring, structured, and responsible, but she wasn't very hungry for spiritual things. She went to church, read her Bible, prayed when she had time, and lived her life in a moral way. But she is pretty much where she was when I first met her. Her only problem back then, in her mind, was a crazy husband. And now she feels that life is better because he is better. I often tried to talk to her about her own hurts and issues, and she basically shut it all out. She just wasn't hungry. Even though she has a basically good life, she touches no one deeply and lets no one in, including God. Her children are distancing more from her as they grow, because there's nobody inside. She is getting busier and busier having lunch with friends and shopping.

The more broken we are, the more God can grow us up.

SPIRITUAL POVERTY HELPS US ENDURE THE PAIN OF GROWTH. Spiritual growth is hard work. It requires sacrifice, suffering, loss, and commitment. It is the narrow gate that relatively few enter (Matt. 7:13–14). It means losing your life, including all the old comfortable patterns, to find your life in Christ (Matt. 16:25). It is hard sometimes to see why we need to continue in our small group or face our issues or even pray or read the Bible. Yet growth is the only solution to our brokenness. Ultimately, the pain of growth is more bearable than the pain of our poverty.

Poverty makes it hard to go backward in the process. Once your eyes are opened to your need, it is difficult to live as though you had none. It is as if a door has been opened that can't be shut.

I was counseling a woman who had made a commitment to grow spiritually. During the process she discovered that what she had thought was being loving to her family was actually rescuing them from growing up and taking ownership of their problems. She realized that her rescuing was hurting both them and her. So she set limits with them, and they gave her a lot of grief about it. She went deeper in her prayer and group study life, and she realized that the roots of her rescuing had to do with her own dependent mother, for whom she had to be the "strong" one. As she dealt with this, she began to feel the lonely, isolated emotions she had had as a little girl when she had needed a grownup mother and didn't have one. These times were painful for her, both relationally and internally. Yet she never wavered in her spiritual growth commitment.

As I saw her go through all this, I said, "Do you ever wish you hadn't started this process?"

"I used to," she said, "but I've realized I could never go back. This is hard work for me, but at least God, reality, truth, and my friends are with me. I don't see how I could pretend as if what was wrong is really right anymore. So I actually feel blessed to be in this position in my life." She endured the pain of growth because her spiritual poverty kept her involved in God's ways.

SPIRITUAL POVERTY KEEPS US LIVING RELATIONALLY. Spiritual poverty and brokenheartedness drive us to emotional connectedness, both to God and to safe people. Coming to the end of ourselves reduces us to a childlike state of need and helplessness, which Jesus said is good: "Truly I say to you, whoever does not receive the kingdom of God like a child will not enter it at all" (Mark 10:15 NASB). Children by nature are relationally oriented. When they are in trouble or pain, the first thing they do is reach out for a protective, comforting parent. They instinctively seek out relationship without even thinking about it. They don't say to themselves, *I'll be strong and ride this one out,* or *I'll just think positive thoughts.* They ask for help from someone outside themselves.

One of the blessings of spiritual poverty is that it helps restore to us God's design of a relationally based life. We learn to receive comfort, support, and acceptance from others, which then strengthens us to continue. Relationship is the fuel of life. We need to internalize great amounts of relationship all during our lifetime to persevere and grow.

SPIRITUAL POVERTY HELPS US ENTER THE DEEPER LIFE. Our brokenhearted state also provokes us to move beyond spiritual immaturity into a deeper walk of faith. Although we all begin our spiritual lives as babes (1 Peter 2:2), God did not intend for us to stay in that stage of development forever. We are to move from elementary things to maturity in Christ (Heb. 6:1). The deeper walk takes us into many areas: the mystery of God's nature; the wonders of the Bible; the complexities of our own character, personality, and issues; and the intricacies of intimate relationships with others.

SPIRITUAL POVERTY DOES NOT ALLOW US TO STAY SHALLOW. Once we are on the path to growth, we are called to continue it at new levels: "Deep calls to deep" (Ps. 42:7). We don't "arrive" in the faith, though we do mature and change. We are always moving forward or backward. Ask yourself if you are disconnected, complacent, or bored with your spiritual life. Ask others if you seem that way to them. If this is the case, it may be a signal to ask God to help you become poor in spirit and thereby find him at deeper levels.

SPIRITUAL POVERTY GUIDES US TO SPECIFIC GROWTH AREAS. Spiritual poverty helps us find the right issues to heal. Physically hungry people are not always hungry for the same things. They may desire meat, vegetables, or fruit. In the same way, spiritually hungry people are not always hungry for the same things. Spiritual poverty can help us find particular areas of need and growth.

It is disheartening to hear stories of people who take their needs and problems to a Christian leader who says something like, "Your problem [meaning this is what I tell everyone who comes to me] is simply a lack of faith/secret sin/lack of surrender/lack of being in the Word/etc." Although we all need to address these issues, sometimes the problem is different. An old Chinese proverb says, "Beware of the man whose only tool is a hammer, for he sees every problem as a nail." In the same way, beware of trying to deal with your spiritual poverty by a "one size fits all" formula.

How does our poverty lead us to specific areas of need and immaturity? By making seekers out of us. Seekers tend to look in many directions for answers and help. They pray and ask God for insight and wisdom about their condition. They search the Bible. They ask mature people for counsel. And God promises that in his timetable they will find what they are looking for. He loves for us to seek. Jesus said, "So I say to you: Ask and it will be given to you; seek and you will find; knock and the door will be opened to you" (Luke 11:9).

Some people may find their poverty leads them to realizing an incompleteness in being loved and emotionally connected. The Bible teaches that we are to be "rooted and grounded in love" (Eph. 3:17 NASB). Yet those who have lived lives devoid of comfort and support do not have this grounding. Other people find that they are broken in the area of self-control and responsibility. They allow themselves to be controlled by others, or they have an area of life, such as eating, that is out of control. They are poor in spirit in taking ownership of their lives. Still other people become aware of their own hatred of and judgment for their imperfections. They find that they cannot make mistakes without experiencing harsh feelings toward themselves.

Poverty accomplishes its task by helping people ferret out these often painful insights and realizations. When people find these arenas of growth, they can work them out in the spiritual growth process we describe in this book. Identifying the areas is an important key—areas such as these:

- Establishing a loving and worshipful relationship with God and his ways
- Maintaining deep, vulnerable relationships with others
- Being free to make decisions based on values rather than on fear or guilt
- Knowing what we are and are not responsible for
- Accepting our badness and weaknesses as well as those of others
- Functioning as an adult rather than as a child in life and relationships
- Achieving competency in some job or career area
- Having a clear and balanced morality

(Some of these topics are covered in *Changes That Heal* and in the character aspects of *Raising Great Kids*.)

HOW TO DEVELOP SPIRITUAL POVERTY

BECOMING POOR IN SPIRIT is one of the most unnatural things we can do. It is the opposite of being victorious and having it together. Yet it is our only hope for spiritual growth. Actually, our task is more realizing our poverty than becoming poor, as we are already in need whether we know it or not. It is better to seek this quality ourselves than be forced to face it by difficult circumstances. Let's look at some ways that we can develop this internal capacity.

ASK GOD. Being in touch with your spiritual poverty is a gift from God because it brings forth things he wants to see in you and because it accomplishes his purposes. He will gladly show you where you are weak.

As you are reading this chapter, you may identify with my friend in the beginning who thought there are two different kinds of groups in the church—one for "healthy" people, and one for the "unhealthy." You may be a spiritual, loving, responsible person who has never dealt deeply with your ongoing sins, weaknesses, and brokenness. Or you may be leading a church, Bible study, small group, or ministry where the norm is not to have problems. If so, get on your knees—and get your ministry on its knees—and ask God to bless you with spiritual poverty, for "theirs is the kingdom of heaven" (Matt. 5:3). He will give you and yours the sense of incompleteness and need that keeps you close to him.

BECOME AN HONEST PERSON. Do an honest review of your past and present life. Look for patterns of avoiding pain, denying problems, staying away from truthful people, and trying to put a positive spin on negative things in your life. Be honest about tendencies to shy away from need and to move toward pride and self-sufficiency.

Look closely at those negative things you might be avoiding. Seeing the reality of your state can go a long way toward promoting your growth in spiritual poverty. Ask God for the grace and love to help you tolerate what you find inside (Ps. 139:23–24). Here are a few categories of issues:

- **Sins.** Look at selfish, rebellious behaviors and attitudes. Although you have been forgiven for them, they still require confession and repentance. Look especially beyond behaviors into dark motives of the heart: withdrawal of love, vengeance, envy, and blaming. (We say more about sin in chapter 16.)
- **Hurts and losses.** All of us not only have sinned, but also have been sinned against and injured. Look at significant people in your life who have hurt you. Also, look at failures and losses in life, such as medical, financial, or career losses.

- **Weaknesses.** Identify character flaws that hamper your life, things you do that you can't stop doing. This might include irresponsibility, control, fragility, people-pleasing, and perfectionism.

Try not to be too legalistic with this short list, as there is much interplay between categories. Irresponsibility, for example, can involve both sin and weakness, and it can be influenced by hurt. For growth purposes, however, this list can help you see your need for God.

READ THE TEACHINGS OF THE BIBLE ON THE TOPIC. Look up terms such as *poor in spirit, needy,* and *brokenhearted,* and learn what the Bible teaches about them. Look at the dynamics of God's relationship with Israel in the Old Testament. When she was complacent or rebellious, he was hard. When she was poor and hurting, he was tender. Study the differences in how Jesus addressed those who were wanting and those (like the Pharisees) who thought they had it together. The Scriptures give overwhelming evidence that spiritual poverty is an essential element of growth.

GET FEEDBACK FROM OTHERS. One characteristic of hungry people is that they surround themselves with others to help them with their dependency. For them, the normal Christian life is one in which people get together, share vulnerabilities, and fill each other up. If you are just entering into a position of poverty, however, ask those you trust if they think you are needy and poor in spirit. The honest ones will understand and will graciously let you know the truth.

My wife, Barbi, and I started a tradition in our family we call *character time.* During our regular family night, in which we meet to talk about the upcoming week, deal with problems, read the Bible and pray, we have character time, during which we help each other remain poor in spirit. Every member of the family—including our sons, Ricky and Benny—has to own an issue or weakness that needs the help of God and others to work out. Here are character issues that have come up over the years:

- Selfishness
- Withdrawing when upset and not talking about it
- Irresponsibility in household chores

- Working too much and not playing with family enough
- Chronic lateness
- Annoying someone and not stopping when the person asks us to
- Not coming when called
- Nail biting
- Getting angry too easily
- Taking kids on errands and calling it "quality time"
- Problems having regular devotional time
- Making promises and not keeping them
- Fighting instead of talking about problems

I hope you don't think we are hopelessly dysfunctional when you read this list! Anyway, we don't simply assign our self our own character issue. We must ask the other family members, "What do I do that really bugs you?" Then we all discuss ways to work on the issues, and we pray for each other. The next week everyone reports on his or her progress. Again, we can't leave out others in evaluating our progress. Rather, we ask, "How did I do this week?" Then we take it from there: we either work on a new issue or keep working on the same one. Most of the time it takes a while to change.

Our sons hated the idea at first, thinking it was just another way for their parents to control them. When they learned that Mom and Dad would participate in the process, they liked it. And while everyone certainly has his or her struggles, it has really helped the entire family hold onto a humble, brokenhearted position of need. Mutual support, vulnerability, and ownership have all happened during our character time.

SEEK A WHOLEHEARTED EXPERIENCE OF BROKENNESS. Poverty of spirit requires more of us than cognitively admitting we are incomplete and needy. It also affects our entire self, especially the heart. Realizing our condition before God is an overwhelmingly emotional experience, involving feelings such as dependence, grief, and remorse. Psychologists call this "being integrated," having the heart and head in alliance with each other. Seek this experience in the same way you seek God: "But if from there you seek the LORD your God, you will find him if you look for him with all your heart and with all your soul" (Deut. 4:29).

God reminds us, time and time again, that he likes neediness. Our life experiences might tell us to avoid need. If so, take a faith step and open up your soul to God and safe people. Spiritual poverty is the only way to be filled with what he has for us.

When we become more attuned to our spiritual condition, we can better understand the importance of the subject of the next chapter: obedience.

TIPS FOR GROWERS:

- Realize that spiritual poverty, though it sounds negative, is actually a blessed state and the only way to receive God's growth and healing. Adopt that attitude toward yourself and God.
- Review your life experiences and look at ways you may have entered spiritual poverty—through losses, failures, or simply a hunger for God and an awareness of your incompleteness. See how God used these experiences to bring you closer to him.
- Be aware of your brokenheartedness, and be mindful that this is not a sinful state, but a state of being sinned against or simply hurt by a broken world system. Learn that your brokenheartedness was not meant to be borne alone or just with God, but also with others.
- Bring up to God and people you trust your weakness, brokenness, and immaturity. Confess these, admit you can't change them in your own power, and admit you need outside resources to help you.

TIPS FOR FACILITATORS:

- Help your growers see that spiritual poverty is a requirement for spiritual growth. Help them see the benefits of experiencing their incompleteness and neediness.
- Work with them on the sin of self-sufficiency, and help them see that, though it looks like the right thing, it will cut them off from God's growth resources. Confront the mentality of "I'm okay, I don't have needs or issues." When your group is maturing, use safe feedback to help those with that mindset hear what others really see about them and their lives.
- Help the brokenhearted not to feel guilty over being hurt or wounded. But help them also to be able to take responsibility for their hurts and to take the initiative to bring their wounds into contexts of growth. Don't let them stay polarized in either denial or the victim role.
- Show your growers that spiritual poverty leads them to a deeper walk with God and with others.

15

FOLLOWING THE GARDENER: OBEDIENCE

Obedience, for spiritual growth purposes, is to be God-directed, not self-directed.

Obedience sounds so simple. You will hear people say, "Just trust and obey," "Just follow Jesus," or "Just obey the Bible." However, most people who have been into growth for any length of time know that these statements are more accurate when you remove the word *just*. This is because, although God helps us to obey him, obedience is anything but simple.

A Tale of Three Wives

To illustrate, look at the stories of three wives. All three were good-hearted, decent Christian women who loved God and wanted successful marriages. All three had marriages with control and communication problems. All three wanted to obey God and resolve their problems biblically. But the three differed greatly on their view of obedience and how it affected their marriage problems. Consequently, the conclusions of their stories are far different from one another.

Jackie

Jackie's husband would lay down the law on the subject at hand (finances, parenting, or mealtime) and then refuse to open up his heart or hear hers. For example, one evening they were discussing ideas for their upcoming date night. Jackie's husband wanted to go to dinner and then home to watch television. Jackie, however, wanted to see her favorite musical, which was in town. When she mentioned her desire, her husband immediately said, "You can go to dinner with me, or the musical alone. Let me know." Jackie was hurt, as she had wanted to talk to him about what she loved about the musical, but the emotional door was shut.

Jackie wanted to connect; he would detach or become angry and shut down. Being passive and compliant, she didn't know how to get past his walls. It broke her heart, as she loved him and wanted to be loved.

Jackie had a deep commitment to God and his Word, and she faithfully practiced spiritual disciplines, such as prayer, Bible study, and confession. Her approach to helping her marriage was, she believed, based on the Bible and supported by her pastor and Christian friends. Basically, her approach was to enter the spiritual life more frenetically. Jackie threw herself more and more into prayer and Bible study. She surrendered her life to God and asked him to control her. She confessed all known sins and asked for enlightenment on unknown ones. She went to several worship services and teaching groups a week. She let Jesus into every aspect of her life.

Not only that, but Jackie tried to obey God specifically as a wife. She tried to be submissive, loving, and attentive to her husband. She apologized for any sins against him. She prayed for him and his life. She shared her spiritual lessons with him.

Some time has passed, and Jackie is still married; however, her marriage is still unfulfilling. Her husband thinks she is a religious fanatic and she preaches too much. He sees her attentiveness to him as simply his due as a husband, and he feels no need to respond to her. More and more, Jackie has withdrawn from him and has retreated into her church and religious life. She does feel very close to God and experiences love from him, yet she feels as if all her devotion to God hasn't paid off. She struggles with depression over the emptiness in her marriage, but she tries to give it to God. She is deeply dedicated to God and her spiritual growth, but she misses how it all relates to her everyday life with her husband.

Jackie's view of obedience is devotional and external.

Kim

Kim and her husband had essentially the same dynamics, with her being the compliant, nice partner and him being the detached, controlling one.

Kim tried Jackie's spiritual approach for a while and concluded that it wasn't working. She saw the biblical teaching as legalistic, rigid, and unrealistic. So instead of throwing herself into Bible studies and devotions, she sought growth and help from sources other than the Bible. She read books on marriage and relationships. She joined support groups for women with struggling marriages. She uncovered her own growth struggles and issues, such as fears of confrontation and abandonment, and gained insight into her husband's fears of closeness and loss of freedom. These resources genuinely helped her to understand what was going on.

Kim took her knowledge and insight home to her husband and suggested marriage counseling. He was open to counseling, and they went for a while. There was some growth in the marriage. He became more emotionally accessible, and she became more able to take initiative with him. Over time, however, Kim's husband grew tired of the counseling and said he'd had enough. He was a better person for it, but he really wasn't as dedicated to the growth process as she was. She became discouraged and thought her life and love were being wasted in this marriage.

At the same time, Kim slowly lost touch with her faith. It wasn't that she was rebellious or defiant. Rather, biblically based Christianity just didn't seem real or pertinent to her and her explorations into growth and marriage. She saw her Christian girlfriends as fake and tied to traditionalism and rigidity. She also saw them as being slavishly dedicated to substandard marriages and not getting what they could out of life. She could not understand how a loving, caring God would relegate her to the limbo of an empty marriage.

Over time, Kim met a man at work who was attentive and emotionally deep. They ended up having an affair, and she ultimately left her husband for the new man. They married, but the marriage has not been easy. They deal with tremendous scars and struggles from the aftermath of the affair. Kim is still involved in personal growth and discovery. She believes she and God are at peace now. She has reconciled her past disappointment with God by shifting her idea on who he is. She sees him as guiding her via her heart and the relationships she enters. As she grows deeper emotionally, she says she sees more of him and his nature.

Kim did a lot of good things. She grew emotionally and relationally. However, her view of obedience centered more on God's role in her emotions and relationships. She interpreted his ways and will as that which would lead to self-actualization. In a way, she saw God as the growth process itself, not the Author of it. That is, Kim saw neither his personal nature nor his transcendence as much as she saw the fruits of what God creates: love, growth, and connectedness.

Alison

Alison had similar problems in her marriage, and she was committed to making her marriage work. However, Alison took a different approach to obedience as a means of resolving her struggles.

As both other women did, Alison first sought out the Lord and asked for his help, committing her life to following his ways. Like Jackie, Alison spent much time in prayer, studying the Bible, attending church, and being with supportive people. She made sure that her life revolved around God and that she was in tune with his paths and people. Also like Jackie, Alison asked God and her husband for forgiveness for any sins she may have committed in the marriage.

But Alison went further than Jackie in her path of obedience. She searched her heart for character issues, immaturities, weaknesses, and brokenness that might be contributing to her marital struggles. She prayed, read the Bible and books on marriage and personal growth, and joined spiritual growth groups at a healthy church with supportive people who comforted her and gave her balanced feedback. Like Kim,

Alison identified her own personal issues underlying the marital problems, such as people pleasing and fear of letting others down. She took responsibility for these issues and worked on them. Over time, Alison became more separate, honest, and free with her husband.

The couple also entered counseling, and Alison's husband, like Kim's, went for a while and then lost interest. This disheartened Alison. She wanted desperately to have a good marriage, God's way. But her husband didn't have the same hunger she did.

At a similar point in her marriage as the other two women, Alison took a different turn. She didn't retreat in discouragement from her marriage into her religious activities as Jackie had. Nor did she escape into a new relationship, rationalizing her sin, as Kim had. Instead, she stayed deeply involved in the growth process with God through prayer, Bible study, and confession. She stayed involved and vulnerable with her growth-oriented friends. She kept her commitment to her marriage firm and permanent. And she determined to be as healthy a wife as possible. Alison learned to love her husband deeply and give him time, respect, and support. Yet she also learned how to confront him when he was hurtful, set limits with him, and avoid rescuing him.

Alison is still married. While her husband is not on fire for growth the way she is, he feels love from her and respects her. He is slowly getting more involved in deeper growth issues, but at a different pace from hers. And while she is very committed to him, she keeps a full life of growth activities and relationships, ministry, and fun that keeps her balanced and fulfilled.

Her deepest desire—that her husband be her soul mate—has not yet been met, but things are moving in that direction. If this desire is not met, she will feel very sad, but at peace. Her life is not based on his coming around, but on her orientation to God's ways and life. That focus will sustain her no matter what happens.

Alison's view of obedience took the best parts of the other two women. She stayed with the traditional disciplines and requirements of her faith, yet she also entered the character and relationship work that the Bible teaches (Ps. 139:23–24). Her obedience runs through her entire life. And this path is bearing good fruit for her.

These three women exemplify the approaches toward the Christian life that we see in the world. The Jackies hope that closeness to God will solve problems. The Kims grow personally and don't see how their faith is relevant. And the Alisons believe that both processes—closeness to God and personal growth—are spiritual and necessary for growth. We agree with Alison, and this chapter on obedience explores that approach.

THE NATURE OF OBEDIENCE

FEW CHRISTIANS WOULD DISAGREE that obedience is central to spiritual growth. Yet, as in the examples above, Christians often misunderstand what biblical obedience really is. One of the central meanings of "to obey" in the Bible is "to hear." Hearing and doing what God says are deeply interrelated: "It is the LORD your God you must follow, and him you must revere. Keep his commands and obey [hear] him; serve him and hold fast to him" (Deut. 13:4). When we hear God as he is, rather than as we desire him to be, we move toward true obedience.

A LIFE DIRECTION. A basic definition of obedience, for spiritual growth purposes, is "to be God-directed, not self-directed." Obedience is to look outside ourselves for our purpose, values, and decisions. This essential stance of life admits that God knows better than we do how to guide our steps. And it is the only way to truly live, for he is life itself. One of God's great desires for us is "that [we] may love the LORD [our] God, listen to his voice, and hold fast to him. For the LORD is [our] life" (Deut. 30:20). Therefore, we cannot grow spiritually without obedience. We cannot live apart from God. He is our life.

For many people, however, obedience means "to be deprived and withheld from." It means they have to adhere to rules and be self-disciplined. In their eyes, God basically says, "Be really good, and don't do any fun stuff," with no real benefit, except maybe in heaven. Jackie felt this way.

Nothing could be further from the truth. Obedience leads to very good things for us. As we travel down God's paths of conducting life, we reap many benefits. In fact, both survival and prosperity—major aspects of a good life—depend on obedience: "The LORD commanded us to obey all these decrees and to fear the LORD our God, so that we might always prosper and be kept alive, as is the case today" (Deut. 6:24). The results of obedience and disobedience are very different: "If you are willing and obedient, you will eat the best from the land; but if you resist and rebel, you will be devoured by the sword" (Isa. 1:19–20).

How is this so? God designed life to be lived a certain way. When we follow his way, life works better. Consider, for example, the statement, "A simple man believes anything, but a prudent man gives thought to his steps" (Prov. 14:15). Who has not experienced the suffering of naively trusting the words of a deceptive person? And who has not reaped the fruit of taking time to consider before rushing into a decision? Obedience is for our own good.

ALL OF LIFE. Some people compartmentalize obedience into their religious or moral lives. For them, obedience is relating to God and doing what is right. However, this view misses the full and comprehensive path God has for life. The Bible teaches and guides on all areas of life: gifts, ministry, money, sex, love, and so on. This is why people pursuing spiritual growth often feel as if they have "come alive" when they see, as Henry and I have seen, that God speaks to their emotional, personal, and relational lives as well as their spiritual lives.

ALL OF US. Not only does obedience deal with all of life, but it also encompasses all of us, both inside and out. Obedience is far more profound than simply refraining from external sins such as lying, stealing, and committing adultery, though it certainly includes those. Obedience has also to do with submitting our values, emotions, and hearts to Christ's lordship. God asks for no less than total commitment: "Love the Lord your God with all your heart and with all your soul and with all your mind. This is the first and greatest commandment" (Matt. 22:37–38). There is nothing more important, and nothing more demanding. In fact, it requires our lives, which then saves our lives (Mark 8:35).

This external and internal nature of obedience helps us to grow up spiritually. It helps us integrate various parts of our character that are either in conflict with or alienated from one another. Take, for example, the man who avoids intimacy because he has difficulty trusting people. This avoidance causes him problems in his marriage, work, and friendships. Part of him wants to be vulnerable, but he is afraid he will be hurt or controlled. Part of him wants to be distant and safe, but he gets lonely. His entire life oscillates between these two poles. This condition disrupts his life and hurts people around him.

Suppose the man enters the spiritual growth process with some good people. He becomes aware of these two conflicted parts of his heart. Here is where the two types of obedience help heal him. Customarily, when he grows closer to someone emotionally, he quickly distances himself by getting busy or watching TV. This is a safe escape from feeling his needs. So he is encouraged to call a member of his group on the phone when he feels the need to isolate. He commits to an external behavior: staying in contact with people (Heb. 10:25). This commitment keeps him from withdrawing and thus avoiding the tension of his feelings.

At the same time, he is internally obeying by confessing his fears of closeness and his desires to be free and distant (James 5:16). As he does this, the understanding and safety of the members of his support group help him integrate his two conflicted parts. He learns to set good limits so he won't be controlled. He learns to be vulnerable and yet free in his relationships.

Thus, the external obedience keeps the tension of his feelings contained and tolerable while the internal obedience heals his conflicts. This is a simplified description of the process, but it shows the value of a comprehensive view of obedience.

Obedience also helps us deal with both the causes and the fruits of spiritual immaturity or deficit. For example, suppose a couple is having financial struggles: The husband is an impulsive spender, and the wife is a frugal saver. In trying to help them, if you concentrate solely on external obedience (creating a financial plan), their characters will tend to sabotage any arrangements. If you concentrate only on the dynamics (he spends to anesthetize his anger, she oversaves to feel in control of herself), you run the risk of their financial struggles ruining their marriage before their internal issues are resolved. It is important for you as a helper to learn when you need to impose external structure and when you don't have to. A good rule of thumb is to set up controls on out-of-control behaviors that can't be stopped with support, confrontation, and awareness.

TASKS CHANGE AS MATURITY INCREASES. Spiritual growth also encounters another dimension of obedience. We are all called to follow God in the basic requirements of life: loving him and others (Matt. 22:36–40), seeking God (Amos 5:4), being just, kind, and humbly walking with God (Micah 6:8), and living by faith (Hab. 2:4). All of these great commands are related at their core in that we are being directed by God and his ways instead of by our own.

We all need to obey these commands; however, as we grow, our tasks in these areas change. Spiritual growth has stages and levels of development (1 John 2:12–14). Take the growth of relationship, for example. Someone who is very detached may be working on simply being emotionally present with others. Another person who is able to be close might be growing in his ability to be empathic with others. Obedience is not a "one size fits all" proposition. God deals with us where we are and shows us our next step of growth.

FAILURE. One of the more obvious results of the Fall is that obedience is not continuous. We sin and fail in many ways. However, God's spiritual growth process takes this into consideration so that we can be restored and continue on the path. Even more, God uses our failures to help mature us.

Two realities, when taken together, are bad news for us: failure is inevitable, and failure is our fault. (These two realities relate to God's sovereignty and our free will—a major philosophical question we do not have space to deal with in this book. However, it is worth studying on your own at some point.) Even as believers, no matter how hard we try not to, we will fail. Sin and immaturity cause us to miss the mark of God's standards for life. And even though failure is inevitable, it is still our fault and our problem. Although this may seem unfair to some, it is a reality.

Several spiritual growth approaches try to resolve this dilemma. One school of thought says that we don't have to fail. We can always be "victorious in Jesus" by making him truly Lord of our lives. Therefore the person who fails has not totally surrendered to God. Although this can sometimes be the case, the reasoning here denies the reality that we are sinners throughout life (Rom. 7:15–19). Adherents to this school of thought do not recognize struggle as normative and expected.

Another group teaches that the presence of sin is a sign of spiritual immaturity. It is not a surrender issue, but a growth issue. As you grow more, you sin less. Therefore the mature believer doesn't sin a lot. While we would agree that we should become more righteous as we mature, the Bible teaches that personal sin will always be present, as in the case of the chief of sinners, the very mature apostle Paul himself (1 Tim. 1:15).

Still another group tries to resolve this dilemma by addressing the nature of failure itself. Although they will admit that failures happen, they will say that failure isn't so bad and that sin and mistakes don't carry a lot of moral weight. They have what is called a weak view of sin. They ignore the gravity of sin and failure (Rom. 6:23).

A similar teaching is that though we fail, it is not really our fault. It is the fault of others who have made us what we are: our parents, hurtful relationships, society, the Devil, or even God himself. So when you fail, realize it is others who are to blame and try to heal from those hurts. As you heal and forgive, your failures resolve. We would certainly agree that our experiences with others, both loving and hurtful, greatly influence who we are and how we turn out in life. We would also agree that learning to forgive is very important. Yet we often fail simply because we choose to, and we are ultimately accountable for our decisions and choices (2 Cor. 5:10).

Our view of the Bible's teaching is stricter than the above four approaches. It is a pretty desperate situation to realize that we must fail, that our failure is a bad thing, and that we are held accountable. However, the good news is that this dilemma leads us straight into the arms of Jesus. We have a problem we cannot solve. His death is the solution for those who put their personal trust in his sacrifice for their sins. And all through life and growth, we learn to have faith in his love, forgiveness, and grace without resorting to our own devices. In this sense, our failure bears fruit in a deeper walk with him.

We fail in many ways. We sin in thought, word, and deed (Gal. 5:19–21; Eph. 4:31; Col. 3:5), such as when we fly into a fit of rage or follow selfish ambition (Gal. 5:20). We fail because of our ignorance (Acts 17:30), such as when we unknowingly intrude on people and cross their personal boundaries. We fail because of weakness (Heb. 4:15), such as when we are not honest about our feelings because we fear rejection. In spiritual growth, we need to be aware of all failure when it arises, and be in a safe place to address it.

REPENTANCE. In spiritual growth, therefore, learn to expect failure. Don't be surprised by it, because God certainly isn't. Peter denied three times that he knew Jesus (Luke 22:34). Deal with failure as Peter did, by repenting. When we sin and stop obeying, we then obey by repenting. Repentance, the proper response to our failure, brings forth more growth, love, responsibility, and fulfillment. Peter went on to become one of the most powerful preachers of all time. Repentance was also a hallmark of the teaching of John the Baptist and Jesus (Matt. 3:2; 4:17).

Repentance, simply put, is *a change of direction*. It is a movement away from the destructive path back toward God's ways. It requires a great deal of humility, because we have to admit we are wrong. However it happens, in repentance our eyes are opened to our own sin, failure, and weakness, especially as compared with God's nature, and we gladly change our ways to better follow his paths.

Repentance can be a response to many things we experience:

- The Lord's nature (Job 42:2–6)
- His holiness and grandeur (Isa. 6:1–5)
- His provision and love (Ezek. 36:24–31)
- His power (Luke 5:8)

Some people see repentance as simply changing one's mind or opinion: *I am wrong about my fear of confrontation.* Some see it as remorseful emotion: *I am sorry I hurt your feelings.* Others see it in behavioral terms: *I will stop drinking.* However, while these are all essential to repentance, they are incomplete in and of themselves. In its most integrated form, repentance involves the whole person—mind, heart, and behavior.

Here is an example of repentance of the entire person. In his Bible study discussion group, a man realizes he has been overinvolved at work and has been failing as husband and father. The lights come on inside. He feels sad and remorseful as he thinks about the lost opportunities with his family and how his withdrawal has hurt them. He prays about and discusses with close friends his workaholic background and performance-oriented family of origin. He sees how these have contributed to his problem, and he works on his longtime need to gain approval and validation through work. He accepts the approval of God and his inner circle of friends. His drivenness starts to diminish.

For a while the man becomes more anxious about relationships, as he is not used to being close to people. But in time this resolves. He becomes more able to relate on a personal level instead of a task level. As a freer person, he then sets limits on work time and connects on heart levels with his family. He is a better person for all the growth work. This repentance as a way of life is the way to deal with any and all failures in spiritual growth.

SOURCES OF OBEDIENCE

OBEDIENCE REQUIRES AN OBJECT—that is, we need to know what and whom to obey. There are several sources to help us with our obedience.

BIBLICAL COMMANDS. The Bible has a great number of universal commands and principles for conducting our lives. However, the Ten Commandments (Ex. 20:3–17) and Jesus' two Great Commandments (Matt. 22:36–40) sum up the law. Learn these foundational laws as well as the many more specific principles found in Scripture. This is why Bible study and reading are so valuable, as they help unearth these principles of living.

THE HOLY SPIRIT. God's indwelling Spirit not only brings verses to light for us to obey, but also directs those who seek his guidance to specific obedience (Mark 13:11). For example, he may direct a person to take a risk in relationship and deepen emotional intimacy in some area.

AUTHORITIES. Growth has a hierarchy of authority. We should follow the leadership of church leaders and teachers, for example, as long as it is biblically appropriate. This can be a healthy part of spiritual growth. For example, a Bible study leader might have insights and suggestions that can help us work through personal issues.

FRIENDS. God speaks to us in safe relationships through which he may direct us to confront an issue, deal with a problem, or confess some brokenness. (See our book *Safe People*.) Make sure your friends are balanced in the same way that Alison's were, and listen to them.

CIRCUMSTANTIAL LEADING. Be aware that God may arrange events to direct you. Attend to the possible interpretations of what is happening in your life. This should be done in consultation with a wise mentor, counselor, or pastor.

Remember that these different sources of instruction are not in conflict or fragmented. God is One (Deut. 6:4); he is integrated without conflict or contradiction. If you sense conflicts in the above areas and you don't know how to obey, ask God to help you find his voice among the many.

TASKS FOR THE GROWER

THE PERSON WHO IS growing needs to understand the importance of obedience. Here are a few of the essential tasks for the grower.

SURRENDER TO THE LORDSHIP OF CHRIST. Life works better if it belongs to God. The more you surrender your life to his authority and care, the more you are living life as you were designed to. For some of you, making Christ lord of your lives is a clear and defined decision. For others, it is a gradual process of increasingly surrendering your life to him. Either way, spiritual growth leads you toward making him the center of your life.

FOLLOW HIM DAILY. Look at obedience as a daily and continuous process. Watch out for compartmentalizing your growth, going from one small-group meeting to the next. Keep your heart always attentive to what God might be saying to you in the Bible, by the Spirit, from his people, or in circumstances.

DEAL WITH YOUR CHARACTER ISSUES. One of the outworkings of a decision to obey God is learning about your character weaknesses and dealing with them. Obeying God, for example, is owning your perfectionism, confessing the insecurity and pride that drive it, working on being accepted as you are and being honest with others about your frailties, and grieving over the safety of being a perfect person, which

TIPS FOR GROWERS:

- Realize that obedience is more than simply adhering to specific commands, but rather a way of life that will bring you good fruit and success.
- Understand the natures of both external and internal obedience. When you encounter a personal struggle, look at both dimensions of obedience to see what is awry.
- Ask God to tell you what your specific growth tasks of obedience are, so that you may know how to follow him in your maturing path.
- See the reality of falling from obedience as normal, and know how to use the processes of confession and repentance to get back on the road.
- Look at obedience relationally: How is your life affecting God and others? What obedience might you enter to be more fully reconciled to them?

TIPS FOR FACILITATORS:

- Help your growers to see that a life of obedience is the only way to have a life of growth, meaningful relationships, healing, and success. Help them to see that obedience is for their good.
- Help them see obedience as what happens as they connect to God, and how disconnecting from dependency on him is always the primary disobedience.
- Deal with people's tendency to miss the internal aspects of obedience— for example, while a person may not be acting out sexually, his heart may nevertheless be far from God.
- Confront the psychobabble view that only the internal world is important, and remind people that we are responsible for both the internal and the external aspects of obedience.
- Work with them on an inventory of what areas of life need to be connected in obedience to God, and how they can begin that process.

has protected you from self-criticism and condemnation. You "take captive every thought to make it obedient to Christ" (2 Cor. 10:5).

RESPONSIBILITIES OF THE HELPER

IF YOU ARE HELPING people grow, you can do several things to make obedience an integral part of the process.

POSITION OBEDIENCE AS ENCOMPASSING ALL OF LIFE. Help your "growers" see that obedience is about much more than the religious, moral, or ethical life, but it is about hearing God in all aspects of life. Make obedience and spirituality relevant to daily existence.

TEACH OBEDIENCE AS BRINGING GOOD TO PEOPLE. Help them see that a "sold-out" life to God does not mean automatic martyrdom or deprivation, but instead leads to a better, richer, and less dysfunctional life.

DEAL WITH OUTSIDE AND INSIDE. Note people who are like Jackie, whose obedience was devotional and externalized only, and people who are like Kim, whose obedience extended only to emotional growth, but not to the absolute parameters of the Bible. Make Alison the model. She did not ignore inner heart obedience, nor did she diminish the importance of adhering to scriptural standards of life. Remember that keeping both helps create a structure inside a person that develops character and integrates divisions within the soul.

Obedience, or God-directedness, is a lifelong process central to spiritual growth. Stay close to what God says regarding your ways, relationships, and inner issues. Those who follow God's voice generally realize that it is ultimately the only way to go, as did the apostle Peter, who said, "Lord, to whom shall we go? You have the words of eternal life" (John 6:68).

When we learn the ways of obedience, we enter the path of growth. Yet that path is not without danger. We need to understand how to handle the problems of sin and temptation, as we discover in the next chapter.

16

PULLING THE WEEDS: THE PROBLEM OF SIN AND TEMPTATION

We are not only responsible for our sin, but also powerless to keep from sinning.

Back in the 1980s I (Henry) remember listening to a minister give his opinion on the recovery movement, which was becoming popular in the church. He was angry. People were getting off too lightly, he thought, and he was not going to stand for it. I can almost still hear his words today: "What's all this stuff about people being 'powerless' over their addiction? Don't you know? This is not what the Bible says! People are free moral agents and responsible for their sin! Don't give me all this stuff about being powerless. People choose to sin, and they are responsible for their choices! It's just sin, period."

The minister was obviously upset at hearing people in recovery talk about Step One in the Twelve Step Process: "We admitted that we were powerless over alcohol—that our lives had become unmanageable." To him, powerlessness was a cop-out. He thought this was letting people off the hook; they needed to admit they were choosing wrong and begin to choose right. They were sinning. They are not supposed to sin. So to him the answer was clear: Stop it!

I remember thinking about all the addicts I knew who were listening, and I felt sorry for them. His was a message I was sure they had heard before, and it had not helped them very much.

At the same time I thought about both the truth and the error in what the preacher was saying. He was not wrong about addicts' choices being sin; virtually everyone agrees on that. But his statement that "people are free moral agents and responsible for their sin," is a loaded one. In this single statement lies much of the problem in how people both look at sin and try to help those struggling with it. The preacher was only half right. People *are* responsible for sin. People *are* moral agents.

But this is only part of the truth. The Bible does teach we are responsible and accountable for our sin. It is our problem and no one else's. But—and this would have been a surprise to the preacher—the Bible's message is much *more* devastating and convicting. For the Bible says not only that we are responsible for our sin, but also that we are powerless to keep from sinning. Think about that for a moment: we cannot change, and we are held responsible for not being able to change. This can only lead to one conclusion: Anyone need a Savior?

I understand what the preacher was thinking, for it would seem that seeing ourselves as powerless and unable to change our lives would get us off the hook, a little like having a genetic illness (hemophilia) versus one caused by an unhealthy lifestyle (cirrhosis of the liver). We usually find ourselves having more immediate empathy for someone with a genetic problem than we do for someone who has made destructive choices and has contributed to his own illness.

But when we add in the other half—that we are responsible for that which we can't change—we find ourselves in a much worse shape than the jail cell to which the preacher wanted to send people. In his thinking, people should go to "jail" for making bad choices, but they could avoid jail, if they truly wanted to, by choosing differently. And they could get out of jail by repenting and becoming better people. His "tough stance on sin" had a strange kind of hope in it. If we are agents who can choose, then let's just choose differently! Why allow any pattern in our lives to ever rule us again. Let's just do better! You can almost hear the motivational speech gathering steam in the pews. "Stop being stupid! Don't let sin ruin your life anymore. Choose life! Make right choices and be successful."

In the "powerless *and* responsible" view, you both go to jail and have no hope of getting out because you are unable to do better. And that is both what the Bible teaches and what any addict will tell you. No matter how many times someone with a compulsive behavior or an internal character problem tries to "just make better choices," it doesn't work. (Ask anyone who has ever been on a fad diet; it may work for a while, but give it time and it will fail.) And they still find that they are held responsible for the reality of the problem and its devastating consequences: relational, health, career, etc.

The Bible tells us that we cannot avoid the problems we find ourselves in, we cannot change ourselves once we are in them, and we are held totally responsible and accountable for them. In short, we are in prison or, as the Bible says, we are "slaves to sin." As Paul explains it, "I know that nothing good lives in me, that is, in my sinful nature. For I have the desire to do what is good, but I cannot carry it out. For what I do is not the good I want to do; no, the evil I do not want to do—this I keep on doing" (Rom. 7:18–19).

We make choices, but all the while we don't really have freedom. And we are held responsible. That is a much more brutal message than the tough preacher was delivering. But gracefully the Bible does not leave us there. When we are thrown into prison with no chance of parole, when we are asked, "Anyone need a Savior?" the Bible gives us one. For it is exactly into that prison that Jesus comes and tells us he will break us out. This is Good News indeed. When people realize that they are both powerless and responsible, they get serious about seeking help from outside themselves.

So, to summarize:

1. We have a problem, and the problem is sin.
2. We are responsible and accountable for our sin.
3. We cannot do anything about it in a fully significant or sufficient way.

4. Trying to "do better" does not work, so we need help because the sin is hurting us or someone else.
5. Help has come in the form of the gospel.

The goal of this chapter is to give a few thoughts on how the problem of sin works in our lives and how the gospel is the answer to this problem in all areas of growth.

FIRST, A WARNING

WHENEVER WE TALK ABOUT sin being a problem in the world of personal growth, we have to make sure you know what we are not saying. We are not saying that a person's individual sin is the cause of all the struggles or problems he or she might have. All too often in the church, people are blamed for pain and struggles not of their own making.

Job was a great example of this. He had losses and pains he had absolutely no part in creating. In fact, it was the opposite. It was his righteousness that placed him in the cosmic contest between God and Satan. He was not suffering because he was bad, but, it could be argued, he was suffering because he was good. Who knows the reason for his suffering, really? It is too complex to ever fully understand. Yet we do know that his pain came from losing his family, his work, and his health. These losses were not his doing. He, like all of us, lived in a fallen world where there is suffering we cannot understand. Jesus once said, when asked whose sin caused a certain man to be blind from birth, "Neither this man nor his parents sinned, but this happened so that the work of God might be displayed in his life" (John 9:3). Some things we just don't understand.

In addition, people suffer because of the sin of others. We have all experienced—or have had someone close to us who has experienced—long-standing suffering because of the abuse of another. In the story of the Good Samaritan Jesus told us how to respond to this kind of pain. In that story, a man suffered at the hands of a robber who beat him up. A Samaritan came by, dressed and bandaged his wounds, and paid for his room in the inn and the innkeeper's care for him. We are to reach out and help those who have suffered at the hands of others. (We will take a closer look at this in the section about the "sin of others" at the end of this chapter.)

So, as we look at the subject of sin, let's first understand that everyone suffers and sometimes lacks growth for other reasons besides their sin. If we don't understand this, we may fall into the trap of blaming the hurting person, as Job's friends did. If we do that, we too will be "worthless physicians," and the best thing we could do would be to be "silent" (Job 13:4–5).

What Doesn't Work

IN CHAPTER 4, ON the God of grace, we looked in depth at the law and at its failure to change lives. In this chapter we would like to start with a brief reminder of what the "law of sin and death" is about and why it doesn't work. As we deal with sin, this will keep us from trying something that is futile over and over again.

Being "under the law" is the system of having a commandment and then choosing to follow this commandment to be good and acceptable, or not following the commandment and being condemned. This simple formula is no problem. If we know what we "should" do, we should "just do it," and then we have cured the problem of sin.

And this *was* true, once upon a time. When Adam and Eve were in the Garden, they were free to do the right thing and avoid the wrong thing. If they had done that, we would have "no problem," but they did not, and now we have a real problem. Part of the problem is that we are *no longer free,* in ourselves, to do the right thing, no matter how much we want to. Now, instead of freedom, we possess a "sinful nature" (Rom. 7:5). This nature has a passion for things that are not good for us ("Get behind me, apple pie!"). We have a penchant for doing unhelpful things as well as sometimes doing downright destructive things.

But it is even worse than that. Not only do we have a passion for doing those things that are against the law, but the law itself arouses in us a passion to do the very thing we shouldn't do! (Rom. 7:5, 8–10). This is double jeopardy. We have the sickness, and the fact that we *ought* to be healthy makes us act out our sickness even more. Listen to the apostle Paul: "For when we were controlled by the sinful nature, the sinful passions *aroused by the law* were at work in our bodies, so that we bore fruit for death" (v. 5).

We have the sin nature, and this nature gets "sprung to life" by the commandment (v. 9). This is most easily seen in the young child who is told "no" for the first few times. Forbidding a child to do something seems to almost "make" him do it again. It is not as obvious with adults, but upon close inspection, it is as much present. We want to do what we shouldn't do.

This is one reason why the three most common forms of the "law" in Christian circles fail so miserably with those caught up in something they can't stop:

1. Harsh, angry preaching against sin with the injunction to repent
2. Legalistic rules to keep people in line
3. Telling people (even lovingly) that the "way" out is to make better choices

While all of these contain some truth, none of them work, because all of them assume a person's ability to choose rightly. But the Bible teaches that this alone will not work for the two reasons above (the sin nature and the fact that the law itself arouses a person to sin). Therefore, if we are going to help people, we have to do better than tell them they are wrong and they should do right. This is what the law does, and it is ineffective in changing people (Heb. 7:18–19; Rom. 8:3).

To compound the problem more, these interventions produce in people the emotions of the law as well. When people are caught up in the law, they will have three very predictable responses: guilt (condemnation), anger (rebellion), and fear. The law produces these emotions in people, and the Bible talks about our need to be freed from their effects (Rom. 5:9–10; 20–21; 6:14; 8:1–2; 1 John 4:18). So we can see that if we just tell people to do right and don't give them the whole gospel, we reap results we are not looking for: failure and bad feelings. (No wonder many people don't like church, for they might have gone to one that produces these emotions.)

Remember my friend's friend (Dirk in chapter 4) who was struggling with his weight? It is easy to see why he failed to lose weight. All he had working for him was the law. He had the standard, the "should." He made a commitment to lose weight, he would fail, and then he would feel guilty and condemned. As a result he would gain instead of losing weight. Then he would repeat the cycle. This is a good picture of law and sin at work.

A BETTER WAY: REPENTANCE AND LIVING BY THE SPIRIT

BUT THE BIBLE GIVES us a better way. As Paul says,

> For what the law was powerless to do in that it was weakened by the sinful nature, God did by sending his own Son in the likeness of sinful man to be a sin offering. And so he condemned sin in sinful man, in order that the righteous requirements of the law might be fully met in us, who do not live according to the sinful nature but according to the Spirit (Rom. 8:3–4).

While the law (and all of our versions of it) cannot help, Jesus can. He replaces living by the law with living by the Spirit. This is the answer to all the problems sin can ever throw at us.

Thus, while the standard is good and the need to make good choices is real, there is only one way to do that: Live according to the Spirit. This means to live according to a relationship and a process that empowers us (Gal. 5:16, 25). So there we are again, back to dependency on God.

To change the areas we want to change, we first have to admit to them (confession) and admit we are unable to change them by ourselves. ("Blessed are the poor in spirit" [Matt. 5:3].) Then we have to be set free by establishing a relationship with Jesus, which takes care of the guilt and condemnation of the law. (As Paul says, "there is no condemnation" for those who have a relationship with Jesus. As we said in chapter 9, guilt and condemnation must end for any change to take place.) Dirk did not change until he knew he was accepted and loved just as he is, weight problem and all. Then Dirk needed a change of mind and a change of direction about the seriousness of the sin. He finally realized that if he did not lose weight, he would likely have a heart attack. *His change of mind is what the Bible calls "repentance" (an entire changing of direction and thinking about the problem).*

Then, as the verse says, to be set free we must live according to the Spirit. Here is where most failure takes place. People think they only need to confess and lean on God for help, but as we saw in chapter 6, *there is a lot more to living according to the Spirit than that.* Living according to the Spirit includes many other things we have to ask God to do for us through his Spirit, such as the following:

- To make known that he is always with us and we need to abide in him (Ps. 139:7; John 14:18; 15:5–8)
- To search our hearts and show us what we need to change (Ps. 7:9; Prov. 20:27; Rom. 8:27; 1 Cor. 2:10)
- To give us abilities to do what we need to do when we are unable (Ex. 31:3; Deut. 34:9; Judg. 14:6; 2 Sam. 23:2; Mark 13:11)
- To lead us and guide us in life (1 Kings 18:12; 1 Chron. 28:12; Neh. 9:20; Ps. 143:10; John 16:13; Acts 13:4; 16:6)
- To show us and teach us (John 14:26; 15:26; 16:13; 1 Cor. 2:13; 1 John 2:27)
- To counsel us and help us (John 14:26; 15:26; 16:13)
- To help us to live the life we need (Rom. 7:6; 8:2, 4–6, 9, 11, 13, 26)
- To fill us and control us (Rom. 8:6; Eph. 5:18)
- To complete us (James 1:4)
- To correct us and convict us (Ps. 139:23–24; John 16:8; Rom. 9:1; 1 Cor. 4:4; Phil. 3:15)
- To change us (2 Cor. 3:18; Gal. 3:3; 5:16–25)
- To give us gifts to help each other and put the Body together around us (1 Cor. 12:7–12)
- To heal us through himself and others as they use his gifts (Ps. 147:3; Is. 61:1; Eph. 4:16; 1 Peter 4:8, 10)

In other words, winning the war over sin includes the entire growth process itself as we live the life the Spirit provides. We have to be doing many things to achieve the victory we need. Significant problems like addictions and other patterns of behavior do not give way to simple formulas such as "That is sin. I won't do that anymore." To achieve victory we need to change fully in all of life as we commit to the life of the Spirit.

This truth also explains why patterns of behavior that have not given way to those formulas do give way to the process outlined above: When we admit powerlessness, ask God and others for help, repent, continue to stay plugged into a supportive environment, seek healing for the hurting parts of ourselves, and receive deep forgiveness, give that to others, and obey God—when we do all these things, long-standing patterns of problematic behavior change. This is the way the Bible has described the process we need.

Too often Christians have a much too shallow view of sin, both in our ability to deal with it as well as the depth at which it must be dealt with. We cannot stop sin; we have to be *saved* from sin. And that means a much deeper healing process than just "stop being bad." In fact, as Jesus spoke of his mission, he said it just like that—as a mission of "healing":

> "For the Son of Man came to seek and to save what was lost" (Luke 19:10).

The word translated "save" in this statement is a word that actually means "healed" or "made whole." Being "saved" from sin means being restored and healed at a much deeper level than we sometimes offer to people. People need more than just "Stop that!" They also need "and God and we will help you." The biblical process of overcoming sin provides a deep healing. Anything else will fall short.

So the Bible's commandment regarding sin is and always has been: Repent. But many times people think "repent" means to stop sinning, and it does have that aspect to it. The reality is, however, that "repent" means to have a total change of mind, to think differently—and that involves an entire turning around of our entire life, not just behavior. It means to think differently about sin, to see it as destructive and producing death. It also means to think differently about how we are going to deal with it. It means to change one's mind and to begin to live according to the whole life of the Spirit, as we have just seen. "Repent" is not a shallow commandment. It is a total life change to the life of the Spirit and all that entails.

REBELLION

BUT, LEST WE BECOME a little too comfortable in our "we are just sick and powerless and want to be healed" thinking, let's look at another side to sin. It is not just our inability to keep from sinning that gets us into trouble. We are sometimes very able to keep from sinning, and we choose not to. We rebel, as Adam and Eve did *before* they had a sin nature. Even though we have the sin nature, at any given moment we do have control over some areas of our character, yet we choose not to exercise this control. There is no other word to use for this than *rebellion*.

Take the example of Sara and Joe.

Sara and Joe had had a rocky relationship for the five years they had been married. After the initial "falling in love" and mutual idealization of each other, they had gotten married. Not long after, they began to argue intensely. Sometimes they argued over significant issues, but most of the time they argued over Joe's temper.

"I don't know what to do," Sara said, sobbing in my office one day. "I am not trying to control him or hurt him, but he lashes out at me in such a rage. I can't take it any more." She said she was feeling herself grow cold inside, since she had been hurt so many times by him. I feared she might not stick it out.

Until then, Joe had tried to make his case to me about how difficult Sara was to live with and how his anger was justified. As he put it, "You would go crazy with her too." I would try to get him to look at his side of things, to no avail. But on this particular day, when the depth of Sara's pain showed itself, Joe gained a different perspective. In the Bible's words, he "repented." He changed his mind about his own behavior. He no longer saw it as justified, but as destructive and hurtful. He was hurting the person he loved and needed.

So Joe finally agreed to work on his anger. For a period of months, he and Sara would come back in when he was not able to control his anger. But these sessions were different from the previous ones. We were now working on his real anger problem and not something to be justified. He was going to a good support group, meeting with a prayer partner, and exploring with me the hurt and history behind his anger.

Slowly Joe changed as the "life in the Spirit" took hold. As Paul describes, he bore the "fruit" of the Spirit. He exhibited self-control, love, and patience (Gal. 5:22–23). (This is another example of how "fruit" works. He had cultivated the garden—his life in the Spirit—

and now the fruit was coming.) More and more he became the loving husband Sara had desired.

One day, however, something happened. They had had a difficult weekend and had gotten into an intense argument. Sara was obviously wounded. When she described Joe's behavior, I was shocked, for I thought we had made more progress than that. My first feeling was one of empathy not only for her, but also for him, for his having been "caught in a sin" again (Gal. 6:1). I wondered what had snapped inside of him or what had overcome him.

As I listened to Joe, my empathy gave way to anger. And as I asked myself why I was angry, it became clear. Nothing had snapped in Joe. Nothing had overcome him. He was perfectly capable of not acting as he did—but he did anyway. What I saw was pure and simple "meanness." So I confronted him.

"Don't give me any of this 'my issues came up' psychobabble," I said. "The truth is that you just chose to be mean instead of restraining yourself. This was not weakness. This was a choice, and it is nothing but ugly sin."

I never will forget the look in Joe's eyes and the expression on his face. He was caught. Then he got sheepish, shied away a little, and said, "You're right. You're right. I was mad, and I took it out on her. And that was wrong." I could see his spirit softening.

He then turned to Sara and said, "I'm sorry."

Sara softened as well. She accepted his apology, and they were able to go on from there.

It was a powerful lesson for him, however, and one that affected many of his other patterns of behavior. He learned that some problems in life are not about things we are "unable" to do, but about things we are "unwilling" to do. He simply rebelled against what he knew to be right and loving. It felt good to him for the moment, but as is true of all sin, that was only for a moment. He paid the price in alienation afterward.

Sometimes we are unable to do what we are supposed to do at any given moment. In those areas we need more work of the Spirit and need to flee the temptation and run to get help. But sometimes we do not use the abilities we do possess, and we willingly, willfully choose to sin. As David put it, "Keep your servant also from willful sins; may they not rule over me. Then will I be blameless, innocent of great transgression" (Ps. 19:13). We do have the ability to do the wrong thing on purpose.

The solution to this is confession, remorse, repentance, making amends, and reconciliation with whomever we have hurt. There is a lot going on in the name of growth today that is just sin in need of repentance. One doesn't need the fruit of "self-control"; one just needs to exercise it.

When Joe was confronted with this reality, he took the confrontation from me into his soul, and it became a part of him. He now had the ability to confront himself—to say "don't do that" to himself. He owned his sin, was sorry, repented, and was reconciled to Sara. From that point their relationship grew deeper, as Joe had a new dimension to his growth—the realization that he now had more freedom and, with it, more responsibility.

No Excuses

I LISTENED ONE DAY to a man talking about the affair he had had; we were working through its aftermath in his marriage. The affair had been devastating to his wife, and he seemed to have little insight into her feelings. In our sessions he caught a glimpse of the pain he had caused, but just when we were getting a little deeper into how the affair had devastated her, he changed the focus.

"But all of this makes me sad for another reason," he said.

"What is that?" I asked.

"Well, if she had been meeting my needs in our relationship, I wouldn't have had to go somewhere else to get those met."

I thought I was going to throw up. I did not condemn him for his failure. Often in working with him, I had been reminded of Jesus' response to the woman caught in adultery. Jesus had showed nothing but grace and acceptance. So that was not what made me sick.

What made me sick was the blame. He basically said that his wife was responsible for his affair. It had never occurred to him that he could have responded in a thousand ways to her other than by being unfaithful. He could have responded redemptively instead of destructively.

But then I had to become aware of something else. I have blamed others for my own behavior at times too. I have felt that familiar "Well,

I wouldn't have done that if you hadn't. . . ." Then, as I was feeling humbled, I remembered something else from the story of Adam and Eve that helped me. When Adam sinned and God came to confront him about it, Adam responded as this man had. He said, "The woman you put here with me—she gave me some fruit from the tree, and I ate it" (Gen. 3:12). In one sentence Adam blamed both God and Eve. He said he would not have been in trouble if God had not given him the woman or if the woman had not given him the fruit. After this we see that blame knows no gender. When God confronted Eve, she blamed the serpent.

Blame is part of the natural order of fallen humankind. We do not "own" our behavior; instead, we automatically shift responsibility. I have a friend who, when she makes a mistake, imitates a kid and says, "No one told me." As if she would have done her duty if someone else had done his or her job. Blaming is human.

But death is human too, and the Bible says that to the extent that we continue in blame and continue to explain our sin away, we will die. Sin kills us, and blame gives life to sin. Blame keeps sin breathing and thriving in our lives.

Much blame goes on in therapy circles as well. People use their past—what happened or didn't happen in their growing up years—to explain away behavior. "I do that because my mother. . . ." As we will see in a moment, getting to the roots of the motivations of our behavior is very important. Many motivations or driving forces are not our fault. *But this does not mean that our behavior is not our responsibility.* If a man's father had been mean to him growing up and that man now hates and resists all authority, the father's meanness would explain part of his motivation. He would certainly have anger and hurt. *But having that background does not explain why he chose to deal destructively with that hurt.* The only thing that can explain that is a fallen nature.

A spiritual response would be to submit that hurt and anger to the healing process described above and work it out without returning "evil for evil" (Rom. 12:17, 21). If that person were working it out in the right way, he would be getting healing for the hurt, getting resolution and forgiveness for the anger, and seeking reconciliation as much as possible with his father.

So when dealing with our own hurt, lacks, and other motivators of behavior and those of the people we help, we have to remember that there is a difference between what happens to me and how I deal with it.

SIN IS MORE THAN EXTERNAL DEEDS

THE ABOVE EXAMPLES BRING us to another point about sin. Sin is not just something we do; it is not just behavior. It encompasses the roots of behavior as well. Too often we think of sin only in external terms, not internal. Jesus warned, "Now then, you Pharisees clean the outside of the cup and dish, but inside you are full of greed and wickedness. You foolish people! Did not the one who made the outside make the inside also?" (Luke 11:39–40).

The two examples above—the man hurt by his wife and my hypothetical example of someone hurt by a parent—show the importance of dealing with internal motivations. Unresolved anger and hurt can turn into bitterness or lust. Hatred for authority has probably ruined more careers than lack of training. And many other monsters lurk in the shadow of the human breast. Consider this list:

> "What comes out of a man is what makes him 'unclean.' For from within, out of men's hearts, come evil thoughts, sexual immorality, theft, murder, adultery, greed, malice, deceit, lewdness, envy, slander, arrogance and folly. All these evils come from inside and make a man 'unclean'" (Mark 7:20–23).

Many illnesses, failures, addictions, relationship difficulties, and destructive behaviors originate in these motivators. As Jesus said, the fruit comes from the tree (Matt. 12:33–35). Looking inside ourselves and resolving the issues we find there is the key to having the outside be good. If we are full of "crummy stuff," then we will exhibit crummy behavior; the same holds for good stuff.

The truth is, though, that all of us have crummy stuff within us. It is part of the fallen nature, the "sickness" of sin, as Jesus put it (Mark 2:17). If we are ever going to get well, we have to have the safety to look inside, confess what we find there, grieve it, repent of it, and "put off [our] old self, which is being corrupted by its deceitful desires; to be made new in the attitude of [our] minds; and to put on the new self, created to be like

God in true righteousness and holiness" (Eph. 4:22–24). We have to be made new from the inside out, and that begins with facing how ugly things are inside.

We all need a place where we can say, "You won't believe how sick I am! Let me tell you about this thought I had today." We need to make this kind of confession normal. Then we can begin to clean up our insides.

FROM MORALLY NEUTRAL TO MORALLY BAD

NOT ONLY THE UGLY stuff can lead us to sin, but also the good stuff. We saw earlier how a boy's hatred of and revenge against his father led to resisting all authority later. But what about the legitimate hurt in the soul of that young man? Forget the hatred for a moment, and look at the hurt. What if someone like that does not act out the anger, but also never deals with the hurt? What happens?

Unresolved hurt is going to do just that—hurt. The person who is brokenhearted and not getting healed is in pain. Often this person will do something to ease the pain. He may feel strong "cravings" for sex or food or alcohol to make himself feel better. He may feel driven to work and achieve at the expense of his loved ones. He may lust after material things, or he may strive for power to cover up his feelings of being small. Whatever the "drug of choice," unresolved hurt can tempt a person to sin. The hurt is not the sin. *The sin is the way that the person deals with the pain and emptiness.* It is a result of trying to meet a valid need in a sinful way.

This is an often overlooked aspect of temptation about which the Bible teaches us. We read in Luke 4 that Jesus was led into the desert to be tempted. For forty days he was deprived of all things human— no companionship, food, or meeting of basic needs. *And when he was in this state of deprivation, Satan tempted him.* Satan went to Jesus and offered him ways to feel "better" when he was at his weakest point.

This is exactly how temptation occurs. Satan tempts us at our weakest moments and in our weakest areas. We need something, or we are in pain. And the temptation answers both of those *for the moment.* If someone needs love or is lonely, the deceptive sin of illicit sex (the lust of the flesh) can momentarily masquerade as love. If someone needs validation, the lure of power and the "boastful pride of life" can trick him into feeling as if his existence is worthwhile because of that power. If someone is feeling "not good enough," the lure of materialism and the "lust of the eyes" can momentarily dull that pain. In those three areas, John tells us, "Do not love the world or anything in the world. If anyone loves the world, the love of the Father is not in him. For everything in the world—the cravings of sinful man, the lust of his eyes and the boasting of what he has and does—comes not from the Father but from the world" (1 John 2:15–16).

The world has its solutions to need and pain, and we can all be tempted to resolve our hurts with those. The age-old story of the Bible is that we try to meet with our own idols the needs God is supposed to meet. We depend on man-made gods instead of the one true God. Again, it is a problem of *dependency. Sin is failing to depend on God and not saying yes to his grace in all its various forms.* Meeting our needs our way is idolatry and never works. Our model is Jesus, who in his deprived state did not meet his needs through sin, but by dependence on God. Hebrews tells us, "For we do not have a high priest who is unable to sympathize with our weaknesses, but we have one who has been tempted in every way, just as we are—*yet was without sin*" (Heb. 4:15).

So, sometimes we fail to understand that deprivation can be the weak state that makes us susceptible to carrying out what the sin nature tells us to do. Christians can try to deal with someone's sin by dealing just with the bad behavior and not dealing with the need or the pain driving it. We deal with the "bad," but we do not add the "good." *Overcoming sin is never just about doing away with badness; it is always also about adding goodness.* Jesus came to do away with death, but he also came to give us life. This is why the Bible tells us to "put off the old" and "put on the new" (Eph. 4:24; Col. 3:10, 14). It is part of what Jesus was saying when he said he did not come into the world to judge the world, but to save (heal and restore) it (John 12:47).

Therefore we need to respond to people's sin by looking beyond the sin nature to what is motivating and driving the sin. The ultimate reality is that sin is driven and perpetuated by being cut off from "the life of God." This formula motivates sinful behavior, according to the apostle Paul. He tells believers not to think like other people:

They are darkened in their understanding and *separated from the life of God* because of the ignorance that is in them due to the hardening of their hearts. Having lost all sensitivity, they have given themselves over to sensuality so as to indulge in every kind of impurity, with a continual lust for more" (Eph. 4:18–19).

When we are "separated from the life of God," we don't have a life at all, and we seek to fill that vacuum in other ways. The life of God includes, among other things, support, connection, honesty, talents, healing, confession, repentance, correction, and discipline. So if people are hurting, they need to find the healing God provides through himself and his people. When that happens, and the hurt is dealt with, the temptation subsides. The need is no longer there, and the ability to resist is greater. Strength and life have replaced neediness.

If people's hearts and minds were full of the life God provides, there would be a lot less room for temptation. I was talking with a thirty-year-old single woman who said she couldn't separate from a hurtful boyfriend. She was sleeping with him even though she knew that was destructive. She said she finally hit bottom and reached out to God, and then his Spirit and his people began to meet her needs. She was able to separate from the hurtful boyfriend, and the sexual temptation went away. God and his way of life met the need and healed the pain. She dealt with the sin, but to do that, she not only repented, but she added the "good" things she needed as well.

So, some of what is behind "badness" is not so bad after all. It is a well of good needs and hurt and pain that people try to "medicate" in bad ways. This excuses none of the sinful answers we seek, and neither does it excuse the partial gospels we give to people as answers to their sin. If we and the people we help are going to have victory, it has to come from all God has offered, and that includes taking care of the needs and the pains that are not connected to his life.

AVOIDING SIN

NONE OF THIS HAPPENS very easily, however. In the meantime, temptation is still around. It does not go away, and we are not to sit idly around and wait for it to subside while we are "getting well." The Bible has a strategy about avoiding it. Let's just remind ourselves of this strategy, as follows.

Pray

"And lead us not into temptation, but deliver us from the evil one" (Matt. 6:13).

"Watch and pray so that you will not fall into temptation. The spirit is willing, but the body is weak" (Matt. 26:41).

Flee and Escape

No temptation has seized you except what is common to man. And God is faithful; he will not let you be tempted beyond what you can bear. But when you are tempted, he will also provide a way out so that you can stand up under it (1 Cor. 10:13).

Flee from sexual immorality. All other sins a man commits are outside his body, but he who sins sexually sins against his own body (1 Cor. 6:18).

Flee the evil desires of youth, and pursue righteousness, faith, love and peace, along with those who call on the Lord out of a pure heart (2 Tim. 2:22).

We don't have to say a lot about these strategies as they are self-evident. The problem is that a lot of people do not practice them. How common is it to see people taking sin seriously enough to pray consistently to avoid it? And fleeing is drastically underrated. The Bible puts a huge emphasis on getting away from the temptation. It talks about fleeing it so that we don't fall prey to it. It implies that it is a very dangerous place to find ourselves, and the best advice is to run from it. While we are to resist temptation when we do encounter it, it is better not to flirt with it at all. So if you have a weak area, or you are working with someone who has one, encourage fleeing.

People tempted by sex should flee situations in which they will be tempted, like being alone with someone who is dangerous for them. Alcoholics should flee the bar. People with weight problems should flee the ice cream store. Pornography addicts should stay off the internet in private places. These are just examples, but the principle is clear: Get away from tempting things *before* the temptation, not after. "Run" is the advice of the Bible. If you are not there, you can't be tempted. And when you find yourself in danger, don't just stand there and try to win. Instead, run from it—flee it—treat it as dangerous.

REMEMBERING WHAT SIN IS

FINALLY, WE ARE TEMPTED to forget what sin actually is. Remember the theology lesson in chapter 2? God created humankind to be connected to him in specific roles. We were to be *in relationship* and *under* his lordship, staying in our own roles as creatures, not the Creator.

Instead, we tried to usurp God's role and become our own god. And that is basically what sin is, to live independent of God, trying to be him. When there is a sin problem, we are likely to find problems in these areas:

- Independence—moving away from dependence on God as the source of life and trying to meet our own needs apart from God and his people
- Loss of relationship—isolation from God and others
- Boss—not submitting to God and obeying him
- Control—trying to control others or things we can't control, resulting in a loss of self-control and a failure to yield to God's sovereign control
- Judging—moving away from being real and experiencing life and others, and moving toward judging self and others
- Self-rule—trying to design life on one's own terms

Sin always appears as some form of independence from God and a taking over and usurping his roles. So don't get confused by the distraction that individual acts of sin can cause. There is a deeper sickness that only humbling oneself before God can cure. In that one move, relationship is restored, and we once again become who we were created to be, humans and not gods.

ONE MORE NOTE

WE CAN'T DEAL WITH sin and temptation without confession and repentance (see chapter 9). They are assumed in everything this chapter talks about, for it would be impossible to overcome sin and temptation without them. We have seen in this chapter, though, a deeper meaning of repentance, and we have reserved two separate chapters to go more deeply into the processes of confession and also obedience, which is also part of repentance. So make sure you include those in your understanding of the above.

THE TWO GREATEST COMMANDMENTS

In thinking about sin, it is so easy to get "religious" instead of spiritual. But religion never did a lot for overcoming sin, as we have seen. Instead, the Bible calls us to true spirituality in our fight against sin. Ultimately this has to do with love. Becoming spiritual is to realize the two great commandments of loving God and loving your neighbor as yourself (Matt. 22:36–40). In fact, Jesus said that all the commandments rest on these two. So what does that have to do with dealing with sin?

Well, as we have seen in this chapter and others, to love God means that we begin to obey him as well as do things his way. That goes a long way toward curing the problem of sin. But also, we need to mention that loving others is also part of the cure to many sins of the self. We often think that to love others cures the sins of how we treat other people. For example, if we are mean, like Joe, loving others means to stop being mean. That is quite obvious.

What is less obvious, however, are the ways that loving others cures our own problems as well. Take the example of Dirk from chapter 4. Remember him? He was trying to lose weight and was dealing with that sin by feeling guilty and making a deeper commitment. We talked about the deeper repentance needed to free him from that behavior and about all the other aspects of grace that would help him. But there is also another element that would lead to his ultimate healing: loving others.

Remember that Dirk had children. His weight was becoming a health danger, and so there was a real possibility that he might one day fall down with a heart attack. What I suggested to his accountability partner was to have Dirk begin to stop thinking about his guilt and commitment program and instead think about loving his wife and children. I suggested he think about what it would be like for small children to lose a father at a young age. I asked him to get Dirk to think about how daughters become promiscuous later, if they are looking for a father's love, or withdraw from relationships with men altogether. I asked him to have Dirk write a story about what his wife's and children's lives would be without him for the next thirty years and how it would be different if he disappeared. Where would their income come from? Where would their guidance come from? What would happen to their lives? Could he see them in their pain and struggle?

The reality was that his sin of overeating and not getting healthy would not only be a sin of the "self" that hurt him, but also a sin that could devastate the lives of others, all the way to the marriages of his children and their children. The fears of abandonment that they might carry forward as a result of his death could affect them for life. If Dirk could begin to think of things that way, then eating and not exercising become more than the sin of laziness and gluttony. They become the sin of a lack of love for many people.

If Dirk could think of that, then love could constrain him just as our love for God constrains us also not to cause grief to him.

This is proven true by prison programs that get criminals eye to eye with the victims of their crimes. When the criminals see the pain they caused, they change. Love does its work where rules and commitment could not. That is why Jesus said that all the other laws and rules depend on love.

Therefore, in your fight against sin, no matter what it is, remember the law of love. No matter what someone is struggling with, most likely someone else is being hurt by the sin. Addictions hurt the family. Lust hurts the marriage partner. Irresponsibility hurts many people. And on and on. There are no victimless crimes, and in helping people with sin, the Bible affirms a strong message: Think of how your behavior is affecting other people, and that will motivate you to stop when rules won't. Remember, all the Law and the Prophets rest on the ultimate Law of Love.

GOOD OLD-FASHIONED RELIGION

AS YOU READ THIS chapter, it might seem a little strange to hear so much about sin from psychologists. After all, didn't psychology explain away sin with early childhood deprivation and other reasons for behavior, such as abuse, unresolved grief and pain, and genetics? Not from our perspective. We strongly believe that if any one of us is going to grow personally, we must deal with our own sin, as well as the sin of others. For those are the two ways that sin affects our lives: sin by us and sin done to us.

The formula for dealing with sin we commit has been around for a long time: confession, forgiveness, and repentance for the "bad stuff" in our own souls. Also, as we have seen, with repentance comes a turning to the life of God and a filling up the soul with the "good stuff" of his life.

Likewise, the formula for dealing with the sin done to us is similar: confession, granting forgiveness, healing the wounds through God's life, and reconciliation, if possible. Both kinds of sin require the grace of God, facing the truth about oneself or others, receiving the life we need, receiving and granting forgiveness, and reconciling as much as we can.

There are no new ways of dealing with sin, for God gave us the Way a long time ago. We think this is very encouraging as we look at the prospects of growth from a biblical perspective. There is no rocket science, only the gospel. But what a gospel it is! It is the medicine for the sickness we all possess, and that really is good news.

TIPS FOR GROWERS:

- See yourself as both powerless and responsible for your sin. Die to any model of thinking that says that willpower will suffice and that if sin is ruling over you, you can just "do better." That is deluding yourself.
- See the seriousness of your sin and its destructiveness. Find the ways by which you have denied how it is keeping you from experiencing all that you want to have in life and with God and other people.
- Take responsibility for your sin—honestly and squarely.
- Realize that personal sin is not the cause of everything bad in your life, because you live in a fallen world. See also where other people's sin is responsible for bad things in your life.
- Get rid of the law in your life and the cycle of trying harder, failing, going into condemnation, and then trying harder, in contrast to living by the Spirit.
- Enter into the whole process of spiritual growth as you fight against sin and not just willpower, or leaning on God or even other good things apart from all that he gives us in the life of the Spirit. Make sure that you fight sin not with a few of the weapons God has provided but rather than with the whole arsenal.
- Face rebellion directly. It is one of the worst sins there is, and it will destroy you.
- Have an overall orientation toward repentance.
- Give no excuses for your sin.
- Make sure you have a view of sin that is not just external but also internal, and that you have a place that encourages you to deal with internal sin with God and others.
- Face and deal with the needs and deprivations that may be driving some sins. Find where you are separated from the life of God.
- Ask yourself where you are not avoiding or fleeing temptation. God has promised a way out. Make sure that you begin fleeing instead of thinking you can withstand temptation.
- Take a deeper view of sin—as in chapter 2—whereby you see the effects of original sin and how it is operating in your life. See where you have disconnected from God as the source of life, God as the Boss, relationship as primary, and the roles humankind is supposed to play. Deal with these roots in your life.

TIPS FOR FACILITATORS:

- Teach a deep view of sin. Teach it as something people are powerless over, yet deeply responsible for. Do not sugarcoat its seriousness. Crush the idea that people can "just stop" whatever is ruling over them, and get them to a point of powerlessness and poverty.
- Provide opportunities in grace to face the seriousness and destructiveness of sin. Teach about the power of denial. Encourage a culture where responsibility for sin is seen as the way to live.
- Avoid the trap of blaming all suffering on personal sin, and provide contexts for people to deal with the sin of others and with the pain of suffering that is not the result of anyone's sin but of living in a fallen world.
- Teach, as the Bible does, against seeing the law as a method of change and instead as a way of realizing our need for grace. Be aware of the subtly of teaching the standard line: confronting failure, giving forgiveness, and then just trying harder without giving growth and plugging into the process of life in the Spirit. Avoid commitment and willpower as the only tools available, and avoid other truncated views of dealing with sin. Where there is failure in dealing with sin, see if something is missing from the process, such as support, dealing with deprivation, confrontation, structure, or any of the other elements of life in the Spirit.
- Confront rebellion directly and teach about its destructiveness. Provide a context for facing up to it.
- Teach that sin is internal as well as external, and provide experiences, contexts, and activities in which people can confess and deal with the internal sins as well as the external ones. Make sure that grace rules.
- Deal with deprivations that are driving sin, and provide for what is missing. Help people understand that sin might be driven by something they are lacking and that this part of them must be connected to the life of God.
- Teach on the value of avoiding and fleeing temptation.
- Monitor how the deeper view of sin presented in chapter 2 is operating in people's lives. Make those issues a constant focus to be overcome, and make sure those issues are being confronted: disconnection from God as the source of life, God as the Boss, relationship as primary, and the roles humanity is supposed to play. Deal with these roots in your life

17

FACING REALITY: HOW TRUTH DEEPENS GROWTH

When we learn that truth is our friend, growth deepens.

I (John) recently had an encounter with truth that helped me grow. Before I left for work in the morning, my wife told me, "You're sort of distant and preoccupied." She said I seemed unavailable to her and wanted to know what was wrong. I told her everything was fine. At work, a client mentioned I didn't seem to be emotionally present in the session. I told him it was probably only his perception. A friend at lunch said, "You're here, but you're not here." I told him I was as here as I had ever been. By that time I was getting irritated at the annoying people in my life.

That evening, while I was reading my Bible, I came across 2 Corinthians 6:12: "We are not withholding our affection from you, but you are withholding yours from us." As I meditated on the verse, I realized I had been bombarded with the same truth from several different sources. I also realized I had been preoccupied with a difficult business problem lately, and I had indeed gone inside myself and lost contact with others in my life. It was humbling to see how many different people God used to tell me the truth before I got the message. At the same time, I felt grateful he had not given up on me and had kept sending emissaries until I woke up.

Although we don't always receive it graciously, truth is one of God's essential tools for growing us up. As we will see in this chapter, he gives us many types of needed truth from different sources. We touch on various aspects of truth throughout this book. Chapter 10 deals with the specific use of the Bible to give us the truth we need. Chapter 13, on discipline, shows us the value of truth in correcting us. In this chapter we deal with truth in general (which includes the Bible and discipline) and how it relates to spiritual growth.

If you have been hurt by truth not spoken in love, or are afraid of it, one of our greatest desires is that you will learn to love and seek it. Truth is sometimes painful, but it is always our friend, because it comes from the Lord, whose love and truth protect us (Ps. 40:11). He dispenses it to us out of a heart of compassion and grace. Like anything else from God, truth works *for* us, not *against* us.

WHAT IS TRUTH?

TRUTH IS A GLOBAL concept that is difficult to get our arms around. The most basic way to understand truth is that *truth is what is;* that is, truth is reality, what exists. Something can be truly good (like love) or truly bad (like deception), but both are part of the truth. Conversely, what doesn't exist can't be true, even if we want it to be.

We see this latter idea in spiritual growth a lot, especially when we wish that something bad wasn't true or that something good that doesn't exist was true. For example, a person might want to see herself as not having selfish parts (a bad true thing), but instead as being a totally giving person (a good untrue thing). We sometimes try to squeeze reality and truth into our own framework. This always fails.

Biblical scholars have categorized truth in different ways to help with the bigness of the concept. One way is that there is "ontological" truth, which refers to all of reality, and "propositional" truth, which is a set of integrated statements about that reality. For example, the Bible is propositional truth, and it describes the ontological realities God wants us to understand. In spiritual growth, when someone in the Body supports a friend's struggles, that person's caring act is an ontological reality. When the Bible says, "Carry each other's burdens, and in this way you will fulfill the law of Christ" (Gal. 6:2), it is a propositional truth that describes the process.

Another important classification of truth is *revelation.* Revelation means "unveiling." It describes those realities God wants us to understand for us to grow. Scholars speak of special revelation, which comprises the truths of the Bible, and general revelation, which is the realities of observed life. Attending to both types helps us learn what is good for our lives.

THE MANY FACETS OF TRUTH

THE BIBLE USES THE word *truth* to describe different aspects of reality as well as what is true in general (1 Tim. 2:7). The first reality is that of God himself. God is called "the God of truth" (Ps. 31:5). Jesus calls himself the Way, the Truth, and the Life (John 14:6). The Holy Spirit is also called the Truth (1 John 5:6). This illustrates the deeply personal and relational nature of truth. It is much more than a set of facts and rules. Truth lives and breathes in the essence of God.

When it is seen in this personal light, we can come closer to the truth. It is more than memorizing a list in our heads. Since truth is part of God's nature and since we are made in his image, truth is a deep part of our hearts as well: "Surely you desire truth in the inner parts; you teach me wisdom in the inmost place" (Ps. 51:6). We not only are to know truth, we are to experience it. For example, in my story about being occupied for a whole day, I had an emotional as well as an intellectual grasp of what God was telling me. This is the nature of truth.

The Scriptures also refer to themselves as a whole as the truth. For example, the Bible uses the phrase "the word of truth" to describe itself (Ps. 119:43; 2 Tim. 2:15). Jesus said that God's Word is truth (John 17:17). When we read the Bible, we expose ourselves to God's complete guide of the necessary truths of life and growth.

The Bible also describes a desirable character quality in people who are aligned to truth, that of honesty and righteousness. For example, Jethro instructed Moses to pick "men of truth" (Ex. 18:21 NASB), who stood against falsehood and for uprightness. We are to think on whatever is true, noble, and right (Phil. 4:8); love "rejoices with the truth" (1 Cor. 13:6). People who love truthfulness instead of falsehood are living right.

Finally, the Bible uses the word to refer to the specific body of facts regarding Jesus' atoning death for us, which reconciles us to God. This is the gospel, the most important truth of life: "the message of truth, the gospel of your salvation" (Eph. 1:13 NASB).

So truth is many things to God. But these many things do not conflict with each other. Truth is always consistent with itself, as God cannot be a part of lies (Titus 1:2).

ITS SOURCES. We can find truth in many places. God uses them all to help us grow in him:

- His Spirit and presence (1 John 5:6)
- The Bible (2 Tim. 3:16)
- People (Prov. 15:31)
- Our conscience (1 Tim. 1:19)
- Circumstances (1 Cor. 10:1–6)

WHAT TRUTH DOES

TRUTH PROVIDES A PATH FOR LIFE. Truth plays several different roles in spiritual growth. The first is that it provides a structure for the process of growth. To mature, people need a path or guide to know the way. Truth is that path: "I have chosen the way of truth; I have set my heart on your laws" (Ps. 119:30). Without truth's guidance, growth would not happen. Think about how a child requires instruction in all parts of life: relationships, tasks, emotions, and faith. A child who has not been exposed to and instructed in truth is often a child who is out of control or is allowing others to control him.

We see this same idea in spiritual growth circles. When people are given the truth as a guide, they know how to order their steps to complete the process. For example, for many people the commands to love

God and our neighbor (Matt. 22:38–39) provide a constant way to think about how to govern everyday life as well as their long-term values.

TRUTH IS MARRIED TO LOVE AND GRACE. Relationship requires a structure. The Bible often puts love and grace together with truth to show their closeness (Ps. 40:10; John 1:14; 2 John 3). When love is separated from truth, people cannot grow. For example, a husband wrote to me the other day that his marriage was in trouble because he loved his wife deeply but for years had been afraid to tell her unpleasant truths. He would avoid telling her when he was frustrated with her or hurt by her, so issues weren't being resolved between them. She had now lost respect and love for him, and the relationship was shaky.

Sometimes we divide love from truth. This is a problem, as they were never intended to be split up. Our love must be honest, and our truth must be for the other person's best. Like that husband, some people fear that being honest is not being loving. God is not that way, however. He is fully loving and fully truthful with us. In fact, in a beautiful picture of how integrated God's character is with love and truth, Psalm 85:10 says that his righteousness (truth) and peace (relationship) "kiss each other." Love and truth are not enemies. They need each other to be complete. In my experience, the most spiritually mature people, like the Lord, are full of love and full of truth.

TRUTH SAVES AND GIVES LIFE. Truth both preserves and provides a life for us. It protects us, and it also guides us into activities and relationships that are life-giving. For example, truth warns us of the danger of not following God's ways. A person who naively puts her trust in others without diagnosing their character can be really hurt. If, however, she heeds the truth and requires facts about a person's background from him and other people, she is more likely not to be jeopardized. Don't be afraid to ask people about their lives. Those who take offense at being questioned often are more concerned with appearance than with the truth.

More than protecting our lives, the truth also gives us life. When we seek out truth, we get involved in what is important for our lives. We search the Bible to solve problems. We go to trusted friends with our struggles, dreams, and desires. The truth gives us answers, hope, and solutions.

Think about the last time you received insight from a friend who was very valuable to you. I remember a man who suffered greatly because he was not sure of God's love for him. He had a constant anxiety that some failure on his part would cause God to disconnect from him. He studied both the truths of God's secure love—that no one can snatch us out of God's hand (John 10:28–29)—and the realities of his own experiences. People who were important to him had left him, and he had difficulty trusting that anyone would stay connected to him. As he internalized both sets of realities, he was better able to see why he had the fears he had. The truth also freed him to grieve his deep losses and receive love he would not lose from stable people and from God. This became a new life for this man, and he is now involved in many meaningful relationships and ministries with his newly developed assurance of love.

TRUTH SEPARATES WHAT IS REAL AND WHAT IS NOT. Truth is a divider and separator. It helps us clarify the real and the not-so-real (Heb. 4:12). For example, a couple may think they are of one mind on an issue—say, finances—because one of them is not forthcoming with his or her opinion. When the truth emerges, the couple realize that they do have different values and feelings, and then they can solve any problems. When the truth is hidden, many problems can arise.

TRUTHS IMPORTANT TO SPIRITUAL GROWTH

SEVERAL CATEGORIES OF TRUTHS are important to people in the spiritual growth process. As you learn them, or lead them in others, growth bears fruit.

THE TRUTH OF GOD'S DESIGN. We need to know that God has designed a structure for our spiritual growth that will give us a good life: "'For I know the plans I have for you,' declares the LORD, 'plans to prosper you and not to harm you, plans to give you hope and a future'" (Jer. 29:11). This structure is the subject matter of this book. We are to understand and live out the truths of God's plan for growth—for example, seeking him, being poor in spirit, and taking ownership of our lives.

THE TRUTH OF OUR CONDITION. Our condition is that we all have to grow. Everyone has weaknesses, sins, immaturities, and brokenness. Most of us are aware that we aren't perfect people. However, true growth occurs when we are able to discover what our own particular issues of growth are, which areas of our lives need God's healing and maturing.

In other words, all of us need to be in the path of living the life of God: dependence on him, relationship with others, productive jobs and careers, ministry, and character growth. This is universal. At the same time, we need to find out what areas we have fragility or a pattern of failure in and bring those into the growth process also. (For an in-depth look at these, see *Changes That Heal* and *Hiding from Love*.)

THE TRUTH OF OUR RESOURCES. Spiritual growth requires certain ingredients to work correctly. Here are some of the things people need:

- A spiritual context where God is seen as central to growth
- Abiding human relationships that are loving and truthful
- Experience and competence in the particular areas of growth
- Enough time for the process to take hold
- A structure or framework that fits the needs of the growers

If you are a growth facilitator, work on creating a growth environment in which the resources are plentiful enough for the needs of the people.

THE TRUTH OF THE TASKS REQUIRED. Whatever people are working on, they need to know what activities to engage in to bring about the fruit of growth. We need not only to know the truth about ourselves, but also to act on it (James 1:22–25). The next chapter provides more detail on the tasks involved in growth.

THE TRUTH OF THE OBSTACLES TO GROWTH. Everyone in spiritual growth needs to be aware of the problems they will face in the process. Learn about the wiles of Satan, the resistances within your own heart, and the problems people in your life may cause as you become a person of light. Many people in spiritual growth become discouraged and disheartened when they encounter problems in growth (Matt. 13:20–21). Remember that struggles sometimes mean you are doing something right.

THE KINDS OF TRUTH WE NEED FOR GROWTH

AS PEOPLE HAVE DIFFERENT needs, issues, and struggles, truth also plays several roles in how it is applied to our lives. Here are some of the principal ways.

ILLUMINATION. We need insight and wisdom for our inner lives. God brings all sorts of truth to us to help us see how best to handle life. A dark part of our lives may need to be exposed and matured. Or we may be ignorant of an issue that needs to be looked at. At times, illumination is simply part of the learning process, such as is found in a good Bible study. At other times, it is what is called an emotionally corrective experience, when a person has a flash of insight on what is driving a problem.

For example, a friend of mine who was having struggles emotionally connecting with his children began exploring his own childhood and discovered, to his surprise, very similar problems with himself and his dad. He felt that a light shone on his entire inner world. Many emotions arose as he revisited these years, and he experienced much healing as he learned to open up that part of his heart to others. He received great help from the truth that God is a father to the fatherless (Ps. 68:5), and ultimately he was able to give to his kids what he had newly received. This powerful experience of truth illuminated his life.

COMFORT. Comfort is the emotional supply we receive from God and others and then pass on to those who need it to bear the pains of life. Comforting words can bring us through many trials and help us grow.

When someone understands our pain and struggle at a deep level and can communicate that understanding to us, we are comforted. I once saw a woman in a growth group provide healing comfort to a man in three words. He was talking about his job frustrations, and he was very angry. He protested his treatment by others and protested that he was not going to put up with it anymore. The woman listened for a while and then said, "You've been hurt." The man stopped ranting and raving and was silent for a few seconds. Then he began to cry, as her comfort helped him safely move away from rage into the sadness and loss he truly felt. Although we don't naturally associate truth with comfort, it does much to soothe us: "My comfort in my suffering is this: Your promise preserves my life" (Ps. 119:50).

CLARIFICATION. Another major task of spiritual growth is learning to clarify things in our lives. We need to understand which of our struggles are our fault, which are the result of someone else's sin, and which are the result of living in a broken world. We need to clarify what is our problem in a relationship and what is not. This is where the truth comes in. For example, suppose a woman struggles with allowing others to control and manipulate her. As she explores her soul, she may discover the following clarifying truths:

- An inability to stand up for the truth in relationships that developed in other significant settings, such as her family of origin (someone else's fault)
- The loss of a supportive, healthy church when she had to move away because of her husband's employment problems in the industry in which he worked (a broken world)
- A resistance to becoming a truth teller because she is more accustomed to a pattern of going along with the wishes of others (her fault)

This woman would be greatly helped in her growth by these clarifications of the truth. For example, she could begin the forgiveness process toward her family of origin. She could begin grieving the relationships she had moved away from and start getting reconnected to new people. And she could confess to God and safe friends her resistance to being honest. Clarification shows us resolutions to particular growth issues.

GUIDANCE. Sometimes the truth gives us a direction to take in our growth and life. Often we stumble through life like little children in the darkness, not knowing how to operate in relationships, in work, or in faith, or even how to guard our hearts. For many people the adult years are very painful, as they feel lost and unsure of their steps. God provides many truths to make our paths straight: "Your word is a lamp to my feet and a light for my path" (Ps. 119:105).

Some of these guiding truths are general principles that apply to all universally, such as the law of empathy for others (Luke 6:31) or the principle of seeking God's kingdom first (Matt. 6:33). Many complicated life issues can be unraveled when we look to see how these principles apply.

In other cases God provides individual and specific guidance, such as a nudging of the Spirit, a Scripture passage that applies to our situation, or the advice of a trusted friend. None of us are lone rangers, and guiding truths are welcome allies in times of indecision.

I spoke with a friend recently whose teenaged daughter was becoming alienated from her. The more my friend tried to point out the right things to her daughter, the more the daughter felt smothered, and the more she moved away. Finally a wise woman told my friend, "Let your husband get more involved, and you back off." This was hard for both of them, because the husband was more of a task-based person and the wife was a relational problem-solver. But they both changed. The father worked on being more direct with his daughter, and the mother started biting her tongue and just listening. In a short time the daughter was reconnecting with her, and things got better. This specific guidance helped reconcile their hearts.

CORRECTION. People also need to be confronted with truth when they stray from God's path of righteousness. It is sad but true that we always need to be receptive to correction, as we saw in chapter 13.

Here is a word of caution: If you are a growth facilitator, remember to help your people be exposed to all these types of truth. Some systems of thought only use one, especially the correction type, and provide an unbalanced way of growing people up. In fact, correction used improperly can seriously wound people. When people are corrective without kindness, for example, a person can become discouraged from his faith in the Lord: "For the despairing man there should be kindness from his friend; So that he does not forsake the fear of the Almighty" (Job 6:14 NASB). Use a full menu of truth, according to the character, maturity, and circumstances of the people you are helping.

HOW WE SHOULD APPROACH TRUTH

OUR ATTITUDE TOWARD TRUTH makes all the difference in the world in terms of its results in our lives. Here are some stances that can best maximize the healing, growing effects of truth.

LOVE TRUTH. When people understand that truth can save and preserve their lives, it is hard not to love it. When you love something, you pursue it and want to be around it. Seek God's truth. Hang around honest people. Invite safe people to tell you the truth about yourself. Don't take a passive role with truth: Hunt it down. Pray David's prayer: "Send forth your light and your truth, let them guide me" (Ps. 43:3).

Struggles in learning to love truth are of two types. Some people have been hurt by truth divorced from love, such as those who have had harsh criticism. Or they have been hurt by inconsistent truth, so they never are sure whether the truth is to help them or to punish them. These people are afraid and hesitant about truth. They need to experience loving truths from God and others so that they can start trusting and loving it.

Other people have experienced more permissiveness than truth. Truth has not challenged their wills and perceptions, so they often end up willful and self-centered. From their perspective, truth has little value because it only hinders them from seeing life the way they want to see it. These people often need to experience the fruit of a life lived by their own rules instead of by God's truths; eventually they will see the damage it causes. This can help them to see that although truth is not always comfortable, it helps their lives to become more of what they were designed to be.

ENDURE THE PAIN OF TRUTH. Truth is often hurtful and uncomfortable. Like the surgeon's knife, its healing power comes with pain. One of the most valuable tasks for anyone in spiritual growth is to learn to tolerate the discomfort of the truth, in light of its great power to help us. Here are some of the painful experiences associated with truth:

- Facing the reality of our failings
- Living life God's way instead of how we would like to live it
- Loving others when we are aware of their imperfections
- Having truthful conversations with people we love
- Holding onto our values when others judge us wrongly
- Learning new ways that are not easy or natural for us in which to conduct our relationships

This is a difficult list. Yet, remember that the fruit of truth is always worth what it costs us. God is with us when we are with the truth: "But whoever lives by the truth comes into the light, so that it may be seen plainly that what he has done has been done through God" (John 3:21).

RECOGNIZE HOW LOVE HELPS THE PAIN. Truth's pain carries some hopeful realities. The first is a little formula: *The more love we internalize, the more truth we can bear.* Love gives us the support and grace to tolerate difficult realities. Well-loved people can face their souls without going all-bad or becoming deeply discouraged, for they have been rooted and grounded in love (Eph. 3:17). If you find that truth hurts too much, you may need to increase or deepen your support base.

This formula also means that as we are loved more, we see things more and more clearly. We are able to look deeper into our souls and see brokenness and sins we may not have been able to tolerate before. You will often find that over time the truths people work with are darker than those with which they started. For example, many people who start spiritual growth begin with an external crisis: a divorce, a dating relationship, a financial or medical issue. It may look as if the person is innocent and is simply the unfortunate recipient of bad times or bad people. Yet, as they become connected, taught in God's ways, and strengthened and do the work of growth, they take ownership of their part of the crisis and solve it. The crisis goes away, but growth doesn't stop. We look more inward, where much more work needs to be done. Truth we couldn't initially bear becomes the stuff of growth.

Also, as we are more loved, we just don't go into bad places when people we trust tell us the truth. A good friend of mine told me one day that I had been pretty unlovable recently. He was very direct, and then, concerned he had wounded me, he asked me how I was feeling about what he had said. I thought a minute and replied, "We're too close. You just can't hurt me." Maybe he could say something that would really injure me, but it would be difficult at this point. We are just used to the fact that each of us is "for" the other person. We all need relationships so knit together with love and truth over time that we can take in who they are and what they say without the risk of injury: "Wounds from a friend can be trusted" (Prov. 27:6).

BE SENSITIVE TO TRUTH AND UNTRUTH. The more a person takes a stance toward truthfulness, the more discerning he becomes about truth and untruth. God designed us to live in reality. As we immerse our lives in this, we see more and more clearly what is and is not true. Darkness and light become more distinct from each other (John 1:5).

How bank tellers are trained to detect counterfeit money is instructive for us. For many hours they handle only real money to the point

TIPS FOR GROWERS:

- Examine your preconceptions about truth. Do you experience truth as harsh or critical or condemning? Rework your approach to truth to see it as a giver of life and as your friend.
- Look for ways to internalize truth, including scriptural teachings, promptings of the Spirit, safe people, and circumstances. See your relationship with truth as connecting to your people relationships and growth.
- Become aware of your resistance to certain types of truth. For example, some people are more comfortable dealing with the truth of their hurt and weakness, but averse to connecting with the truth of their selfishness and rebellion. For others, it may be the converse.
- Learn both to receive and to give truth graciously and humbly. See the value of making truthfulness a part of your deepest relationships.

TIPS FOR FACILITATORS:

- Develop in your growth settings an attitude that truth is a normal and required part of the growth process. Watch for tendencies only to comfort and encourage as well as tendencies only to confront with truth. Keep the balance of truth without judgment, and grace without license.
- Make confessing painful truths about ourselves part of the process as well as being able to receive others' insights and perspectives. Help your growers not only to be available to hear truth, but to actively seek it out.
- If you see a grower getting stuck in defensiveness with a particular truth about himself, back off and provide grace, comfort, and empathy, to see whether the problem is that the person does not possess enough love inside to tolerate the truth. If you do this and the problem remains, deal with a possible tendency to see oneself as a "good" person rather than an honest and broken person. Help restore that person in a spirit of gentleness.
- Help your growers live in the tension of the mystery of God: that we will not have all the answers to our problems, nor can we make him predictable.

that they are so familiar with the real that, when they are given the unreal, they know something is amiss. This is the same in spiritual growth. People become so steeped in the truth that they become more aware when they are not being honest with themselves, God, or others. They sense when someone in their life is being untruthful. And the converse is true, too: Deceptive people, because they live in shadow, are also more and more self-deceiving.

I know a woman who had lived her entire life so afraid of conflict she was unable to see faults in other people. She entered the spiritual growth process and committed herself to admitting and seeing reality, no matter how painful it was. Things began to change. First, she became aware of her own self-deception, attempting to make life comfortable for those in her life. After that, she woke up to her husband's financial irresponsibility and deception, which she had never been able to face. In time, her courage, along with the love she had for him, helped him to get help. It got to the point that when he would slip up and lie about money issues, she could read it in his face, which was good for both of them: "For you were once darkness, but now you are light in the Lord. Live as children of light" (Eph. 5:8).

BE RECEPTIVE TO ALL STYLES OF TRUTH. People learn and grow in different ways. Some of these ways have to do with their early experiences, some are brain hard-wiring, and some are preferences. For example, some people understand linear, logical truth more easily, while others do better with intuition. While understanding cognitive styles is helpful, what is more important is to work on being receptive to all types of reality. This gives God and the process more freedom to work within us.

LEARN TO LIVE WITH MYSTERY AND THE UNKNOWN TRUTHS. One more aspect to the role of truth in spiritual growth is learning to live with what we do not, and sometimes can never, know. God alone knows all truth, as he alone can bear the weight of it. It is a mercy from him that we don't know everything about ourselves and the world. At the same time, we are a curious race, and we sometimes feel entitled to have all the answers.

This attitude has all sorts of applications in spiritual growth. There are lots of unknowns we must accept, live with, and move on from, for example:

- All facts about our childhood and past
- Reasons people in our lives did the things they did
- Reasons we did everything we have done
- Why God allowed certain things to happen
- Exactly when we will be through with a particular issue

Some spiritual growth systems give the impression that everything is in black and white and we can have answers for all questions. The Bible teaches, instead, that we need to make space for not knowing: "Then I saw all that God has done. No one can comprehend what goes on under the sun" (Eccl. 8:17). We indeed need to pray for wisdom, as Solomon did (1 Kings 3:7–9). But we need also to learn to be dependent on a loving God who dispenses the truths that heal us in the seasons when we most need them.

CONCLUSION

YOU DON'T HAVE TO be afraid of the truth, even when it hurts. Seek reality and become a person of the truth.

The next chapter, dealing with activity, will help you to take initiative in that seeking and growing process.

18

PUTTING ON THE GLOVES: THE IMPORTANCE OF ACTIVITY

God designed spiritual growth to be an active partnership with him.

Glenn and Anne, a married couple in their thirties, came to see me (John) for counseling. They were not in a crisis; rather, they wanted to make sure they were getting the most out of their relationship with God and with each other. They came for a checkup more than an overhaul. So we went to work.

One thing that always emerges when a couple works on their relationship is that the couple is actually made up of two distinct individuals, each with his or her own experiences, past, hurts, and ways of looking at life. A relationship cannot grow without each member understanding the individual issues of each person. It would be like trying to improve a recipe for spaghetti without knowing about pasta, tomato sauce, and meat.

Over time, Glenn's and Anne's souls became more distinct in counseling. We noticed two major differences between them.

First, they differed in the degree to which they struggled with character issues. Glenn had some hurts and conflicts, but his were not major and they did not severely affect his life. He had problems in being vulnerable and open emotionally and in being as clear and assertive as he needed to be. But he loved Anne and the children, had good friends, liked his job, and enjoyed his church involvement.

Anne's situation was tougher. When she was a little girl, her parents had been emotionally distant and unavailable. They also had controlled and manipulated her. Part of the fruit of this background was that Anne struggled with significant depression, had great difficulty trusting others and opening up, and had a hard time being clear and defined in her boundaries. She went through life with more pain and difficulty than Glenn. But, like him, she loved her family, friends, work, and church.

Second, Glenn and Anne differed in the degree to which they sought spiritual growth. While Anne sought out spiritual and emotional growth, Glenn was passive. They also used growth moments in very different ways. For example, when we met each week, Anne would respond to what had happened at our last session. She was evidently working on her growth in between our meetings.

In one session, while she was talking about how much she enjoyed her church, all of a sudden she felt a deep sadness. We didn't have time to get into her feelings then, as other things were going on, but we remarked on how suddenly the feelings had cropped up. In the next session Anne brought up the incident. She had prayed and searched her soul since we met last, and she had traced this experience down to the fact that when she was a little girl, God had been her only refuge in a world of emptiness and pain. She used this insight to bring out her deep feelings of being unloved and take them to God, Glenn, and others who cared for her and comforted her heart.

Anne was also in a women's Bible study, and she was never satisfied with learning theology for its own sake, but always wanted to know what the passages meant for her growth. She took many risks in telling others the truth, whether it hurt or not, because she knew she had to live in the light of reality. She surrounded herself with growing people who supported her and held her hand through her darkness.

By contrast, though he was a good person and had a serious faith, Glenn was less involved in the growth process. He had a hard time making it to our sessions on time, and he would often cancel for business reasons. He would have difficulty remembering what we had talked about in the previous session or how his issues tied together. Sometimes he would sit down in the chair, look at me, and say, "So what will we discuss today?"

"Let's look at why you need to ask me that question," I would respond.

As their time with me was wrapping up, we reviewed their growth—what had been done and what they needed to do in the future. Anne had shown much change. She certainly wasn't perfect, but she was a long way from where she had been. Her emotional connectedness to God and others was much stronger; she was also much more able to be clear about her values and feelings when she was in conflict with others. She was bearing much fruit.

While Glenn showed progress, he was vague about his changes. He was also more emotionally accessible and more assertive, but he was still fundamentally the same, passive person who was letting life happen to him instead of taking hold of life.

I am not trying to paint Glenn as the bad guy or Anne as the good girl. However, it is instructive to see that the person with more damage to her soul grew more than the person who was less damaged. The real difference was their level of active involvement.

GOD WORKS, WE WORK

ACTIVITY—BEING ENERGETICALLY INVOLVED in an endeavor—is part of who God is and how we are made in his image. God is constantly working on his own agenda and tasks. As Jesus said, "My Father is always at his work to this very day, and I, too, am working" (John 5:17). Even when the Bible says God "rested" after he finished the creation, the Hebrew word describing his rest is one that refers to completion, not weariness (Gen. 2:2).

God never stops his active search to love and help those who want him. I love the words of 2 Chronicles 16:9—"For the eyes of the LORD move to and fro throughout the earth that He may strongly support those whose heart is completely His" (NASB)—because they illustrate how God takes the initiative to find and help those who love him. Activity has to do with the "doing" parts of life as opposed to the "relating" parts. God constructed life to break down basically into those two tasks: work and love.

Adam and Eve were designed to relate deeply to God and to each other as well as to rule and subdue the earth he had assigned them. A good life always reflects both dimensions. Spiritual, relational people also have meaningful, active lives of purpose. They are deeply connected emotionally and have jobs, ministries, and hobbies that make life fuller.

Activity and love are intertwined. Love is the fuel of activity; love is also its purpose and goal. Loving God and others is the end result and purpose of basically any good activity. Being connected emotionally to God and others requires effort and initiative. It takes work to seek out safe people, open up to them, confess who we are, and receive and give truth and reality to them. Relationship is not at all passive. As most people know, our most precious relationships are those in which we have invested a lot of energy.

SPIRITUAL GROWTH REQUIRES ACTION

ACTION IS ALWAYS AN integral part of growth. Spiritual growth does not "happen" to us; it requires a great deal of blood, sweat, and tears, as we saw with Anne. She put the time into the process, and her life bore good fruit from it.

This doesn't mean either that we must do it all on our own or that God does it all. Sometimes people fear that being active is not being spiritual. They wonder, *Is this all* my *effort? Am I not trusting God?* Neither extreme is the way God designed the process. Our sanctification is a collaborative effort between God and us. We have certain tasks, which we discuss in this chapter. He has certain tasks also, such as preparing our hearts, setting up the circumstances, and bringing forth results from the growth work. The Bible teaches this partnership this way:

> Therefore, my dear friends, as you have always obeyed—not only
> in my presence, but now much more in my absence—continue
> to work out your salvation with fear and trembling, for it is God
> who works in you to will and to act according to his good purpose
> (Phil. 2:12–13).

We work out our salvation, meaning we diligently execute our responsibilities in growth. All the while, in mysterious and often invisible ways, God works in us for his purposes. He does the many things we cannot do for ourselves, for which we depend on him. This co-laboring is not at all as if God is simply doing things to us, like a surgeon operating on an anesthetized patient lying on an operating table. It is more like certain forms of brain surgery, in which the patient is awake and working with the surgeon, telling him what he is experiencing as the surgeon probes and cuts one way, then another. We are partners in our own spiritual surgery.

THE PLACE OF ACTIVITY IN GROWTH

LET'S RETURN TO OUR own role in the partnership. When we grow spiritually, we perform many tasks. Exploring the depths of our souls and seeing what needs to be done is hard and sometimes scary work. This work requires love and support from God and others. Love functions as fuel for us. Energized by those who care for us, we are able to carry out the tasks.

Most of the time, growth requires action. In only one period of our life can we be totally passive, receptive, and dependent, and that is in the womb. For nine months the unborn baby is developed, protected, and fed. But even in the first year of life, babies take part in getting their needs met. They cry to signal they need comfort, food, changing, or warmth. They learn to reach out their arms, kick their legs to show excitement or distress, and engage in eye contact with Mother. As time passes, they take on more complex responsibilities of activity to meet the demands of life.

RECONCILIATION VERSUS FAIRNESS. An active stance toward growth also means that we give more weight to reconciliation than to fairness. Rather than waiting for a person who has hurt us to come to us, we need to take the initiative to reconcile. If someone has something against us, we are to go to him (Matt. 5:23–24). If we have something against another, we are also to go to him (Matt. 18:15). God sought us out and solved our alienation from him even though he would have been justified in taking no more action toward us. He gave up demands for fairness for the sake of relationship.

OWNERSHIP. When we are active in our growth, we tend to take more responsibility for our lives. The experiences of being involved, learning, taking risks, and talking to others about our lives increases the level of ownership we have in the process. When people are passive about their growth, they tend to let others control them and see forces outside of them as being in charge of their lives.

I remember a woman who was stuck in a passive role in her marriage. Her husband was controlling and insensitive to her. He would make financial and scheduling decisions, such as trips and vacations, without even consulting her. She took little ownership of the marriage problems, thinking he would never change and things would always be like this.

Then this woman became involved in a healthy church and a support group. She saw that things would stay the same as long as she allowed them to. She took ownership, not of his life, but of her own growth and her responses to him. She began telling him how she wanted to be involved with him, and if he kept controlling things, she would have to consult their pastor about it, or even a counselor who would help her with the legalities of his financial dealings. She loved him without rescuing him, confronted him without nagging him, and respected him without affirming his sinfulness. The more she saw that she was part of the problem, the more she solved the problem. Ultimately, her husband slowly changed, gave up control, and developed a more intimate relationship with her.

The sobering reality is that, right now as you are reading these pages, there is no meeting currently going on somewhere else, in which the agenda is to make your life better. However, the more you own your life, the more things change for the better.

LEARNING FROM MISTAKES. Being active in growth also means that sometimes we fail. When people seek to grow spiritually, they soon realize that they will be trying new ways of relating to God and others, ways based on love and truth. These new ways can bring them more of the abundant life Jesus promised (John 10:10). Our old ways of life might have been more comfortable, but they were often based on fear or habit, not faith in God's paths. Yet the fact that new ways are new can be unsettling. Like Abraham—who "when called to go to a place he would later receive as his inheritance, obeyed and went, even though he did not know where he was going" (Heb. 11:8)—people discover new thoughts, feelings, and parts of themselves. They don't know much about them at first, and they make many errors.

For example, many years ago I became aware that I was pretty closed off emotionally from others. I had particular difficulty talking about struggles and difficulties. It was easier for me to respond to others' lives and to stay distant about my own. With the help of loving and honest friends I began to understand that this being shut down wasn't good for me and that I was missing out on much of the life God had intended for me within relationships. I decided to become an emotionally honest person. I felt this was a spiritual growth step in authenticity for me. It was a step of active involvement on my journey.

Whenever I would meet someone, even a casual acquaintance, and the person would say, "How're you doing?" I would take the greeting literally and tell him about my problems in relationships, my inner life, and so on. This had two results. One was that this new way of relating opened up things for me with some people. We deepened our relationship; they would also open up; and we would grow together. The second result was that some people were unnerved by my answers to what they thought was a simple, friendly greeting. It was awkward for them, and I don't think it helped our relationship. Some would try to understand what I was saying. Others would change the subject. Still others wouldn't say anything because they had no idea what to say!

So, while I did grow from this experience, I also had to repair some relationships along the way, in my zeal for emotional honesty. I have since learned a lot about discerning the proper time, place, and person for opening up one's heart. These mistakes taught me as much as the good connections did. I probably sounded pretty weird to some friends, but I did learn some things.

THE TASKS OF GROWTH

IF YOU ARE EITHER into personal growth or are helping others in the process, it is important to understand what you need to do to foster your own spiritual growth. The process involves much effort, but brings forth much fruit.

HUMBLE YOURSELF BEFORE GOD. Humbling yourself is seeing yourself as God sees you. Humility helps you assume a position of need, dependency, and obedience, which allows God to best support your growth.

SEARCH FOR AREAS THAT NEED GROWTH. God designed us all to be in the process of spiritual discovery and growth. You need to take initiative to find where you are weak, broken, or immature. Ask God to search you and know you (Ps. 139:23–24), using his presence, truth, circumstances, or other people. Your natural tendency is to avoid pain and not rock the boat, yet the spiritual person stays on a quest for growth.

FIND GROWTH CONTEXTS. Just as plants need good soil, so we need to research and seek out people and places where spiritual growth occurs. Look for healthy churches and groups full of grace and truth that have experience and success in whatever area you wish to work on. A man I know who had some poor financial habits attended a church that didn't have much expertise in helping him with his overspending issues. So twice a week he drove a couple of hours to a church in another city because the right help and group was there. Ask your pastor for advice concerning a good context for your growth.

ASK FOR REALITY AND TRUTH. Take the initiative to get information about your issues from God and others. Be aware of your human tendency to minimize the seriousness of your condition or to want to appear to be like someone who has it all together. Throw all of that on the Cross and be vulnerable to feedback from others.

BRING YOUR HEART TO RELATIONSHIP. Being emotionally present requires action. It takes work to keep your heart available and vulnerable. The human tendency is to withhold or protect. Yet the fruit of growth comes when you let others inside: "We are not withholding our affection from you, but you are withholding yours from us. As a fair exchange—I speak as to my children—open wide your hearts also" (2 Cor. 6:12–13). Face hurt and pain. With the love and support of God and others, experience the realities of your past, your sins, and your hurts. Bring these into relationship so that they may be grieved, accepted, repented of, and comforted. Do not wait for change to happen. Take the initiative to face what you have been afraid to know.

TAKE RISKS IN AREAS THAT NEED STRETCHING. This may involve being more honest than you are used to, being open to feeling close when you are not comfortable, and allowing yourself to sit with a painful emotion when you normally avoid it. These activities are much like the work of someone with a muscle injury during physical therapy; they are the painful stretches and moves that bring repair.

FIXING THE PASSIVITY PROBLEM

MANY PEOPLE STRUGGLE WITH actively pursuing spiritual growth. Like Glenn, they are passive rather than active. When people allow life to happen to them or when they react to others rather than taking initiative, they take a passive role. Passive people who also have dependency needs often have real problems growing. They desire and value relationship and support, which is a good thing, but they seek it only for connectedness, comfort, or safety. They are less able to use relationships as the fuel to solve problems, take risks, or execute responsibilities.

Some people with passive, dependent tendencies will initially come alive when they join a growth group, because they receive support for, and acceptance of, their struggles. They become attached in very good ways to the members of the group; however, the closeness becomes an end in itself. They do not make significant progress in confronting problems, learning new ways of relating, repenting of old ways, and so on. They use the love they receive to protect themselves from life rather than to engage fully in life. Sometimes they develop a bottomless hunger for love that, no matter how much they receive, never leaves them satisfied. This is the problem of the passive position.

Here are some of the causes and solutions of the issue.

Misunderstanding the Bible's Message

God addresses passivity as a problem, not a virtue. In the parable of the talents (Matt. 25:14–30), the master gives money to three servants before leaving town. Two servants actively invest their money while the third passively buries his in the ground. Upon returning to town, the master rebukes the third, saying,

> "Well then, you should have put my money on deposit with the bankers, so that when I returned I would have received it back with interest. Take the talent from him and give it to the one who has the ten talents. For everyone who has will be given more, and he will have an abundance. Whoever does not have, even what he has will be taken from him" (vv. 27–29).

Why was the master hard on the third servant? Because he received no return on his investment. God gives us time, talent, and treasures in life to glorify him in many ways, such as expanding his kingdom, growing closer to him and others, and having fruitful jobs. To develop our souls (his investment), we must take risks and initiative. Passivity negates risk and initiative and, ultimately, growth. The passive position keeps us safe, as Glenn was, but we are not getting all God has for us.

When we are passive, we shrink from the risks of the faith life itself. God's soul takes no pleasure in this (Heb. 10:38). He himself stays actively involved with us, even when what we do causes him pain (Eph. 4:30), because he values his role in our lives. And Jesus' active obedience models the same attitude for us.

However, some Bible teachers believe that activity is a danger to spirituality. They teach that when we "do," we are not trusting God, and that it is far better to wait on him: "Be still, and know that I am God" (Ps. 46:10). I have seen many people be spiritually passive because of this. Singles do not go out and find someone to date, believing they would be taking over God's job of making connections. People in a troublesome relationship are silent and compliant instead of speaking the truth in love. Others suffering from depression will wait for God to give them relief without seeking a wise and godly person with experience in treating depression.

This principle has enough truth in it to be dangerous. The Bible certainly teaches that there is a time to stop striving and to listen to his voice. Relationship is always more important than task. That was Jesus' message to Martha when she was bound up in busyness (Luke 10:38–42). People grow when they attend emotionally to God and their relationships with each other, and this often requires slowing down, listening, and being quietly receptive. But the problem is not that activity is bad in and of itself. Activity is bad when it takes the place of relationship rather than serving the purposes of relationship. Activity was designed by God to involve us in the work of life, not to replace closeness.

Often the problem these teachers address is a real one. God has his job, and we have ours. When we try to do God's or demand that he do ours, we run into problems. An example of the first problem would be someone who tries to use willpower to stop a drinking problem instead of submitting to the spiritual growth process. An example of the second would be the person who waits for someone in his life to become aware that she is being hurtful, without saying anything to her.

This confusion of job responsibilities always needs to be clarified. Study the example of biblical characters who experienced many miracles and encounters with God. They saw and met God in numerous ways. The "let go and let God" teaching should surely apply to them, one might think; yet these people were also very active, involved, and working. Moses judged the people's legal matters. David drew up battle plans. Paul traveled far and wide to preach the Good News. Their lives were full of effort and work. They weren't navel-gazers. Instead, they were people who experienced the holiness and mystery of God, had deep relational connections with others, and lived actively in the real world.

Fear of Failure

Some people are passive because they are afraid to fail. The internal pain they experience when they make mistakes is so great they become paralyzed and unable to take charge of their decisions. People with perfectionist issues often deal with this struggle. They feel all-bad, self-condemned, or a total failure. Thus they stay in a safety zone in their spiritual growth and rarely take a risk.

TIPS FOR GROWERS:

- Look at all the ways God actively works for your betterment. Use that as a model for you to take initiative in the growth process.
- Review your life and consider the times you were passive or fearful and missed opportunities God intended for you. Investigate the reasons behind these, and work on them.
- Be aware of any tendencies to see spiritual growth as something only God does, and look at how you can partner with God. Deal with devaluing attitudes toward activity, such as "it's not being spiritual" or "it's not trusting God."
- In relationships, take initiative in reconciling with people as opposed to waiting on them to approach you, apologize, and so on. Give up fairness for reconciliatory activity.
- Unearth any passive rescue wishes you might have in your heart. Deal with them as unhelpful to you, and work on letting them go, replacing them with your partnership with God and others.

TIPS FOR FACILITATORS:

- Give your growers opportunities to understand that activity serves the purposes of love and growth and must not be separated from them. Otherwise, it is a works mentality. Remind them of the relational nature of biblical activity and initiative.
- Provide your growers with an approach to growth that involves initiative from both them and God. Deal with any prideful passivity that gets passed off as being "spiritual."
- Help them see that growth requires risks and mistakes, and that God's grace and the comfort of the Body will help them to sustain those risks and learn many things from them.
- When they encounter relational conflicts, teach them that no matter with whom the problem originated, they are to take active steps to work out the issue, the way God does.

God has a solution for this problem. When we experience those inevitable mistakes in spiritual growth, we need to know that failure is our friend. God does not condemn or judge us, even when our hearts condemn us (1 John 3:19–20). It simply means that we are experiencing a learning curve. Don't be afraid of mistakes as you try out different ways of living life. God has paid the price for this so that we can keep growing without any loss of love or security.

If you are a growth facilitator, find ways to communicate that failure is okay and something people can laugh about and get over. Tell stories on yourself. Model how failure brings people closer, not makes them more distant.

The senior pastor of my church has this ability. He uses his foibles to illustrate his sermon points. During one message he described how emotionally inattentive he had been to his wife that week. It was a pretty typical "clueless husband" occasion. He said that one day all their kids were somewhere else for the day and he and his wife were alone in the house. His wife said she wanted to spend some special one-on-one time with him. His response was, "Great idea! There are lots of projects we can do around the house."

Looking around the sanctuary, I could see lots of couples laughing and poking each other, as they were able to safely identify with the pastor's story.

When people start living in grace without the fear of failure, they begin to experience freedom. This freedom leads to more activity, because the paralysis of condemnation has been dealt with.

Rescue Wishes

Rescue wishes are early, developmentally young desires for someone to take care of us. All people have them to a greater or lesser degree. People who struggle with this issue have a deep desire for someone who will mother them: we will protect and sooth them. Often these people have in their history someone who loved them inconsistently so that they carry an ache for sustained love. Others have been in relationships in which they were unable to stand on their own, so they do not trust themselves to be competent in the world.

These wishes can keep people inactive in the spiritual growth process. They find themselves enslaved to fantasies of others reading their thoughts and feelings without having to express them. Or they will confuse *help* with *rescue,* desiring others not just to assist them in their problems, but to solve them for them.

For example, a wife may wait for her husband to see that her feelings have been hurt by his insensitivity. She desires that he be so attuned to her that he knows what she is feeling. Her fear is that if she has to tell him, it means he doesn't love her. However, if she takes ownership of this rescue wish and lets her husband know her heart, she is more likely to get the love and connection she needs.

We hope you are learning the benefits of taking initiative in spiritual growth.

Warning: Sometimes active people are impatient and want results yesterday! In the last chapter learn how we need to submit to the process of time in our growth.

19

WAITING FOR THE HARVEST: TIME

The time we spend in the growth path will bear fruit in a changed life.

Robin entered counseling with me to deal with her marriage, her eating habits, and some depression. During my initial interview with her, I found that she was a CPA and had earned her master's degree in business administration. She was a highly trained professional in the business world.

As you might have guessed, Robin was a very hard worker in spiritual and emotional growth. She took it seriously and faced many fears and problems.

One thing I began noticing was her perspective on how growth worked over time. For example, she discovered that many of her concerns (the marriage, the eating, and the depression) had to do with a long-standing inability to grieve, accept her losses, and accept comfort rather than being omnipotent and perfect. When Robin found this out, she asked me, "Now that I know this, what do I do about it?" I told her, "You are going to have to learn how to let go of things, give up the demand to be so strong, and experience your weaknesses without running from them."

She thought about that for a minute, and then said, "Okay, I'll have that done by next session. Then what?"

I started to laugh. I told her, "You can't apply business principles to spiritual growth. It's not like coming up with a project structure and implementing it into the business, hoping that it will have immediate results. Look at this more as how plants grow." Robin loved gardening. We talked about how she sets her plants in the right soil, waters and feeds them, makes sure the temperature and light are right, and keeps them safe from pests. She noted how you don't see results for a long time, then all of a sudden, life begins emerging from the soil.

Robin understood the analogy and said, "I suppose I need to get used to this time thing." And she did. She stopped expecting growth to be immediate, settled in, and eventually received the results she desired.

The most common question I hear from people in spiritual growth is, *Why is this taking so long?* They will often enter the growth process with great hope and excitement and then, somewhere along the way, become discouraged that they aren't achieving results as soon as they would like. Someone is still struggling in a marriage; another is unable to open up emotionally to God and others; still another is unable to set appropriate limits; and someone else may be tormented by the pain of the past.

Spiritual growth facilitators may feel lost, confused, or guilty about the lack of fruit in the lives of the people in their growth group. They may wonder what they are doing wrong, or if they are letting the grower down, or how to even know what "too much time" is.

Spiritual growth should bring forth fruit of one kind or another over time. If it doesn't, it could be a sign that something is breaking down along the way. The purpose of this chapter is to look at the role of the process as well as steps along the path of spiritual growth.

THE PROCESS OF TIME

SO MANY GROWERS EXPECT that, if they read their Bibles and do the right things, they will instantly and permanently change. They are disappointed when this does not happen. They may feel God has let them down or they are doing something wrong, when in fact everything may be proceeding as God planned it. Time is a necessary ingredient of growth.

God originally did not include time in his plan, as he exists outside of time, in eternity. He experiences past, present, and future all at the same time (Ex. 3:14). We, too, were created to live in an eternal state of relatedness and joy; however, when Adam and Eve sinned in the garden, God's wonderful creation was marred. He saw the trouble we were now in and knew the seriousness of our condition. And he knew that two things were necessary to fix the problem. The first was an atoning death to satisfy the requirements of his holiness. The second was a process of repair for his creation to be redeemed and healed from what it had brought upon itself.

This process we call time. Time takes the creation out of the eternal state, as quarantine takes a sick person out of the community. This is so that the disease of sin will not contaminate eternity. When the creation is healed of sin, time will be no more, as its job will have been accomplished. We will again enter the eternal state with God. There will be no progression of day and night in eternity, only a continual day illuminated by God himself (Rev. 22:5).

The gift of time applies also in the lives of individuals. When a person comes to faith in Christ, the guilt of sin is removed from him, and he now has a relationship with God. Yet he is born again not as an adult, but as a spiritual baby. Like an infant, he must now enter the process of growth over time and receive the elements of growth that will one day mature him. This is what Peter means by our growing in salvation (1 Peter 2:2).

We aren't negating miracles by saying all this. The Bible and our own experience show that God does do instant and marvelous things. And we need to ask for these, receive them when they happen, and thank God for them. For example, God can and does instantly remove an addiction to alcohol or a depression. At the same time, however, the norm taught in the Scriptures is a model for growth (Mark 4:26–29; Eph. 2:20–21; 4:15–16; Col. 2:19; 2 Peter 3:18). Teachings that only emphasize deliverances, for example, can create people who become nonfunctional in real life, dependent not on God and his maturing ways, but on an event to heal them. So our suggestion for those you are helping is to work on the process and be open to the miraculous. God is for us in both ways.

SO WHAT TAKES ALL THE TIME?

IF YOU ARE A growth facilitator, you surely have heard the question, "Why is this taking so long?" Although you may understand the big picture of the growth process, it is often helpful for you and those you are helping to understand the specific ways in which time is a necessary part of growth. It is much better to redeem time than to waste it, as the days are evil (Eph. 5:16 KJV).

EXPERIENCE VERSUS INTELLECTUAL LEARNING. Spiritual growth involves the whole person. All of our parts need to be exposed to God's love and healing: heart, soul, and mind (Matt. 22:37). This means that growth is much more than cognitively understanding or memorizing a fact, idea, or principle. Understanding and memorization are simply the mind working, which is a necessary but insufficient component of growth. If that were all that is involved, growth would be a much faster, cleaner, and simpler process. Simply learn a list, and you are healed.

Some growth circles believe something like this. They teach that if you will just know the Bible or their particular set of ideas, you will be matured. While we agree that a thorough understanding of God's ways is certainly a requirement, even the Bible itself teaches that knowing truth is not enough (James 1:22–25; see our chapter 10).

We need to add experience to our intellectual grasp of growth, what people call those eighteen inches between the head and the heart. Experience, by definition, takes time. For example, someone in your group may have an unloved heart. She can't connect at deep levels with others. She is unable to trust and be vulnerable with others. She needs what she does not possess inside: love. She certainly needs to be taught about the grace and safety of God and his care for her. But she also needs to experience God's care in her soul through his hands and feet. You may need to create a safe context in which she can bring her unloved heart to others who can empathize and bring comfort. It may mean allowing her to experience fear and distrust without condemnation, so that she knows she is safe. It may mean letting her confess her pain and disconnection to others, and in turn receive the grace and tenderness from them that she can't manufacture for herself. All these events take time, much more than learning some facts. Yet they are essential.

TAKING IN GRACE AND FORGIVENESS. Of all the principles of growth, internalizing God's grace and forgiveness takes the most amount of time. It is much more natural for people to try to earn God's love or to learn a habit or ritual. This is our heritage in the divine law. It is unnatural for us to live by grace and forgiveness. That which is not natural requires more time.

I know a man in a growth group who, for the longest time, couldn't "get it" that when he failed, God wasn't mad at him. So he would act out in various ways and stay out of relationship with God and the group. When he felt more under control, he would reemerge, thinking he was "okay" with God and the group. Finally he learned that those who loved him most wanted to know when he failed, so they could help restore him (Gal. 6:1). But this reality took time, as the law had such a hold on him.

REPEATED EXPOSURE TO THE ELEMENTS OF GROWTH. Another reason we need time to grow is that it takes more than one "inoculation" for us to mature. A single lesson or experience (as described above) is not enough. Growth often requires repetition to sink into our heart and character. The Bible calls this "practice": "But solid food is for the mature, who because of practice have their senses trained to discern good and evil" (Heb. 5:14 NASB). Psychologists refer to this as a learning curve.

Why is repetition necessary for growth? There are several reasons. One is that we have many parts to our soul, and we may grow in one part but not another. For example, suppose you are teaching the value of confession in your group. A man who has been very emotionally detached understands this and confesses, "Sometimes I feel like I don't fit in." After a period of time in the group, however, as he opens up more and gets in touch with his inner parts, he may confess, "When I feel how empty I am inside, it seems like I am falling through a hole in myself, and it frightens me." Clearly, he has begun working on a deeper level.

A second reason is that we are often afraid of truth and light, and we will resist it. We may deny some reality about ourselves until we are safe enough to handle it. For example, someone who has not wanted to see that she is married to a rageaholic may, in time, admit it. This has to do with the fig leaves we wear to protect ourselves. The fig leaves she uses might be rationalization ("he's not that bad"), guilt ("he gets angry because I provoke it") or defensive hope ("I know he will get better if I pray and think positively"). (For more information on this subject, see *Hiding from Love*.)

Add to this the reality that often we are on another path than God's in the first place. Left to our own devices, our nature is to do life on our own rather than to bend the knee to God's ways. So often we are already moving in some direction, only it's the wrong one. When we encounter growth principles, they may require that we turn around 180 degrees. And, just as turning a boat around in the water takes time, so does turning our soul around. It involves trials, risks, and failures.

I see many courageous people who have conquered emotional hurts because they repeatedly and unashamedly failed as they tried out new ways of life. One of them emailed me recently that she has always tried to please others rather than God (Gal. 1:10). Now that she is in the growth process, she is working on living by God's ways, not by her fear of letting others down. She still finds herself taking back her truthful words or not speaking up, yet she is constantly learning from her failures. It takes time—time richly worth the investment.

Don't be afraid to have your group or ministry encounter the same principles again. For the above reasons, they may need to soak things in more than once as they grow.

INTERNAL VERSUS EXTERNAL CHANGE. Remember also that if you are helping others in the sanctification process, you are working with internal changes of heart and life. This change causes true character growth. It is from the inside out, not from the outside in. As hearts are transformed, they also transform the external life. But this takes time.

It is easy to focus on external, behavioral change. While our actions are indeed important, and we are responsible for them (Matt. 16:27), we must ultimately focus our character growth on our hearts.

I was in a growth group with a woman who struggled with her weight. It bothered her greatly, and she had done many things to deal with it, mostly external: diets, exercise regimens, and diet pills. But nothing ever stuck. Then, in the group she dealt with her fear of closeness and vulnerability. She had never let anyone truly know her, and her weight helped her stay distant from others. Over time, she shed her fears and let others inside. And this time the diet she was on became a permanent thing. This time the weight loss became a long-standing part of her life. The internal work took longer, but it had more lasting effect.

If you are working with a group and encounter a crisis—an addiction, an acting-out sin, a marriage breaking up, or the like—don't ignore it in favor of the internal issues. Rather, deal with both at the same time. Provide resources to help the crisis, such as people and places with specific experience in these matters. Simultaneously keep working on whatever in the person's soul is driving these struggles.

DETERMINING LENGTH OF THE GROWTH PROCESS

PROBABLY THE SECOND-MOST-OFTEN-ASKED QUESTION I encounter is, "How can I know how long it will all take?"

The first answer to this is that *it generally takes more time than you thought* (as Henry showed in chapter 1). Many of us get into the growth process hoping to get some quick answers and comfort and then resume "normal life." However, this is not God's way. For him, normal life is being in the growth process for life. Issues and struggles may and should change over time, but growth is not a season. Rather, it is at the heart of life itself: We "are being built together to become a dwelling in which God lives by his Spirit" (Eph. 2:22). So help your group get over the idea that because an issue has been resolved, they are "done." They may just be beginning.

Beyond that, several indicators can help give a sense of how long specific growth or repair issues take to resolve. Put together, these indicators can help people get a sense of time for their work.

SEVERITY OF THE ISSUE. People come to growth in varying stages of immaturity and injury. Generally speaking, the worse the issue, the longer the time required to resolve it. For example, a person who is slightly perfectionistic might deal with tendencies to be self-critical and have problems accepting her badness. However, someone who has deeper issues in this area might experience harsh self-condemnation that paralyzes her, and she may be unable to look at her bad self without falling apart emotionally. Expect the person with the worse battle to take longer.

ONSET OF THE ISSUE. As you get to know the people in your group, find out when their particular struggles began. Life has a way of continuing to injure already existing weaknesses, and it can become unclear where things started. Generally, the earlier the problem, the more time it will take to deal successfully with it.

For example, a man who has just come out of a painful divorce may have trouble trusting others and opening up. He may be withdrawn and avoidant. At first blush, it may seem that the wounds from the divorce are the sole cause. However, as his life unfolds, it may turn out that his childhood relationship with his mother was marked by her detachment and preoccupation with things in life other than him. This set the tone for his struggle with reaching out, and the divorce exacerbated an already existing injury. This man will assuredly be able to heal; however, his path will be more intricate than that of a person who came out of childhood secure in love and who then has a bad divorce.

AVAILABLE RESOURCES. Although the work of spiritual growth is, at its heart, a miraculous act of God, it still requires resources, such as a healthy support system, a balanced church, good materials to study, appropriate leadership, and frequent meetings. The more resources available, the less time is needed.

As you help people grow, you may find that many of them have spent a great deal of time addressing their weaknesses and struggles with little to show for it. Much of the time, they may not have had the right resources. Some may have been in a legalistic environment. Others may have lived in unsafe relationships. The availability of resources is a critical issue.

A woman I know lived in a town in which she simply could not find enough healthy resources to help her grow. She finally pulled up stakes and moved to another town that had more resources. I saw her recently, and her life is blooming. She told me she does not think she would be where she is today if she had not made that radical move. This is certainly no prescription to leave town; rather, help your people unearth and use the good growth resources in your area.

SPIRITUAL POVERTY. We have already addressed this component chapter 14, but we need to say here that, of all the factors, this one has the most effect on the length of time growth takes. Those who are truly aware of their need and hunger for God and growth will, like the woman above, go and get it. They will fervently beg God for help. They will read the Bible and anything else healthy on the subject. They will find growth environments and regularly participate, letting nothing in life stop them. They will unveil their soul, expose their weaknesses, accept comfort and correction, and try their mightiest to grow in God's ways. And they will grow and resolve issues!

Those without the hunger may have less severe issues, yet take longer to resolve them. For excruciatingly long periods of time, they may find themselves stuck in lukewarmness, blame, denial, or avoidance of pain. Help your people see the value of spiritual poverty in reducing the time needed for growth.

THE PLACE OF THE PAST

TIME IS ALSO IMPORTANT in terms of the role the past plays in our growth. As with the man who had suffered relational injuries both in childhood and divorce, the past is very important to understand in the process. Here are some of the key principles.

AN UNRESOLVED ISSUE MAY MEAN THAT PART OF A PERSON'S SOUL IS STILL "IN THE PAST." When a person struggles, he experiences some aspect of himself as split off and lost in an injured or unloved state. This part is still stuck in the original state in which it was hurt. It is as if the person grew up on the outside, but left a part of himself behind, still alone or attacked or overwhelmed.

For example, a man I know suffered harsh criticism from his parents. They loved him, but did not give him grace when he was a boy.

When this man grew up and went to work, he could not tolerate criticism from his superiors. If his boss criticized him, he would immediately feel unloved, persecuted, and attacked. He would say to his group, "I feel like a little kid getting beat up." The part of him that needed security and approval was not adult, but childlike. This issue caused him many lost career opportunities.

Fortunately, the group was able to help him understand that his career problems had roots in his past. He brought out the attacked and persecuted part of himself to the healing relationships. He came to the realization that God was present with him back as a little boy and now when he still felt the hurt. From his group he received the grace he hadn't gotten as a child. In time, he was able to receive criticism without losing a sense of love and security.

From this example I hope it is clear that we don't believe that for someone to work through their past, they literally have to go "into their past." This is impossible, though some schools of thought teach that this is what happens. All we have to work with is today: "But encourage one another daily, as long as it is called Today" (Heb. 3:13). It is more accurate to say that you help bring parts of people who are experiencing life as they did in the past into a present and more healing environment. This environment begins the process of helping these parts of the soul to grow past their immature or wounded state, which occurred in the past, and to mature and repair, so that they are integrated into the life of the present.

Think of all your group members as having parts inside them that are still in the past, whether or not they are aware of it yet, and help them see where they need to grow in these areas. A good book for understanding this concept is *The Mom Factor.*

MOST SPIRITUAL, EMOTIONAL, AND RELATIONAL ISSUES HAVE A HISTORY. Your people do not generally have struggles out of the blue. Someone's parenting problems, guilt issues, and faith doubts all have roots in the past. For empathy and perspective, know about your people's history.

It is especially important to have this information, as you will see patterns emerge in people's lives. These patterns can be very helpful in helping a person grow in areas of weakness. Often, understanding a pattern will help a person turn major corners in growth.

A single woman came to a growth group complaining that she couldn't find men of character to date. They were all controlling and self-centered. She felt there was no good relational future for her. After some time in the group, one of the members said, "Charlene, you have a passive history. From your parents to your church to your boss to your dates, you have always let others decide your values and how you spend your time." This statement changed Charlene's life. She realized how passive her life patterns had been; she had let controlling men pick her. This awareness gave her much fuel to change.

FORGIVENESS REQUIRES A PAST. One of the most important elements of helping people grow is forgiveness, which is covered in greater detail in chapter 9. When we forgive, we cancel the debt of another, and we are free to live without the need to exact revenge on another. When we receive forgiveness, we experience God's freedom from our sin and guilt.

However, if the past is not relevant, there is nothing either to forgive or to be forgiven for. Some Christian circles teach that we are to forget the past and press on. They quote Paul's personal story of "forgetting what is behind and straining toward what is ahead" (Phil. 3:13) as an example of not dealing with the past by looking ahead. Yet, in that same passage Paul talks about all the things in his past he had to deal with, such as self-righteousness, pride, and contempt for others (vv. 4–8). Help your people see the value of understanding their past both factually and emotionally as a key to forgiving.

TRAUMA. Often, as people feel safe in a growth context, their past will come back to them with a vengeance. The safety of love, grace, and structure makes it possible for them to bear what was previously unbearable. Old traumatic hurts, feelings, memories, and terrors may resurface. The people will experience these not as happening yesterday, but as if they are happening right now in a flashback.

This is an intense example of the past's importance. When trauma is re-experienced, past and present are one. If you see that someone in your group is showing signs of this, hook her up with someone who has specific experience in that area. The goal is to help the person turn the flashbacks into memories that are not disruptive and frightening.

Trauma problems are amenable to help, and people can resolve them and go on in their lives.

THE PATH OF GROWTH

GOD USES THE PASSAGE of time as one element of growth for his people. Within time, growth follows a defined order that shows that spiritual movement is occurring. We don't believe that the process is a structureless journey you can't know or understand. Rather, God wants you to be a co-laborer in this process (Phil. 2:12–13). Let's look at the essential aspects of this path so that growth facilitators can be aware of what to expect.

NEED, OR BAD FRUIT. The process of spiritual growth begins in most people with either a recognized need for God or growth, or some struggle or problem that needs God's help (Matt. 7:18). As we saw in chapter 14, both are authentic ways to start the process. These tend to begin the process because they indicate that *we do not possess all we need*. Therefore it must come from outside our skin, from God and his resources. The people you are helping will have one or both of these indicators. For example, some will come in saying, "My life is okay, but I want to make sure I'm on the right path." Others will say, "I have an issue that I can't resolve by myself." Both of these people belong in the growth process.

Here is a partial list of "fruit" struggles—the types of struggles people might bring into a growth setting that are actually the fruit of deeper spiritual issues:

- Marriage or dating conflicts
- Depression
- Doubt
- Addictions
- Family problems
- Anxiety
- Career failures
- Troublesome emotions
- Hurts from the past

Remember, however, that symptoms are not the problem, but a signal of a deeper soul problem.

A RELATIONAL ARENA FOR GROWTH. Spiritual growth doesn't occur in a vacuum. It happens within intimate, vulnerable relationships with God and safe people (Eccl. 4:9–12). As people open up, confess, and receive what they need to follow God's ways, someone must be around to supply all of this. If you are a group facilitator, make sure that relatedness is a high value with your members. If people don't feel they are being connected with, not much will go on at a deep level.

IDENTIFICATION OF ISSUES. Character injuries and immaturities are the central issues that drive the fruit, or symptoms. Here are some key issues to help your people identify.

- Lack of bonding and trust
- Problems being separate and setting limits
- Problems controlling others
- Inability to deal with one's badness
- Problems accepting the failures of others
- Struggles in relating to the world as an adult

(For a more thorough treatment of these issues, see *Changes that Heal.*)

As you can see from this list, people have differing issues, and we need to treat them as individuals (1 Thess. 5:14). A group that treats everyone as having the same kind of problem—whether the problem is self-image, position in Christ, codependency—will be ineffective. It is important also to realize that different issues can drive the same symptom. For example, depression can be a fruit of any of the above list. So always look for the issue underneath what is going on in the outside life.

OWNERSHIP. As people become educated about their particular issues, they will need to take responsibility for them. Understanding the past helps them to see what parts are their fault (denial, rescuing, fear of loss), what parts are others' fault (control, withholding of love, nonacceptance), and what parts are the product of living in a fallen world (death of a loved one, a chronic illness). However the percentages end up, though, ownership means that the person comes to the realization that her life is her problem and that her growth is the solution. This

---

Tips for Growers:

- Make the adjustment from an instant results mentality to a biblical process of growth that bears fruit over time. Understand why growth takes time, and understand the purpose of time in that process.
- Confess and repent of any performance-based, perfectionistic, or grandiose tendencies to be in control of the time involved in your growth.
- Understand the part time plays in moving from intellectual "knowing" to heart "knowing."
- Be a person who uses the ingredient of time to be willing to expose yourself to the same growth experiences repeatedly until you internalize them.

Tips for Facilitators:

- Help your growers to stay away from the "time heals all" mentality. Without involvement in the tasks of growth, time can just be a marker for spiritual stagnation.
- Help them to use their growth time responsibly. Let them know that they can speed up or slow down the process by their involvement in growth, but that it will still take time.
- Give them perspective on why their growth takes the time it takes in terms of the severity and origin of the issue, available resources, and spiritual hunger.
- Provide people with a biblical perspective on the past: They need to see its part in their lives so they can learn, ask forgiveness, and forgive, but they also need to accept, grieve, and move on to today.

---

process often takes time, as people sort out their feelings about the nature and cause of their issues. Be patient with them during this phase.

REBUILDING TASKS. Here people begin using the love, support, and structure of others to develop what they do not possess inside. For example, someone who is disconnected may learn to experience needs for love in his group. Or a person who is dependent learns to stand up for what is right. This is like people going to a physical therapist to take care of an injured muscle. Exercising, risk, and practice with injured parts in the context of safe relationships help people grow.

FORGIVENESS AND GRIEF. At some point, having owned the issues, people need to let go of debts, feel sadness about the past and losses they can't change, and receive forgiveness for what they have contributed. This is often a sign that they are well on the road to resolving a particular issue, as grief means they now have enough love inside them to tolerate letting go of someone or something they have lost.

GOOD FRUIT. As the inside grows, so ultimately should the outside. You should see better relationships, emotional experiences, and connectedness to God. These aren't signs that one is done growing, but they are certainly signs that things are moving in the right direction.

DEEPENING. Growth never ends on this earth. People will find new areas of growth as God helps them search their hearts (Ps. 139:23–24). Often you will find that the process may begin with some external crisis (such as a marriage conflict or an emotional issue). As that crisis is resolved, some people will think growth is over. But the wise ones will know that the real work is just beginning, and they will look long and hard at the person in the mirror (James 1:23–25) and go deeper inside their soul, bringing more and more to the light of God's healing grace.

GROWTH FOR LIFE

The other day I met a woman who had been trained many years ago to disciple women in the basics of the faith and spiritual disciplines. She told me she had recently decided "just for fun" to mentor young women "on the side." She had been working with a young college student who was in turn training other young women in the faith.

"How's it going?" I asked.

"It's been very interesting," she said. "Nothing like I had planned."

"What do you mean?"

"Well, I was all prepared to go through some materials on the basics of the faith, doctrine, the spiritual disciplines, and all of that other good stuff I was trained in, but I found I'm an expert in something no one wants anymore. I'm going to have to go and relearn it all."

"How so?"

"I was prepared to talk about doctrine, and she wanted to tell me about her life. She wanted to talk about her struggles with her boyfriend and about what she should do next. She wanted to talk about her family and how her relationship with her mother had affected her choice of boyfriends. I was sitting there trying to figure out how all of this connected with following the Holy Spirit, praying, and the like. I know it does, and in many ways I know *how* it does, but I was just not prepared."

"I totally understand," I said. "All the organizations I work with who do ministry with people say the same thing. People are looking for not just doctrine, but real-life applications of the faith. Sounds like a good idea to me. That's the way it ought to be anyway."

"I know. That's what I believe and the way I live. I'm just not prepared to teach it yet!" she said, laughing.

What she was describing is what all of us long for. We want to know our faith and the major biblical doctrines. We want to know what the Bible says about itself, God, and the spiritual life. We want to know about orthodoxy and the spiritual disciplines.

And we want to know what in the world these things have to do with our real lives. We want spirituality to be practical and real, from dealing with marital problems to overcoming difficulties reaching our goals, from dealing with depression to disciplining our children. We want God and real life to come together.

The woman I met expressed what we have tried to do in this book. We have taken an in-depth look at the major doctrines of faith from Creation to Sin to Redemption. But we have also looked at real life in light of those doctrines. When you put God and his doctrines together with the struggles of your life, you will find that growth in both your faith and your life has no boundaries.

And that has been our prayer for you as you have read this book. We have enjoyed writing it, trying to live its principles, and continuing to learn about them each and every day in our own lives. We hope you find this book helpful and fruitful in your life and in your work with others.

We encourage you to continue down this path. Get to know God better, and take him and what you learn into every life situation you encounter. For then, we believe, you will realize Jesus' promise: "If you hold to my teaching, you are really my disciples. Then you will know the truth, and the truth will set you free" (John 8:31–32).

Learn his teaching, and hold on to it as you live. Then you will really know it, and it will set you free to love God, to love others, to be all you were created to be, and to find the path God has ordained specifically for you. This is how people grow—grow for life.

God bless.
Henry Cloud, Ph.D.
John Townsend, Ph.D.

INDEX